The Jesus Lifestyle

NICKY GUMBEL

Published in Nashville, Tennessee, by W Publishing Group, an imprint of Thomas Nelson. W Publishing Group and Thomas Nelson are registered trademarks of HarperCollins Christian Publishing, Inc.

Illustrations by Charlie Mackesy

ISBN 978-1-938-3-2894-7

First Printing 2007 / Printed in the United States of America

23 24 25 26 27 LBC 11 10 9 8 7

Contents

Foreword

One of the great challenges for the church today – made harder, I suspect, because the world seems largely to have given up the attempt – is to hold together teaching and ethics.

The Sermon on the Mount is Jesus' teaching on how to conduct our lives. It is his answer to the question, 'How exactly can we fulfil our calling to be "in" the world but not "of" it?' What could be more important for us in our generation than an earnest attempt to understand and apply this teaching of Jesus?

As we move towards the so-called 'post-Christian' era, Nicky Gumbel's choice of material, combined with his experience of life, his humour, and his passion for bringing practical sense and sparkle to biblical teaching has produced an invaluable book for today.

It will prove equally useful to both mature and new Christians, provides excellent follow-up material to Alpha, and will help the church to 'shine before others, that they may see your good deeds and glorify your Father in heaven' (Matthew 5:16).

Bishop Sandy Millar
Former Assistant Bishop in London

Preface

'Astonishment' is probably the best word to describe what we have felt as Alpha, developed in our local church, has spread all round the world. Now running in 169 countries, in over 110 languages, over 27 million people have completed the course and millions are attending it each year.

As Alpha continues to grow, one of the questions we are asked over and over again is: 'What happens after Alpha?' In response to the demand for follow-up material, we first produced *A Life Worth Living* and then *Challenging Lifestyle*. I wrote *Challenging Lifestyle* over twenty years ago. Recently I gave a series of talks on the Sermon on the Mount at HTB. Inevitably, as the culture has changed and time has passed, the material has developed so much that it seems appropriate to give it a new title. There is a great deal of continuity and therefore I have left the word 'lifestyle' in the title. But the word 'Challenging' no longer seems strong enough. The only appropriate words I can think of to describe the teaching in the Sermon on the Mount are, 'The Jesus Lifestyle'.

To seek to follow the teaching in the Sermon on the Mount is to seek to follow Jesus. The words of Jesus are the greatest words ever to have fallen from the lips of a human being. They are the kind of words we would expect God to speak; they authenticate Jesus' own understanding of his identity as a man whose identity is God. Since I first encountered Jesus in 1974, I have tried to live by the teaching of Jesus. Often, I have failed miserably and continue to do so. However, I love Jesus and I love his words. This book attempts to meditate on them and explore how they can be applied to our lives in the twenty-first century.

I am so grateful to the many people who have helped with this project. In particular, I would like to thank Kitty Kay-Shuttleworth, Chris Smith, Julia Evans, Mark Knight, James Orr and Kate

Crossland-Page for their help and advice on the text. I would also like to thank all those who have been involved in the filming of the talks; Archie Coates, Martin Bennett, James Wynn, Mark Elsdon-Dew, Lisa Carlson, Jo Soda, John Butterworth, David Groves, Dan Lawson Johnston, and Katie Markham.

Last, but by no means least, I would like to thank Rosalyn Suni who has overseen the whole project in addition to numerous other projects with an extraordinary combination of hard work, dedication, commitment, patience, good humour, grace and total unflappability.

Introduction

Now when he saw the crowds, he went up on a mountainside and sat down. His disciples came to him, and he began to teach them.
Matthew 5:1–2

Our culture is obsessed with lifestyle. There are numerous magazines devoted to clothes, health and fitness, dieting, sexual performance, homes and gardens, and other aspects of lifestyle. They place style above content, and are preoccupied with how things look. Jesus is much more interested in what is underneath.

Jesus' teaching in the Sermon on the Mount presents a challenge to our lifestyle in the West. However, it also offers an alternative lifestyle. We are called to develop the Jesus lifestyle. The question often asked by our culture is not so much 'Is Christianity true?' but 'Is it real? Does it work?' The world is watching. This is the challenge set before us.

As I have preached and worked through the eighteen chapters of this book over the last few years, on every occasion I have found myself profoundly challenged by Jesus. I only hope the reader will be as challenged as I have been.

The standards of lifestyle set by Jesus are very high. The Christian leader John Wimber put it like this: 'Jesus is insatiable. Everything we do pleases him but nothing satisfies him. I have been satisfied with Jesus. He has not been satisfied with me. He keeps raising the standards. He walks in high places. He is generous but uncompromising in his call.'

The Sermon on the Mount has been described as 'the supreme jewel in the crown of Jesus' teaching'.[1] It is the 'Manifesto of the King' and 'The Magna Carta of the Kingdom'. To say that this is the greatest sermon ever preached would be the understatement of world history! As one nineteenth-century commentator put it, 'We are near heaven here.'[2]

Jesus chose to give this sermon from a mountainside (Matthew 5:1). Perhaps he had in mind that it was on a mountain that Moses received God's commandments in the Old Testament, or it may have been that this was simply the best place to speak.

There is some debate as to whether the sermon is addressed to his disciples or to the crowds. He appears to begin with his disciples (Matthew 5:1) and to finish with everyone listening (Matthew 7:28). The teaching would seem to be primarily for the disciples, the equivalent today of those who have already encountered Jesus. But it is clearly appropriate that it be heard by the crowds – comparable, perhaps, to those who have not yet encountered Jesus. Jesus continually contrasts the two. He says, 'Do not be like them.' His disciples should be different both from the non-religious, the Gentiles and pagans (the equivalent today of the secular world and the confused world of pluralistic religion) and also from the religious, the scribes and the Pharisees.

Jesus was not laying down a new law to replace the old covenant of Moses; he was teaching his followers how to live out the Jesus lifestyle. Many who would not call themselves Christians claim to live by the teaching of Jesus in the Sermon on the Mount. If they had really read it carefully they would see that it is quite impossible even to begin to live as Jesus taught without the help of his Spirit.

Perhaps that was one of the purposes of the sermon. The Reformers in the sixteenth century used to say that the law sends us to Christ to be justified and Christ sends us back to the law to be sanctified. Reading the Sermon on the Mount should make those who do not know Christ, and indeed all of us, cry out for mercy and help. As we receive Christ and the help of his Spirit, he sends us back to the Sermon on the Mount to learn how to live out our faith. Jesus is teaching us here how to work out what God has worked in.

01

How to Find the Secret
of Happiness

Blessed are the poor in spirit,
for theirs is the kingdom of heaven.
Blessed are those who mourn,
for they will be comforted.
Blessed are the meek,
for they will inherit the earth.
Blessed are those who hunger and thirst
for righteousness,
for they will be filled.
Matthew 5:3-6

How do we find the secret of happiness? Magazines, newspapers
and TV tell us that things like shopping, dieting, plastic surgery and
fame are the means to find happiness. I read recently in *The Sunday
Times* that 'Fame is still the number-one ambition of pretty much
every kid in the iPod world.'[1]

The media also portray wealth and possessions as the means to
happiness. As a society we are three times richer than thirty years
ago and yet surveys have shown that Britain's happiness is in
decline.[2] In the 1950s over half the population said they were 'very
happy'; now only a third describe themselves in this way.[3] A recent
TV programme on BBC2 called *Making Slough Happy*, showed
a group of experts attempting to teach the people of Slough how to
make themselves happier. It offered advice such as, 'Each day give
yourself a treat.'

What happens when we have all these things that the media

promotes? George Michael, the singer, had it all – fame, wealth, possessions. Yet he wrote these lyrics, 'Well, it looks like the road to heaven, but it *feels* like the road to hell'.[4]

'We all want to live happily; in the whole human race there is no one who does not assent to this proposition, even before it is fully articulated',[5] said St Augustine, one of the greatest theologians of the church.

Jesus addresses this natural desire that we all have for happiness in the Sermon on the Mount. The importance of this sermon, of which we probably only have an abbreviated form, is underlined by three phrases in the opening verses. First, Jesus 'sat down' (Matthew 5:1). In Jesus' time, when a Rabbi sat down to teach, it was a sign that he had something of supreme importance to say. Second, 'he opened his mouth' (v.2, RSV). The Greek expression used here conveys solemnity. Perhaps the modern equivalent might be, 'he opened his heart'. Third, as we have seen already, Jesus was 'on a mountainside' (v.1). Mountains were associated with revelation from God, and especially with the law that God had once given to his people from Mount Sinai (Exodus 34).

Jesus then explodes the myth of finding happiness. True happiness is not about how we feel. The Greek word for 'blessed', which appears nine times in the first eleven verses, conveys the idea of happiness, but it means much more than that. The word used by Jesus, *makarios*, means 'blessed by God', or 'receiving God's favour'. The Amplified Bible translates it as 'happy, to be envied, and spiritually prosperous – with life-joy and satisfaction in God's favour and salvation, regardless of their outward conditions'.

Right at the start Jesus teaches us about what matters most in life. So often we judge people by what they do: their jobs, their achievements or even what kind of school they went to. Or we may judge them by what they have: wealth, looks, friends or possessions. Jesus says here that what matters most in life is not what we have or what we do, but who we are. When I was a student at theological college I was no longer 'earning a living'. It was not so much the lack of money that I felt, but the lack of self-worth. When I was working as a lawyer I was paid for giving my opinion. At college no one was the least bit interested in my opinion! I remember telling a wise Christian how difficult I found this. He said something simple yet so profound. He told me that my experience was a good thing because what matters in life is not what you do but who you are.

In the opening verses of the Sermon on the Mount, Jesus shows us that the secret of happiness is to be found in who we are. These eight Beatitudes, or 'beautiful attitudes', as the great evangelist, Billy Graham, described them, show us how our characters can grow. They are like the fruit of the spirit, in that they are for all Christians. They are not just for a spiritual elite; they are for all followers of Christ. The 'you's of the beatitudes are plural. Jesus is helping (or teaching) us to live with others as well as ourselves.

In the opening verses of the Sermon on the Mount, Jesus answers the question: What sort of people should we be? He describes in eight steps the kind of character we should have. The first four steps, which we will look at in this chapter, focus on our relationship with God. The second four focus on our relationships with others, and we will come to those in chapter 2.

1. True happiness comes from being 'depressed'

Jesus said, 'Blessed are the poor in spirit' (v.3). But what did he mean? When I say that true happiness comes from being 'depressed' I am not referring to clinical depression. Rather, I use the word 'depressed' here in the sense of 'being brought low, being weakened'. What Jesus says here is totally surprising and totally shocking. We may be so familiar with the words 'Blessed are the poor in spirit' (v.3) that they don't shock us in the way that they would have shocked the original hearers. Jesus is using the language of paradox, which G. K. Chesterton described as 'Truth standing on her head, demanding attention.'[6]

There are two Greek words for 'poor'. One means 'lacking wealth' and therefore needing to work. The other, which is used here, means 'desperately impoverished' and therefore dependent on others for support.

To be 'poor in spirit' does not mean having no spiritual backbone; rather, it is the opposite of spiritual pride. It is the opposite of saying, 'I have led a morally good life.' The person who says that can only have compared their life with others and not with God's standards. It is also the opposite of saying, 'My life is basically fine'. It means to look at our lives, and more so at the world we are living in, and to recognise

that something is lacking and that something needs to change.

Before I became a Christian I was quite content in many ways. I thought, 'My life is fine. I don't need God. I try to lead a good life. I don't rob banks. I don't do anybody any harm.' But in other ways I was very dissatisfied. I was constantly searching. I felt an emptiness inside and tried to fill it in all sorts of different ways that ultimately did not satisfy. When I became a Christian, this situation was reversed. The more I looked at Jesus and his teaching, the more aware I became of how far I fall short. The more I read the Sermon on the Mount, the more I become aware of my weakness and sinfulness, and all I have been able to say is, 'God, have mercy on me, a sinner' (Luke 18:13).

Jesus' response is wholly encouraging: the kingdom of heaven flings open its doors to beggars, 'for theirs is the kingdom of heaven' (v.3). It is precisely when we feel spiritually desperate or a complete failure that we come under the rule and the reign of God; not just for this life, but for all eternity. The psalmist says: 'In your presence there is fullness of joy. In your right hand are pleasures forever more' (Psalm 16:11, RSV).

2. True happiness comes from 'grieving'

By 'grieving' I don't just mean crying. Personally, I cry very easily. I cry at soppy romantic comedies and even every time I watch *The Sound of Music*! When Jesus said 'Blessed are those who mourn' (v.4), he was not talking about that kind of crying. The Greek word used for 'mourning' is a stronger word. It is frequently used in the Greek translation of the Hebrew Bible for mourning over the dead. It is the word that is used of Jacob's grief when he believed his son Joseph was dead (Genesis 37:34–35).

There are two mistaken views about the Christian life. One is that Christians should never be happy – always carrying the world's cares on their shoulders – and that there should be no smiling or laughter in church. Equally, it is a mistake to think that Christians should never be unhappy. This is the cheerleader approach: 'Come on, guys, let's smile and be happy!' As the writer of Ecclesiastes points out 'There is a time for everything… a time to weep and a time to laugh, a time to mourn and a time to dance' (Ecclesiastes 3:1, 4).

It is not wrong to weep and to mourn at the loss of those we love, just as Jesus wept on hearing that his friend Lazarus had died (John 11:35). We may also weep over the mess we see in the world and in the lives of others. Paul wept over the enemies of the cross of Christ (Philippians 3:18).

When I became a Christian I remember being convinced in my mind that Jesus was alive. After experiencing the power of the Holy Spirit this knowledge dropped from my head down to my heart as well. He gave me a deep inner certainty that Christianity was true and filled me with joy. A few days later I found myself weeping as I realised that if it was true this had implications for those people I knew and loved who were not following Jesus.

Dietrich Bonhoeffer was a German Christian who opposed Hitler in the 1930s. He was arrested, imprisoned and shortly before the end of the war he was martyred for his faith. Bonhoeffer wrote a commentary on the Sermon on the Mount called *The Cost of Discipleship*. Writing about this verse 'Blessed are those who mourn' (v.4) he said, '[Those who mourn] see that for all the jollity on board, the ship is beginning to sink'.[7]

There is great precedent for God's children weeping not simply for themselves, but for the cities they are part of and for the land in which they live. Jesus wept over Jerusalem because its inhabitants were so blind to what was going on in their midst. I am ashamed that I do not weep more when I see pictures of children dying of starvation or AIDS; or images on the TV news of those killed or injured in war. We should weep at these things.

However, Jesus' teaching here is perhaps more concerned with our own sin than the sins of the world around us. He speaks to us about the times when we think, 'Oh no, I've messed up again!' When Peter realised how much he had let Jesus down he wept (Matthew 26:75). Jesus says, 'Blessed are those who mourn, for they will be comforted' (v.4). The word 'comforted' has the same root as 'Comforter', a word that Jesus uses for the Holy

Spirit (John 14:16). When the Spirit of God comes upon a man or woman the experience is sometimes accompanied by tears. Sometimes past hurts are being healed. Often someone is mourning over opportunities that have been wasted, or a sense of spiritual poverty. When the Holy Spirit, the Comforter, comes he embraces us, he comforts us (Acts 9:31), and he pours the love of God into our hearts (Romans 5:5). Out of that love flows a compassion for those around us. This is why the second step to true happiness comes from this grief that drives us into God's arms.

3. True happiness comes from being 'broken'

Jesus said, 'Blessed are the meek' (v.5). The Greek word used for 'meek' does not mean 'weak, spineless, feeble'. Rather it means 'gentle, considerate, and unassuming'. Meekness is the opposite of arrogance and self-seeking. It means 'broken', not in the sense that glass is broken, but in the sense that a horse is broken in when it is tamed. With a broken horse there is great strength under submission. This word is used of two of the greatest men in the Bible. Moses, who led the Israelites out of captivity, is described as 'very meek, above all the men which were upon the face of the earth' (Numbers 12:3, KJV). And in the New Testament, Jesus, who was the saviour of the world, says of himself, 'Learn of me; for I am meek and lowly in heart' (Matthew 11:29, KJV). Jesus was meek because he was under control. He was submitted not only to God but also to his parents and to the law; he even submitted himself to Pilate.

The preacher and writer Dr Martyn Lloyd-Jones defined meekness as 'essentially a true view of oneself, expressing itself in attitude and conduct with respect to others'. He goes on further to say:

> The man who is meek is not even sensitive about himself. He is not always watching himself and his own interests. He is not always on the defensive. We all know about this, do we not? Is it not one of the greatest curses in life as a result of the fall – this sensitivity about self? We spend the whole of our lives watching ourselves. But when a man becomes meek he has finished with all that; he no longer worries about himself and what other people say. To be truly meek means we no longer protect ourselves, because we see there is nothing worth defending. So we are not on the defensive; all that is gone. The man who is truly meek never pities himself, he is never sorry for himself.[8]

He goes on to quote the author and preacher, John Bunyan: 'He that is down need fear no fall.'[9]

When we are in this position Jesus says we will 'inherit the earth' (v.5). Everything we receive is a gift because we know we don't deserve it. When we reach this state we are in a position to know how to receive what God wants to give, both in this life and the life to come – he will give us everything.

4. True happiness comes from being 'deeply dissatisfied'

Jesus says, 'Blessed are those who hunger and thirst for righteousness' (v.6). Most of us in the West have no idea what it means to be hungry. The person who is really hungry (as opposed to having hunger pangs) or the person who is really thirsty (as opposed to feeling like a drink) is so desperate that everything else is excluded from their desires.

William Barclay, who was Professor of Divinity and Biblical Criticism at Glasgow University, describes the thirst a person might experience in Palestine in these terms:

A man might be on a journey, and in the midst of it the hot wind which brought the sandstorm might begin to blow. There was nothing for him to do but to wrap his head in his burnous (a hooded cloak) and turn his back to the wind, and wait, while the swirling sand filled his nostrils and his throat until he was likely to suffocate, and until he was parched with an imperious thirst. In the conditions of modern western life there is no parallel at all to that.[10]

When we are truly desperate, satisfying that hunger or thirst becomes a consuming passion, a grand desire, and an overwhelming ambition.

Jesus says we are to have this attitude towards 'righteousness'. We should long to live in a right relationship with God, to be seen as righteous by him and to see his righteousness in the society around us. In the Greek New Testament text the word for righteousness is in the accusative case and not the genitive. If it were in the genitive case it would mean to desire partial righteousness – a slice of the loaf. As it is in the accusative, it means 100 per cent righteousness – the whole loaf. It means to desire to be entirely righteous. We're not to be satisfied with anything less than a righteous life. It is not enough to live a Christian life when we feel like it and do what we like at other times. A righteous life is one that is righteous twenty-four hours a day. It is an integrated Christian life that is lived out in an ongoing relationship, with God affecting everything we do, say and think. The problem with many of us is that we are not that desperate. We do not want to pay the price. We say 'Lord, make me holy but not completely holy quite yet, if you don't mind'.

When we are really desperate, Jesus says that God will fill us and we will be satisfied. One woman who seems to have grasped the truth of this beatitude is Sister Wendy Beckett. A graduate of Oxford University, Sister Wendy entered the Notre Dame

Community in 1946. She lives simply in a mobile home in the garden of a monastery in Norfolk. All she owns is a fold-up bed, a mattress, a bookcase, a table and chair, and a manual typewriter. She gets up just before midnight every day. Since 1946, when she joined Notre Dame Community aged sixteen, her daily prayer has been, 'Oh God, it is to praise thee that I awake. I start off each day with a wonderful spring of happiness.' In recent years, Sister Wendy has found fame as an art historian and TV presenter. However this has not affected her frugal life. She allows herself four crisps each day. Her great friend Delia Smith used to buy her a box of chocolates for her birthday in February, but stopped doing so once she discovered that there were still some left at Christmas. She spends seven hours a day in prayer and two hours working. Sister Wendy says this:

> It's a great disappointment that I'm too old to die young. Death is the supreme act of faith. I hope that when it comes I'll have long enough to say a total 'Yes!' so that it's a real death, a jumping-off point. Before bed at ten o'clock I put my feet in lovely hot water, I'm very tired, and I say, 'It is you, O Lord, who are my happiness.' And I lie there drifting off into sleep. There's a psalm: 'I sleep but my heart watches.' By two o'clock I'm awake again, a very lucky woman with a very happy life. Looking back, the years in Notre Dame deepened my desire for God. I had a pool of desire when I first started; now I have an ocean full for him, and I couldn't be happier.[11]

How to Change the World Around You

Blessed are the merciful,
*   for they will be shown mercy.*
Blessed are the pure in heart,
*   for they will see God.*
Blessed are the peacemakers,
*   for they will be called children of God.*
Blessed are those who are persecuted
*   because of righteousness,*
*   for theirs is the kingdom of heaven.*

Blessed are you when people insult you, persecute you and falsely say all kinds of evil against you because of me. Rejoice and be glad, because great is your reward in heaven, for in the same way they persecuted the prophets who were before you.

You are the salt of the earth. But if the salt loses its saltiness, how can it be made salty again? It is no longer good for anything, except to be thrown out and trampled under foot.

You are the light of the world. A city on a hill cannot be hidden. Neither do people light a lamp and put it under a bowl. Instead they put it on its stand, and it gives light to everyone in the house. In the same way, let your light shine before others, that they may see your good deeds and praise your Father in heaven.

Matthew 5:7–16

American civil rights leader Martin Luther King once said, 'An individual has not started living until he can rise above the narrow confines of his individualistic concerns to the broader concerns of all humanity.'[1]

There is something very wrong with our society. We only have to open our newspapers to see a nation torn apart by strife. There is an increasing level of violence and other criminal activity. The breakdown of family life cuts across every background, scarring parents and children alike. The sanctity of human life is threatened by abortion and the desire to allow 'mercy-killing'. Traditional bases for morality are no longer accepted. Fiona Gibson spoke for many when she wrote in the *Daily Mail*, 'If there is a moral code it is: Whatever is pleasurable. It is okay to do whatever you feel like doing.'[2]

Sir Francis Richard Dannatt, head of the British Army from 2006 to 2009, said:

> There is a moral and spiritual vacuum in this country. Our society has always been embedded in Christian values. Once you've pulled the anchor up, there is a danger that our society moves with the prevailing wind.[3]

Not only is there a vacuum at the heart of our nation, but there is also a vacuum in the hearts of individuals. The spiritual hunger in the hearts of human beings remains largely unsatisfied: hunger for meaning and purpose; the desire for permanence; the search for an answer to the problem of guilt and the longing for community and belonging.

As we consider the needs of the world around us and the extent of individual unhappiness we must ask, 'Is there anything we can do to make a difference?' In answering this question we have a choice. Either we can make excuses, saying, 'Well, I'm too young',

'I'm too old', 'I'm too busy'. We can live a life satisfying our own selfish desires, in what Martin Luther King refers to as 'the narrow confines' of our individualistic concerns. Or we can look to 'the broader concerns of all humanity'.

We tend to think that the opportunity to bring transformation within our society comes from wealth, political and military power, or position. However, Jesus said to his disciples, 'You are the salt of the earth… You are the light of the world' (vv.13–14). He was in fact saying, to people who were both uneducated and unsophisticated, 'You can change the world around you. You can make a difference.'

Jesus said that the first command was to 'Love the Lord your God with all your heart and with all your soul and with all your mind' and that the second was to 'Love your neighbour as yourself' (Matthew 22:37–39). In the first chapter we saw that the first four beatitudes are about our relationship with God. The next four are about our relationships with others.

5. Don't give people what they 'deserve', but show mercy
Jesus said: 'Blessed are the merciful' (v.7). To be merciful has two slightly different connotations. First, we are to be merciful to those who have wronged us, even when justice cries out for punishment.

When we have been cheated or hurt by someone our natural reaction may be to want to give them what we feel they deserve. However, this is not the reaction that we are called to as Christians.

Stephen Oake, a Special Branch Constable from Greater Manchester, set out one day to arrest a suspected terrorist called Kamel Bourgass. Instead, he was murdered by Bourgass, leaving behind a wife and three children aged seventeen, sixteen and fourteen. His family, who are Christians, were grief-stricken. His wife said that on some days she could not even get out of bed. Yet her faith helped her survive, and the family have prayed for the murderer every single day. Stephen's father, Robin Oake, a retired policeman and devout Christian, said on the day after the murder that he forgave the killer. After seeing the murderer in court he said, 'I'll carry on praying for this man so that first of all he knows that we've forgiven him, and also that he himself might find peace with God.'[4]

Jesus stressed time and again that it is those who show mercy who will receive mercy. It is not that we can earn God's mercy. Rather, the fact that we forgive is evidence that we have been forgiven by God (Luke 7:47). It is not a bargain with God but a virtuous circle. When we see how much God has forgiven us we cannot fail to have mercy on others (Matthew 18:23–35).

It works the other way round as well. John Wesley told of how he once confronted someone who was about to discipline one of his servants harshly. The master said, 'The rascal should have taken care not to have served me so, for I never forgive,' to which Wesley calmly replied 'Then I hope, sir, that you never sin.'[5]

The second connotation of the word mercy is this: we are to be merciful to those who are in need, like the victim in the parable of the Good Samaritan. We are to look out for those who are hungry, sick, outcast, unpopular, or lonely and have mercy on them. Our mercy will lead naturally to practical help. Dietrich Bonhoeffer said:

The merciful have an irresistible love for the downtrodden, the sick, the wronged, the outcast and those who are tortured with anxiety... No distress is too great, no sin too appalling for their pity.[6]

Mercy is a divine quality. It is a characteristic of God himself. Portia described the quality in Shakespeare's *The Merchant of Venice*:

The quality of mercy is not strain'd,
It droppeth as the gentle rain from heaven
Upon the place beneath: it is twice bless'd;
It blesseth him that gives and him that takes:
'Tis mightiest in the mightiest; it becomes
The throned monarch better than his crown...
It is an attribute to God himself.[7]

Those who fall into the category of the first four beatitudes realise how much they need God's mercy. This is the opposite attitude to that of the fault-finder, who is consistently looking for and dwelling on the faults of others. As we have mercy on others we will become increasingly aware of the mercy of God.

6. Don't put on a mask, but be transparent

Jesus said: 'Blessed are the pure in heart' (v.8). Jesus made the point that God is concerned about our hearts, our inward motivation. That is the place where God looks. He is concerned about the inward and moral rather than the outward and ceremonial (Mark 7:1–23). He wants us to have 'pure' hearts. The word for pure means unmixed, unadulterated, unalloyed, like pure clean water.

So we should seek to have integrity, openness, sincerity,

and authenticity in our relationships with others. J. B. Phillips translates this verse: 'Be utterly sincere'.[8] In a world where the pressure to conform is very great, it means being free from putting on masks and having different roles for different occasions. It means being ourselves as God intended instead of play-acting; living life in the open and letting people see right through us. The pure in heart are those who are completely sincere in their relationships. They are totally open and have nothing to hide. As Christians we can sometimes find ourselves acting one way when we have our 'Christian uniform' on, perhaps at church on Sunday or in our small groups, but acting differently for the rest of the week, when we are not wearing our 'Christian uniform'. This applies at work, but is particularly important in marriage and family life.

Shane Claiborne, author of *The Irresistible Revolution* adds:

> I've met a lot of Christians who say, 'If people knew about all my struggles and weaknesses, they'd never want to be a Christian.' I think just the opposite is true: if people knew that idiots like us, in all our brokenness and vulnerability, can be Christians, they'd know that each of them could give it a shot too.

The pure in heart are the same in every situation. The question is, who are we when no one is looking? H. L. Mencken defined conscience as 'the inner voice which warns us that someone may be looking'.[10] This is very challenging – yet Jesus promises that God will reveal himself to people that live with this kind of integrity and that one day they will see God face to face. Deception blinds us, but purity opens our eyes to see God. The merciful hold nothing against their brothers and sisters. The pure in heart allow others to see them as they are.

7. Don't stir up conflict, but make peace

Jesus said: 'Blessed are the peacemakers' (v.9). A peacemaker desires to bring blessing to other people. So many people around us lack inner peace. H. G. Wells wrote of Mister Polly, 'He was not so much a human being as a civil war'.[11] When we reflect on our inner conflict, and on our conflicts with one another, we realise that it points towards our lack of peace with God. This is a call for peace at all three levels: inner peace, peace between people and, most important of all, peace with God.

Jesus says that if we make peace we will be 'called children of God' (v.9). We will bear the family likeness of our heavenly Father because he is the ultimate peacemaker. Through the cross he made it possible for us to have peace with God (Romans 5:1). Jesus' death on the cross broke down the dividing wall of hostility between people (Ephesians 2:14) and made it possible for men and women to be at peace with themselves. This was not peace at any price, but a costly peace; the price was 'his one and only Son' (John 3:16).

We are called to reconcile people to God by sharing the message of Jesus. We implore others to 'be reconciled to God' (2 Corinthians 5:20). We know that this is the only route to inner peace, which is neither superficial nor deceptive, because it is a peace based on the objective reality of peace with God.

We are also called to bring peace between human beings. That is quite different from doing anything for a peaceful life. Sometimes we need to face up to difficult situations. We may even need to confront in order to make peace. But this is our calling as children of God. This may involve bringing people from apparently irreconcilable positions to a meeting of minds and hearts.

A friend of mine was fortunate enough to have dinner with Nelson Mandela, who commented: 'It takes a long time to make peace; a short time to make tension. Many, many people make tension; few people make peace. Wherever you find tension you must make peace.'

As we look at the world, we see many conflicts. Yet peacemaking has to start where we are. Jim Wallis, pastor and reformer, wrote that 'Those who have learned to love their enemies in community are the best persons to offer their experience in the wider political context.'[12] So we must seek peace in our marriages, with our neighbours, in the local church, and between churches.

Rwanda is a small republic in Africa with a turbulent and bloody past. Out of a population of six million, 90 per cent are Hutu. The Tutsi are the ruling minority. In April 1994, there were three months of genocide on the part of the Hutu militia, followed by the revenge of the Tutsi Liberation Army. The war left one million people dead, two million people implicated in these deaths, 250,000 widows, 450,000 orphans, and 1.5 million exiles.

One man, Jean-Claude, lost fourteen members of his family and witnessed their houses being destroyed. After the war he felt called by God to go into the prisons and preach the gospel of Jesus Christ. One day he preached to a man called Kamunzini who had been part of the group that killed his family with machetes. Kamunzini responded to the message, repented of his sins and gave his life to Christ. He admitted to Jean-Claude what he had done and asked

for forgiveness. Jean-Claude told him that he forgave him and said that he hoped Kamunzini would be with him one day in heaven.

Since 1999 Jean-Claude and Kamunzini have travelled the country as peacemakers. They travel to churches and remote areas and tell the story of how their relationship was transformed by Jesus Christ. Jean-Claude says this:

> I go and speak to those people with Kamunzini and I show them the man that killed the members of my family. Jesus tells us that if we do not forgive others, our guilt will not be forgiven either. Jesus even says that we should forgive our enemies – and Kamunzini was my sworn enemy. But I've forgiven him. Kamunzini killed fourteen members of my family and destroyed their houses. When the people hear that, they fall on their knees and they acknowledge that they too must forgive.

Jesus said, 'Blessed are the peacemakers, because they will be called children of God' (v.9). God loves peace. Like any father, he loves to see his children getting on with each other.

8. Don't expect anything in return, except criticism

Jesus says: 'Blessed are those who are persecuted because of righteousness, for theirs is the kingdom of heaven' (vv.10–12).

Righteousness sums up all the previous seven beatitudes, which are to do with having a right relationship with God and a right relationship with others. We might well think that if we live the kind of life that Jesus advocated we would be universally popular. Yet this is not the case. Jesus never guaranteed popularity. In fact, he warns us to be on our guard if everyone thinks highly of us and says that there is bound to be opposition. He never said, 'Come to me and your troubles will be over.' We are the conscience of humankind and that can make us very unpopular. We may have to endure insults and ridicule, or worse.

The early church had a very different attitude from ours in the West when it came to being willing to pay the price of being followers of Jesus Christ. On occasion they found that there was a conflict between their business interest and their loyalty to Jesus Christ. A man once came to the theologian Tertullian (who died around AD 220) with just such a problem. He told him of his business difficulties and ended by saying, 'What can I do? I must live!' In reply Tertullian asked, 'Must you?'

I recently had dinner with Bishop Ben Kwashi from Nigeria. Bishop Kwashi told me that in 1910 missionaries came from Cambridge to preach the gospel in Nigeria and as a result, his whole family became Christians. He said that now he is 'haunted by the graves of these missionaries':

> We have a heritage, not to the Anglo-Saxons, but to the church of God led by the word of God. Because the gospel

> transforms eternities, lifestyles, communities. Pray for the
> grace to endure persecution. It's going to happen if you
> preach the gospel.

Religious persecution does occur in Nigeria. The houses of many
Christians in his area were burnt to the ground. His wife was
physically attacked for her faith in Jesus Christ. Yet it has not
stopped them; they go on preaching the gospel. He said:

> I'm not afraid. I'm not afraid of dying. I died long ago.
> The moment I came to Christ I died to all that... Look at
> the power of the Resurrection – Jesus Christ is risen from
> the dead! Look at the future we have. Look at the future
> you have.

Jesus never told us to seek persecution but he did say that, when it
comes, we are to regard it as a blessing. We are 'to rejoice and be
glad' (v.12) or, as one translation says, 'leap for joy' (NRSV). How
can we rejoice and be glad when we're persecuted, when we're
ridiculed at work? Jesus gives three reasons for doing so.

First, because of our reward in heaven. Those who are
persecuted because of righteousness are 'blessed' because 'theirs is
the kingdom of heaven' (v.10) and in a similar vein he says to his
disciples, 'Great is your reward in heaven' (v.12). Second, our joy
comes from identifying with Jesus. It is 'because of me' (v.11) that
they are persecuted. Third, it is a sign that our faith is genuine, since
the prophets were persecuted in the same way (v.12). Jesus says
that we are in line with all the people of God who went before us.

The eight attitudes Jesus urges on his disciples are a coherent
whole. Matthew uses the literary device of an 'inclusio' to show
this. Both the first and last beatitude end with, 'For theirs is the
kingdom of heaven'. These should be the attitudes of those

whose desire is to follow Jesus. The eight steps can be summarised as follows:

1. Being spiritually desperate for God
2. Weeping over our condition
3. Allowing ourselves to be broken
4. Being hungry for God
5. Receiving forgiveness and being merciful
6. Being completely sincere
7. Striving to bring peace
8. Expecting nothing in return, except persecution

Jesus told this small group of ordinary people that if they lived like this they would change the world around them. And so they did. In the same way, we are 'the salt of the earth' (v.13). In days before deep freezers and fridges, salt was used to keep meat from going bad. Christians are called to keep society from decay. Salt is also a flavour enhancer. We are called to bring out the full flavours of humanity by living in relationship with God and one another. We are also called to be 'the light of the world' (v.14) and to light up the darkness around us.

In order to change the world around us, it is vital, first of all, for Christians not to withdraw from the world into a Christian sub-culture but to get involved in our society. God sent Jesus to get involved in society. He could have remained aloof and safe in heaven but he chose to get his hands dirty and become immersed in our world. Since we are called to be 'the light of the world' (v.14), we must not put the light in a valley where it cannot be seen, but on a hill (v.14). We do not put lamps under bowls but on stands so that they can give light to the whole house (v.15). So, Jesus says, we must be out there in society letting our lights shine before others so that they may see our good deeds and give praise to God (v.16).

Followers of Jesus need to be salt and light in their work environments. That is why we should not give up working in a secular environment unless we are specifically called out of it. We are called to have an influence in the office, factory, police force, hospital, shop, or wherever it is that we are working. This is where frontline ministry takes place.

We are also called to be salt and light in our neighbourhoods, with our friends and families, and in our leisure activities. Sport, for example, offers an ideal opportunity to get involved in local teams and clubs and to pray that we may be able to be salt and light to those around us.

Further, we are called to play our part as citizens. For some this means direct involvement in local or national politics. Perhaps we have become too cynical about politics; Ronald Reagan said, 'Governments do not solve problems; they merely rearrange them.'[13] However, we need Christians in politics. All of us are called to speak out on issues that conflict with Christianity, to fight for justice, freedom, the dignity of the individual and the abolition of discrimination as well as taking

social action to help those who are casualties of our society.

This calling does not end at our own shores. We live in a world with so many needs. Millions have yet to hear the good news about Jesus Christ. Two thirds of the world's population suffer chronic food deficiencies. 30,000 children die each day because of avoidable diseases, or because they live in poverty, and 8,000 people die of AIDS every day in developing countries. Injustice abounds in our world as human rights are violated and the poor remain oppressed. Now more than ever we are aware of the serious threat that irreversible damage poses to the environment, to our world and to the human race. The Bible teaches that both God and human beings have rights in and responsibilities towards the earth, rather like a landlord and tenant. Mismanagement on our part is a sin against God as well as humankind. We all have a responsibility to be ecological stewards of our world.

While it is easy to feel daunted and overwhelmed by the scale of these problems, there is much we can do. Some will be called to devote their whole lives to the alleviation of global suffering and many, like Mother Teresa or Jackie Pullinger, have brought about change far beyond their expectations. All of us can be aware of the problems, advocate the cause of the poor and offer support with our prayers and our money through agencies such as Tearfund that are working so effectively in the sphere of Christian service.

Second, while not withdrawing from the secular world, we must remain distinctive within it. The salt is different from the meat. The light is different from the world. Jesus warned that, 'If the salt loses its saltiness, how can it be made salty again? It is no longer good for anything, except to be thrown out and trampled by men' (v.13). We are called to live a radically different lifestyle from that of the world around us. If we have the character that Jesus describes in the beatitudes, there is no doubt that we will be radically different. It could be summarised as loving God with all our hearts and loving our neighbours as ourselves. Others will see in us humility, openness, truthfulness, hard work, reliability, the avoidance of gossip, the desire to build up and encourage others, unselfishness, kindness and all the fruits of the Spirit (Galatians 5:22–23).

Third, if we are to change the world around us we must let our light shine before others, 'that they may see your good deeds and praise your Father in heaven' (v.16). Jesus, of course, is our example. His praying, fasting and giving were private (as he taught his disciples to do) but his good works were public. He proclaimed the gospel, healed the sick, raised the dead, set the captives free and fed the hungry. It is because the disciples followed his example that they had such an enormous influence on society. If we follow Jesus and live as Jesus encourages us to live, we do have a purpose and we can transform the world around us.

I began this chapter with a quote from Martin Luther King. I want to end with an excerpt from the sermon he preached at Ebenezer Baptist Church on 4 February 1968, two months before he was assassinated, and which was played at his funeral:

> Every now and then I guess we all think realistically about that day when we will be victimized with what is life's final common denominator – that something we call death. We all think about it. And every now and then I think about my own death, and I think about my own funeral. And I don't think of it in a morbid sense. Every now and then I ask myself, 'What is it that I would want said?' And I leave the word to you this morning.
>
> If any of you are around when I have to meet my day, I don't want a long funeral. And if you get somebody to deliver the eulogy, tell them not to talk too long. Every now and then I wonder what I want them to say. Tell them not to mention that I have a Nobel Peace Prize, that isn't important. Tell them not to mention that I have three or four hundred other awards, that's not important. Tell them not to mention where I went to school.
>
> I'd like somebody to mention that day, that Martin

Luther King tried to give his life serving others. I'd like for somebody to say that day that Martin Luther King tried to love somebody. I want you to say that day that I tried to be right on the war question. I want you to be able to say that day that I did try to feed the hungry. And I want you to be able to say that day that I did try, in my life, to clothe those who were naked. I want you to say on that day that I did try, in my life, to visit those who were in prison. I want you to say that I tried to love and serve humanity. Yes, if you want to say that I was a drum major, say that I was a drum major for justice. Say that I was a drum major for peace, I was a drum major for righteousness.

And all of the other shallow things will not matter. I won't have any money to leave behind. I won't have the fine and luxurious things of life to leave behind. I just want to leave a committed life behind.

And that's all I want to say… if I can help somebody as I pass along, if I can cheer somebody with a word or song, if I can show somebody he's travelling wrong, then my living will not be in vain. If I can do my duty as a Christian ought, if I can bring salvation to a world over wrought, if I can spread the message as the Master taught, then my living will not be in vain.[14]

How to Understand the Old Testament

Do not think that I have come to abolish the Law or the Prophets; I have not come to abolish them but to fulfil them. I tell you the truth, until heaven and earth disappear, not the smallest letter, not the least stroke of a pen, will by any means disappear from the Law until everything is accomplished. Anyone who breaks one of the least of these commandments and teaches others to do the same will be called least in the kingdom of heaven, but whoever practises and teaches these commands will be called great in the kingdom of heaven. For I tell you that unless your righteousness surpasses that of the Pharisees and the teachers of the law, you will certainly not enter the kingdom of heaven.

Matthew 5:17–20

If I am honest, there are parts of the Old Testament that I find confusing and hard to understand. Did Noah really live to the ripe old age of 950? What about all the wars and sacrifices? Why don't we sacrifice oxen in our services anymore? What about the way that women seem to be treated? What about all those wives? Some people feel that the God of the Old Testament is scary, angry and judgmental. I have spoken to many people who say that they like the teaching of Jesus, but not the God of the Old Testament. Others, while accepting the Old Testament as part of God's revelation, in practice do not consider it of great importance and never read it. In addition, many modern atheists are scathing about the God of the Old Testament in particular. Richard Dawkins described him as, 'arguably the most unpleasant character in all fiction... an evil monster and a cruel ogre'.[1]

So why don't we just cut out the Old Testament? This is not a new dilemma. It was also faced by the early church. Marcion, who lived in the second century AD, was a wealthy shipowner, son of a bishop and a superb organiser who set up communities over a large part of the Roman empire. His central thesis was that the Christian gospel is wholly a gospel of love, to

" The New lightweight Ma translation "

the absolute exclusion of law. He rejected the Old Testament in its entirety. However, he found that if you reject the Old Testament, you have to reject quite a lot of the New Testament as well. In fact, he rejected all the writings of the apostles except for Paul, who was his hero. Marcion accepted ten of Paul's letters, but not before making some alterations. With the Gospels he was more cavalier. He rejected all but Luke, and since Luke showed every sign of acknowledging the validity of the Old Testament and the Law, considerable parts of this Gospel had to go as well. He demonstrated the principle that once you take scissors to the Bible, it is very difficult to know where to stop cutting.

I have tried to read the Old Testament regularly since I became a Christian. For many years now I have been reading *The Bible in One Year* every day, which includes a passage from the Old Testament, a passage from the New Testament and a psalm or proverb. If you read the passages for each day it is possible to read the whole Bible each year. I have found this invaluable and my experience has been that God has spoken to me through the Old Testament readings as much as through the rest of the Bible.[3]

The Old Testament contains some of the greatest literature in the world, including some incredible stories, such as those of Abraham, Joseph, Moses, Ruth, David and Daniel.[4] Large numbers of films, TV dramatisations, plays and books retell their life stories. In the Psalms we find some of the most beautiful poetry in the world; in Proverbs some of the greatest wisdom. Moreover, in the Old Testament we find some of the most tender descriptions of God's love for us: his grace, his mercy and his kindness.

When looking at the Old Testament our attitude should reflect that of Jesus. Obviously he never read the New Testament; to him the Old Testament writings were the Scriptures. Jesus' attitude to the Old Testament was exactly the opposite of Marcion's. He stamped the entire Old Testament with his seal of authority (vv.17–18). The Old Testament is sometimes referred to as 'the Law or the Prophets' (v.17) and sometimes as simply 'the Law' (v.18). He taught that 'the Scripture cannot be broken' (John 10:35). He read it, quoted it, believed it and lived by it. Theologian John Wenham sums up Jesus' view of the Old Testament:

> To Christ, the Old Testament was true, authoritative, inspired.
> To him, the God of the Old Testament was the living God,

and the teaching of the Old Testament was the teaching of
the living God. To him, what scripture said, God said.[5]

The Old Testament is a rich and complex library of many books of
different literary genres covering over 1,000 years of history. There
are three main ways to look at the Old Testament. The first is to
look at it as the acts of God in *history*. History is 'his story'. We
see the people of God from Abraham to Joseph; from the Exodus
to the wilderness and the Conquest. We read of the Judges and
the monarchy, the Exile and the return from Exile. How are we to
understand all this? What relevance does it have to our lives today?

A second way of looking at the Old Testament is in terms of
promise. The Old Testament is full of hope and expectation. We
read of the promises to Noah, Abraham, Moses and David. Then,
in the Prophets, we see how God spoke to the people of Israel. The
'former Prophets' are the books of Joshua, Judges, 1 and 2 Samuel
and 1 and 2 Kings. They describe the early history of Israel. The
'latter Prophets' include Isaiah, Jeremiah, Ezekiel and Daniel, and
twelve other lesser-known characters: Hosea, Joel, Amos, Obadiah,
Jonah, Micah, Nahum, Habakkuk, Zephaniah, Haggai, Zechariah
and Malachi.

A third way of looking at the Old Testament is in terms of *law*.
It can be helpful to divide the law into different kinds, and some
scholars have distinguished ceremonial law, civil law and moral
law in the first five books of the Bible.[6] The Hebrew word for law,
torah, really means 'guidance' or 'instruction'.

In the Sermon on the Mount Jesus said that he did not come
to abolish the Old Testament but to fulfil it. What did he mean?
The theme of fulfilment runs through the New Testament and it
is especially drawn out in Matthew's Gospel. The Old Testament
is, of course, a Scripture shared by Jews and Christians, but for
Christians the key to understanding the Old Testament is to read it
through the lens of Jesus. Matthew shows how Jesus fulfilled each

of these three views of the Old Testament and in turn shows us how to understand the Old Testament.

1. Get to know the person

The first chapter of Matthew's Gospel indicates to us that Jesus fulfils God's story: His Gospel begins not with the birth of Jesus, but by summarising the Old Testament story in terms of Jesus' ancestry (Matthew 1:1–17). For Matthew, the Old Testament tells the story that is completed by Jesus. He sets out the history of the people of God in terms of three equal periods: the fourteen generations from Abraham to David, fourteen generations from David to the Exile, and fourteen from the Exile to Christ (Matthew 1:17). In the genealogy, biological generations are skipped over (as was quite common in Old Testament genealogy). He is pointing out that Old Testament history falls into three approximately equal spans of time between crucial events. Jesus is the end of the line as far as the Old Testament story goes – the climax has been reached.

This is the story from which Jesus acquired his identity and mission. It is also the story to which he gave significance and authority. As we read the Old Testament it makes a difference to know that it leads to Jesus and that he gives meaning to it. How then are we to understand the Old Testament in light of the fact that Jesus completes the story?

First, the reality of the Old Testament is affirmed. The Old Testament is more than prediction about Jesus. It is the story of the acts of God in human history out of which promises arise and in relation to which they make sense. The stories tell us about a true, real relationship between God and his people and a real revelation of God to them. For example, the story of Abraham being willing to offer his son, Isaac, as a sacrifice to God, gives us the picture of a God who was willing to sacrifice everything that was most important to him for us. The story of the Exodus tells us about

God's care for the oppressed, the poor and the suffering. It tells of his action for justice on behalf of the exploited. It tells us of a God of redemption who sets his people free.

The Swiss theologian, Karl Barth, said this:

> The Old Testament is not an introduction to the real New Testament Bible which we can dispense with or replace... Again and again Paul stresses... that what happened and what was recorded in the Old Testament was 'for our sakes'. It is evident, therefore, that the desire of the evangelists and the apostles themselves was simply to be expositors of the former Scriptures... Christ has risen from the dead and has revealed the fulfilment of Scripture and therefore its real meaning. In the light of this, how can the church understand the Old Testament witnesses except as witnesses to Christ?[7]

Second, Jesus sheds light backwards on the story. We understand a story in the light of its ending. The Old Testament cannot be fully understood without Jesus. Jesus once said to the Pharisees, who knew the Old Testament in the utmost detail, 'You diligently study the Scriptures because you think that by them you possess eternal life. These are the Scriptures that testify about me, yet you refuse to come to me to have life' (John 5:39–40). If we go into a dark room full of furniture, we may be able to make out something of what is there by feeling the sofas, chairs and pictures. When the light is switched on we are able to see the whole room in a completely different way. So with the light of Jesus we are able to see the whole Old Testament with an additional level of significance. As St Augustine of Hippo saw: 'The new is in the old concealed. The old is in the new revealed.'[8] For example, we may wonder what the sacrificial system was all about. The book of Hebrews shows that it was all leading up to Jesus and preparing the way. It was a shadow; the reality was found in Christ.

Third, the Old Testament helps us gain a full understanding of Christ. Just as it is possible to watch the last act of a play and get a great deal out of it, so it is possible to read the New Testament on its own. However, it helps to watch the earlier acts of the play as well if we are going to understand the climax and conclusion. In order to understand Jesus we need to read the earlier acts of God in the story of our salvation. We cannot understand Jesus fully without understanding the Old Testament background. The Messiah figure (Isaiah 9:2–7), the suffering servant (Isaiah 40–55), the 'son of man' (Daniel 7:13), and the 'son of God' (2 Samuel 7:14) in the Old Testament all point to what it meant that Jesus was Lord.

2. Enjoy the promises

Jesus is not only the completion of the Old Testament story at an historical level, he is also the fulfilment of the Old Testament at the level of 'promise'. In the Christian Bible, the Old Testament ends with prophecy, because the early Christians saw the Old Testament as a promise which Jesus fulfilled. Once Matthew has shown Jesus completing the Old Testament story he then moves on to Jesus fulfilling Old Testament prophecy. He ties up each of the five scenes from the conception, birth and early childhood of Jesus to the Hebrew Scriptures, which have been 'fulfilled' by the events described (Matthew 1:22; 2:5–6, 17, 23; 4:15).

Jesus fulfilled over 300 Old Testament prophecies, including twenty-nine in a single day. His birth in Bethlehem, his early life in Nazareth, his healing miracles, his betrayal, his suffering, his death between thieves, his burial, resurrection, ascension and the outpouring of the Holy Spirit were all predicted in the Old Testament and fulfilled by Jesus, spoken by different voices over a 500-year period. After his resurrection, on the road to Emmaus, Jesus took the two disciples through the Old Testament, 'Beginning with Moses and all the Prophets, he explained to them what was said in all the Scriptures concerning himself' (Luke 24:27).

However, when we say that Jesus fulfilled the promises of the Old Testament we mean more than that he did what had been predicted. The Old Testament is more than a series of predictions. The word 'testament' means 'covenant'. At the heart of the word 'covenant' is the idea of promise. The Old Testament is about the promises of God given on his initiative, yet requiring a human response. This can be seen in all the Old Testament covenants, with Noah, Abraham, Moses and the people of Israel and with David. We see the rich array of the promises of God, like different streams leading to a great river. In the end they all combine into a single current, flowing deep and strong: the ongoing irresistible promise of God finding its climax in a new covenant with the life, death and resurrection of Jesus of Nazareth.

The Old Testament promises were made in terms already within the experience and comprehension of those who received them. This is important, since they are not always fulfilled in the literal form originally given. The fulfilment in terms of what God did in Christ is at a different level of reality. Suppose in 1950 a man promised his young son a black and white TV on his twenty-first birthday. When the time came he gave him a colour TV that had not existed at the time the promise was made. Would the son complain that the promise had not been fulfilled? Would he go on looking for a literal fulfilment? No, because the reality far surpasses the original promise.

All the promises in the Old Testament apply to us, only much more so. St Paul says that 'no matter how many promises God has made, they are "Yes" in Christ' (2 Corinthians 1:20). They are more than fulfilled in Christ, as the Old Testament promised. This is true of all God's promises to us – of love, blessing, guidance, protection. They all find their 'Yes' in Christ.

3. Live it out in practice

The third way to look at the Old Testament is in terms of 'law'. Indeed, we have seen that Jesus himself refers to the Old Testament as 'the law' (v.18). How do we live out the law in practice today? In the prologue to his Gospel, Matthew shows that Jesus fulfils the Old Testament story (Matthew 1:1–17), and in the next section he also shows that Jesus also fulfils the Old Testament promise (Matthew 1:18–4:14). In the Sermon on the Mount he goes further, showing that Jesus fulfils the Old Testament by revealing the full depth and meaning of the Old Testament law.

The law was given as part of God's blessing to his people, in the context of the covenant (Exodus 20). The law was intended for their good, to protect them from harm and to bring them prosperity and life (Deuteronomy 6:24). It was not a means of salvation, but a response to salvation. The motive for keeping the law was gratitude for what God had done for them in bringing them out of Egypt (Exodus 20:2). In keeping the law they would be imitating God (Leviticus 19:2).

Jesus does not repudiate the Old Testament law; rather he radically reinterprets the law. In the Sermon on the Mount Jesus was attacking the scribal misinterpretations of the law. The scribes and Pharisees had found 248 commands and 365 prohibitions in the Old Testament. In the Mishnah and the Talmud, which embody Jewish oral law, they added their own interpretation of these laws, in order to put a hedge of protection around the law and to avoid any possible transgression.

The Old Testament law can be divided more or less into three categories. First, there are the ceremonial laws, which include all the laws relating to priests and sacrifices. The New Testament and in particularly in the book of Hebrews tells us that these have come to an end. It is important to study these laws because they reveal the seriousness of sin, and stress our need for forgiveness. They help explain the significance of Jesus' death on the cross. And now that the one perfect sacrifice has taken place, we no longer need to make sacrifices.

Second, there are the civil laws, specifically applying to ancient Israel. The principles of these laws can still apply today, but the details do not. For example, we read in Leviticus, 'When you reap the harvest of your land, do not reap to the very edges of your field or gather the gleanings of your harvest. Do not go over your vineyard a second time or pick up the grapes that have fallen. Leave them for the poor' (Leviticus 19:9–10). This does not mean that we should not use combine harvesters, and that we should not plough to the edge of fields. Yet it does tell us that whatever our business is, we should make sure we remember the poor.

Third, there are the moral laws: 'You shall not murder', 'You shall not commit adultery' (Exodus 20:13–14). These laws still apply to us today, but Jesus widens them further. He does not reverse them, rather he shows their full meaning. In the rest of the Sermon on the Mount, Jesus goes on to show that this meaning is not outward and concerned with external observance, but inward and moral. He interprets them, not by adding new rules, but by showing that at the heart of the law is the law of the heart: the law of mind and motive. He shows what the law really means in terms of anger, lust, fidelity, integrity and care for others. He called his disciples to a righteousness that surpassed that of the scribes and Pharisees (v.20). He was not contradicting the Old Testament, but going in the same direction. He was building on it and surpassing it, whereas the scribal misinterpretations and additions were going in the opposite direction, in that they led to legalism.

Jesus summarised the law as loving God and loving our neighbour (Matthew 22:37–40). We need this summary to keep us from legalism. On the other hand we need the detailed breakdown of the laws to keep us from sentimentality. It is no good thinking that adultery is 'loving our neighbour' when adultery is specifically forbidden. The Highway Code could be summarised as, 'Drive carefully and considerately'. That is what really matters. On the other hand we need the detailed rules to tell us how to drive carefully and considerately.

So Jesus fulfilled the Old Testament law by showing us what it really meant. Jesus also fulfilled the law in the sense that he lived it out. He is the only person who has ever done this because only he has ever lived a sinless life. As German theologian Dietrich Bonhoeffer said about Jesus and the Old Testament laws, 'He has in fact nothing to add... except this, that he keeps them'.[9] He lived a righteous life. Jesus' life is an example of how to keep the Old Testament law.

Jesus also fulfilled the law in that he made it possible for *us* to live a righteous life. Through his death and resurrection he set us free from the power of sin and provided for us a righteousness that comes from God (Romans 3:21–26). He enabled the Spirit of God to be poured out.

What the law was powerless to do in that it was weakened by the sinful nature, God did by sending his own Son in the

likeness of sinful humanity to be a sin offering. And so he condemned sin in our sinful nature, in order that the righteous requirements of the law might be fully met in us, who do not live according to the sinful nature but according to the Spirit.
Romans 8:3–4

So Marcion was wrong. To reject the Old Testament is to reject the clear teaching of Jesus. Jesus did not reject it. He meditated on it. He endorsed and fulfilled it. The gospel of love is not opposed to the Old Testament; rather it is complementary. It sets us free from the condemnation of the law (Romans 8:1), but not from the commands. Rather Jesus gives us the desire and the power to fulfil the real meaning of the law and to live righteous lives. The church understood that Jesus endorses the law. This is why they rejected Marcion; in AD 144 he was excommunicated for immorality and heresy.

To summarise:

> The Old Testament tells the story which Jesus completed. It declares the promise which he fulfilled. It provides the pictures and models which shaped his identity. It programmes a mission which he accepted and passed on. It teaches the moral orientation to God and the world, which he endorsed, sharpened and laid as the foundation for obedient discipleship.[10]

We need to be reading the Old Testament regularly, seeking to understand it, not only in terms of the culture and history in which it was written, but also, ultimately, in the light of Jesus' fulfilment of it. Then we need to go back to the New Testament and reread it with a fresh understanding of who Jesus was and is.

How to Handle Anger

You have heard that it was said to the people long ago, 'Do not murder, and anyone who murders will be subject to judgment.' But I tell you that anyone who is angry with a brother or sister will be subject to judgment. Again, anyone who says to his brother or sister, 'Raca,' is answerable to the Sanhedrin. But anyone who says, 'You fool!' will be in danger of the fire of hell.

Therefore, if you are offering your gift at the altar and there remember that your brother or sister has something against you, leave your gift there in front of the altar. First go and be reconciled to them; then come and offer your gift.

Settle matters quickly with your adversary who is taking you to court. Do it while you are still together, or your adversary may hand you over to the judge, and the judge may hand you over to the officer, and you may be thrown into prison. I tell you the truth, you will not get out until you have paid the last penny.
Matthew 5:21-26

A young girl who was writing an essay for school came to her father and asked, 'Dad, what is the difference between anger and exasperation?' The father replied, 'It is mostly a matter of degree. Let me show you what I mean.' With that her father went to the telephone and dialled a number at random. To the man who answered the phone, he said, 'Hello, is Melvin there?' The man answered, 'There is no one here called Melvin. Why don't you learn to look up numbers before you dial them?' 'See,' said the father to his daughter. 'That man was not a bit happy with our call. He was probably very busy with something and we annoyed him. Now watch...' The father dialled the number again. 'Hello, is Melvin there?' asked the father. 'Now look here!' came the heated reply. 'You

just called this number and I told you that there is no Melvin here! You've got a lot of nerve calling again!' The receiver was slammed down hard. The father turned to his daughter and said, 'You see that was anger. Now I'll show you what exasperation means.' He again dialled the same number and when a violent voice roared 'Hello!' the father calmly said, 'Hello, this is Melvin. Have there been any calls for me?'

A *Sunday Times* article showed that anger is more common than we might think. More than 80 per cent of drivers say they have been involved in road rage incidents; 64 per cent of Britons working in an office have experienced 'office rage'; 71 per cent of internet users admit to having suffered 'net rage'; and 50 per cent of us have reacted to computer problems by hitting our PC, hurling parts of it around and screaming.[1]

"There goes another laptop"

It is easy to justify our own anger and condemn that of others. This tendency was picked up on by the

New Statesman, '*You* are annoyed; *he* is making a fuss about nothing; *I* am righteously indignant.' Many today regard anger as part of self-assertion and anger management courses stress the 'right to be angry'.

But what does Jesus say about anger? Is all anger wrong? Is there such a thing as constructive anger? How should we handle our anger? These are some of the questions I want to look at in this chapter.

1. Consider the cause

Jesus says, 'But I tell you that anyone who is angry with a brother or sister will be subject to judgment' (v.22). Some manuscripts add the words 'without cause'. These words are not in the earliest texts of Matthew's Gospel, but arguably they are a correct interpretation of Jesus' teaching. Not all anger is wrong. Jesus himself was angry at times. Matthew, along with the other Gospel writers, recalls how he overturned the tables of the money-changers in the Temple area (Matthew 21:12). He called the Pharisees 'You blind fools!' (Matthew 23:17). On one occasion, when he saw their 'stubborn hearts' and a lack of compassion for the sick, Jesus looked at them 'in anger' (Mark 3:1–6).

So there is such a thing as righteous anger. In the Old Testament there are twenty different words for 'wrath' and between them they are used 580 times. The prophets and the psalmists use strongly personal terms when they speak of the anger of the Lord (Isaiah 30:27; Jeremiah 23:20; Ezekiel 8:18).

Sometimes people so emphasise the anger of God that there is a suggestion that God has a dual nature – that he is love and wrath. Nowhere in the Bible does it say that God is wrath. However it does say that God is love (1 John 4:16). His anger is part of his holy love, a flame that sears and purifies. There is no moral flabbiness in God. Anger is God's personal reaction to sin. He loves people and he is angry on behalf of the victims of oppression, injustice, and cruelty. C. S. Lewis says, 'Such anger is the fluid that love bleeds when you cut it.'[2]

For the rest of us there is also a place for righteous anger. Indignation against wickedness is surely an essential element of human goodness in a world in which moral evil is always present. How can a person who knows, for example, about the evil of terrorism or the sexual abuse of children fail to be angry? Our lack of anger can reveal a failure to love and to care for our fellow human beings. Therefore there is a difference between righteous and unrighteous anger. Even righteous anger can easily be turned into self-righteous arrogance that tolerates no difference of opinion and opposition.

" This is righteous anger... its allowed "

Anger is an emotion and a natural passion. Physically, it causes many changes in our bodies. Adrenalin flows, hunger disappears, we have a clearer and more focused vision, an increased supply of the male hormone testosterone, and glucose is released from the reserves in our livers. This energy can be channelled in a constructive way. The abolitionist William Wilberforce (1759–1833), for example, channelled his righteous anger against the slave trade towards a constructive purpose. Martin Luther (1483–1546), the great reformer, wrote, 'When I am angry I can write, pray and preach well, for then my whole temperament is quickened, my understanding sharpened, and all mundane vexations and temptations depart.'[3] We need men and women like Wilberforce and Luther today, who will be roused with a passion (which includes anger), who will see the evil that exists in the church and the world and be driven to do something about it.

The difficulty we face as fallen human beings is making sure we do not sin when we are angry. St Paul wrote, 'In your anger do not sin' (Ephesians 4:26). Over 300 years earlier Aristotle (348–322 BC) wrote, 'Anybody can become angry... [that] is easy; but [to be angry] with the right person and to the right degree and at the right time, and for the right purpose, and in the right way – that is not within everybody's power and is not easy'.[4] Our anger tends, on the whole, to be unrighteous. Unlike Jesus, we get angry because we are hurt, jealous, proud or arrogant, our toes have been trodden on or our noses put out of joint. For example, I recently saw on the news anti-war protestors – peace protestors – hurling stones at the police! Richard Chartres, the Bishop of London, has written, 'I have discovered that there are many unwholesomely angry people who claim to be committed to studies in the field of peace and justice.'[5]

The test as to whether our anger is justified or without cause is to work out whether it is based on love for others, or simply love for ourselves. Jesus' anger was directed against sin and injustice; it was the judicial anger of one who was given authority by God to judge. It was always based on love of others; his personal ego was not wrapped up in it. When he was arrested, unfairly tried, tortured and then crucified, 'he did not retaliate; when he suffered, he made no threats' (1 Peter 2:23). When hanging on the cross in agony, attacked, oppressed, exploited, hurt and rejected he did not say, 'I have a right to feel angry.' Rather he said, 'Father, forgive...' (Luke 23:34).

There are several Greek words for anger. The word used in this passage means 'long-lived anger', the anger of a person who nurses wrath to keep it warm. It means 'anger that broods, refuses to be pacified and seeks revenge'. Jesus says that these angry feelings may not be capable of being examined in a human court, but they are accountable in the court of heaven (v.22).

Jesus sees anger as the root of murder. The process starts with angry feelings. If they are nursed, hatred follows, and if unchecked, the fruit is sometimes actual murder. St John makes the same point when he says, 'Anyone who hates a brother or sister is a murderer' (1 John 3:15). What Jesus is concerned with in this passage is the wrong sort of anger – an anger that lies unresolved in the heart, festering until it bursts forth in destructive behaviour. How should we deal with our angry feelings?

2. Press the pause button

In describing the character of God the Bible often tells us that he is 'slow to anger' (Psalm 145:8). Conversely we also read that the 'fool is hotheaded' (Proverbs 14:16), that 'the quick-tempered do foolish things' (Proverbs 14:17) and 'Do not be quickly provoked in your spirit, for anger resides in the lap of fools' (Ecclesiastes 7:9). The third President of the United States, Thomas Jefferson, said, 'When angry, count ten before you speak. If very angry, one hundred.'⁶ Someone else said that we should learn a lesson from the space shuttle and always count down before blasting off!

The danger of email is that it enables people to respond very quickly when they are angry. Bishop Sandy Millar told how his father-in-law, who was a lawyer, always used to say: 'When you're angry, write a letter. Leave it overnight. Read it again in the morning and tear it up.'

Pressing the pause button gives us time to reflect. It also gives us time to talk to other people about the cause of our anger. We should not bury our anger; we should speak with wise friends whom we can trust, who themselves are not quick-tempered.

The book of Proverbs warns us not to make

'One thousand and one, one thousand and two ...'

friends with a hot-tempered person, 'Do not associate with those who are easily angered, or you may learn their ways and get yourself ensnared' (Proverbs 22:24–25). When I became a Christian it was a great help to me that I was sharing a room at university with a friend called Nicky Lee. Nicky is a man of absolute patience who has a wonderful way of handling difficult situations. Since then I have been married to Pippa, who has the patience of a saint! Being around people who model a positive approach to anger and having the opportunity to discuss it has made a huge difference in my life. We are not supposed to push anger down but to talk it out and then to work out a way to respond in love.

3. Watch your words

Jesus warns us that words are powerful and that they can be extremely damaging. He says, 'Anyone who says to a brother or sister, "Raca," is answerable to the Sanhedrin. But anyone who says, "You fool!" will be in danger of the fire of hell' (v.22). The word 'Raca' is an Aramaic term that conveys contempt for a person's mind. It is the equivalent of calling someone an 'imbecile' or an 'idiot'. The Greek word for 'fool' suggests contempt for their heart or character. Some have tried to suggest that these two words that Jesus used are particularly objectionable words. But that is to misunderstand his message. Jesus is using examples of the lightest terms of abuse and warning us of their danger.

Angry words pierce the heart. They are intended to hurt and destroy. They are extremely damaging to relationships and if left unchecked they can even lead to murder. I will never forget hearing a mother of a small child with whom she was very angry, shouting at her, 'I'll kill you!' Jesus is warning here that such words break the sixth commandment and that they are the first step on a road that leads in a dangerous direction.

Of course, loving confrontation is sometimes necessary and children need discipline. Disagreements need to be brought out into the open and truth is more important than a superficial peace. Personal growth involves being willing to learn from criticism as well as encouragement. Jesus is not suggesting that we suppress all feelings and emotions. Rather he is warning against reacting out of anger because we have been hurt in some way.

Nor is this a minor matter. The threat of judgment was part of the Mosaic legislation dealing with murder. The murderer would appear before a human court and be judged. Jesus warns that angry feelings and words are equally subject to judgment. Calling a brother 'Raca' renders the person liable to the Sanhedrin (the highest Jewish court in the land). Calling him a fool puts him in danger of hell. Gehenna, the name Jesus uses here, was the valley of Hinnem, the ravine south of Jerusalem where rubbish was dumped and burned. Jesus often used the word as a picture of the final judgment. The list of judgments is not an escalating succession of threats, but a warning that God is behind all judgment, based on his assessment of the heart and that feelings and words can lead to ultimate destruction. He is not equating angry words and feelings with murder, but using the language of hyperbole to warn of the dangers of vengeful anger.

I love being a part of our church because it is a safe place. It is a blessing to be a part of a Christian community in which we do not need to be afraid that people are going to get angry; rather we are encouraged. Of course, we are far from being a perfect church. But I am privileged to work with people who express love, affirmation, acceptance, forgiveness and grace. This breaks the vicious cycle that anger can cause. Proverbs 15:1 says, 'A gentle answer turns away wrath, but a harsh word stirs up anger.' This is one of the things that is so beautiful about a community of love, where words are used to build each other up in a positive way.

4. Master your mind

'You have heard that it was said to the people long ago, "Do not murder, and anyone who murders will be subject to judgment." But I tell you anyone who is angry with his brother or sister will be subject to judgment' (vv.21–22). Jesus makes a contrast, not between the law given through Moses and his teaching, but between a false interpretation of Moses and a true interpretation. Moses said, 'You shall not murder' (Exodus 20:13) and the word 'murder' indicates a criminal killing. The false interpretation is to limit the command to the physical act of murder. Jesus traces murder back to the secret place of the human heart where the thought processes that lead to murder begin.

So we have to win the battle of the mind. As Philip Henry (1631–96) put it, 'When anger was in Cain's heart, murder was not far off.'[7] Jesus says that the place to begin is early on, with the initial feelings of anger. They need to be dealt with ruthlessly. We have to win the battle of the mind.

5. Count the cost

Jesus talks about the consequences of anger: 'the danger of the fire of hell (v.22)... you may be thrown into prison' (v.25). Our anger can have dire results. In some cases it literally leads to a prison sentence. A cricketer named Bryn Derbyshire who had been given out 'leg before wicket' reversed his car at high speed at the umpire, who hurt his arm as he leapt clear. Members of the opposing team came to the rescue and one smashed the sun roof of Derbyshire's car with a cricket stump.

In court Derbyshire, aged thirty-seven, admitted causing bodily harm by wanton furious driving after the match between his team, Old Park, of Nottingham, and a side from Blyth, Nottinghamshire.

Nottingham Crown Court gave him a three-month suspended sentence and ordered him to pay compensation of £400 to the 59-year-old umpire, Joseph Purser. Afterwards Mr Purser said: 'I stand by my decision. He was out.'

On a more serious note, I read recently in *The Times* an article about an incident that occurred in Fulham, very near to our church:

> This week a female passenger on a bus in Fulham, West London, knocked a 62-year-old woman to the floor, stamped on her face, simply because her newspaper had brushed her arm. The victim needed surgery for her injuries.[8]

Jesus is saying is that this kind of anger sometimes leads to the destruction of relationships, families, and marriages, the abuse of children, violent crime and the breakdown of communities. St Paul says, 'Do not let the sun go down while you are still angry, and do not give the devil a foothold' (Ephesians 4:26–27).

In many ways, anger is like dry rot. A few weeks after Pippa and I moved into our first house, we discovered a small area of rot on a

"I still have ten minutes before I have to apologise"

doorframe. As we began to look for the source, we discovered that the whole basement was riddled with dry rot. Apparently, in the right conditions it can spread up to three feet in a week. For the most part it is hidden behind walls and door frames, and to begin with it is hard to see. If left unchecked it brings sudden devastation. The only way to deal with it is quickly and with drastic action. In the same way, we need to deal immediately with anger in relationships and take drastic action.

6. Pursue peace

The theologian Stanley Hauerwas says that Christians are, 'A people committed to peace in a world at war.' [9] Jesus gives two practical examples about how to deal with situations where anger has caused division in relationships. First, when there is a Christian with whom we are very angry, Jesus says that we are to *settle out of church*. Disharmony destroys the church. When Christians get angry with one another, when they attack and insult their brothers and sisters, the body of Christ is split.

Second, Jesus says we are to *settle out of court*. He takes us from the temple to the courtroom, or rather just outside the courtroom, and says: 'Settle matters quickly with your adversary who is taking you to court. Do it while you are still together on the way, or your adversary may hand you over to the judge, and the judge may hand you over to the officer, and you may be thrown into prison. I tell you the truth, you will not get out until you have paid the last penny' (vv.25–26).

Under Roman law there were certain crimes, such as theft, burglary and kidnapping, for which the offender could be subject to summary arrest. If the criminal was caught red-handed, the offended citizen caught hold of the man's robe at the throat and held him in a stranglehold so that he could not escape. If the defendant was found guilty, he was handed over to the court officer whose duty it was to ensure that the penalty was paid. He had the power to imprison defaulters, who would not get out until they had paid the 'last penny'. The Greek word refers to an infinitesimal sum.

This is not an allegory, so we cannot apply every detail to our own situations today. Rather it is a parable, in which Jesus warns us of the dangers of getting involved in quarrels and especially in litigation. The nineteenth-century preacher, C. H. Spurgeon, commenting on these verses pointed out that 'a lean settlement is better than a fat law-suit', and remarked, 'Many go into the court to get wool, but come out closely shorn.'[10] I know from my own experience practising as a barrister how true this is. I have seen many cases in which both parties would have been far better off if only they could have settled these differences without the need of a court case. Often it is unresolved anger that spurs the parties on, in spite of the consequences.

The way to deal with anger is to engage in reconciliation. We are to take positive steps to restore relationships. Jesus says, 'Therefore, if you are offering your gift at the altar and there remember that your brother or sister has something against you, leave your gift there in front of the altar. First go and be reconciled to them; then come and offer your gift' (vv.23–24).

The lay worshipper brought his gift, along with an animal or otherwise, to the temple for sacrifice. It is implied that he has been in the wrong. Jesus says there is no point in offering the gift until he is reconciled with his brother. Jesus points out that our anger in human relationships erects a barrier, not only between us and other brothers and sisters in Christ, but also between us and God.

It is not just our own anger that creates this barrier. If we are conscious that we have angered someone else we must equally cease worship and seek reconciliation. Ugandan bishop Festo Kivengere told how he was going off to preach after a row with his wife. The Holy Spirit said to him, 'Go back and pray with your wife!' He argued, 'I'm due to preach in twenty minutes. I'll do it afterwards.' 'OK,' said the Holy Spirit. 'You go and preach; I'll stay with your wife.'[11]

Worship cannot be detached from conduct. They are inextricably linked. In one sense, our conduct flows from our worship. In another sense, it is only when our conduct is right that we are in a fit state to worship God. This is what the prophets pointed out over and over again (Isaiah 1:10–17; Jeremiah 7:9–11; Amos 5:21–24; Micah 6:6–8).

The standard Jesus sets in this passage is extraordinarily high. It is his first example of an area in which we are called to a 'righteousness [which] surpasses that of the Pharisees and the teachers of the law' (v.20). We all fall so far short of his standards. As we read this passage, surely we are all conscious of our own failings and weaknesses. We are brought back to the cross to cry out for mercy and forgiveness. The forgiveness we receive gives us the strength to forgive and seek reconciliation. As we see what our offences did to Jesus, it is hard to be angry with our brothers and sisters.

Dealing with anger involves both receiving and giving forgiveness, through the cross of Christ. It requires a determined act of the will to deal ruthlessly with anger and root it out from our lives. This cannot be achieved without the help of the Holy Spirit. Corrie ten Boom, who was involved in the Dutch Resistance and imprisoned by the Nazis in the Ravensbrück concentration camp, describes how all these three are involved in dealing with anger:

> It was in a church in Munich that I saw him, a balding heavy-set man in a grey overcoat, a brown felt hat clutched between his hands. People were filing out of the basement room where I had just spoken, moving along the rows of wooden

chairs to the door at the rear. It was 1947 and I had come from Holland to defeated Germany with the message that God forgives.

It was the truth they needed most to hear in that bitter, bombed-out land, and I gave them my favourite mental picture. Maybe because the sea is never far from a Hollander's mind, I liked to think that that's where forgiven sins were thrown. 'When we confess our sins,' I said, 'God casts them into the deepest ocean, gone forever.'

The solemn faces stared back at me, not quite daring to believe. There were never questions after a talk in Germany in 1947. People stood up in silence, in silence collected their wraps, in silence left the room.

And that's when I saw him, working his way forward against the others. One moment I saw the overcoat and the brown hat; the next, a blue uniform and a vizored cap with its skull and crossbones. It came back with a rush: the huge room with its harsh overhead lights, the pathetic pile of dresses and shoes in the centre of the floor, the shame of walking naked past this man. I could see my sister's frail form ahead of me, ribs sharp beneath the parchment skin. Betsie, how thin you were!

Betsie and I had been arrested for concealing Jews in our home during the Nazi occupation of Holland; this man had been a guard at Ravensbrück concentration camp where we were sent.

Now he was in front of me, hand thrust out: 'A fine message, Fräulein! How good it is to know that, as you say, all our sins are at the bottom of the sea!'

And I, who had spoken so glibly of forgiveness, fumbled in my wallet rather than take that hand. He would not remember me, of course – how could he remember one prisoner among those thousands of women?

But I remembered him and the leather crop swinging from his belt. It was the first time since my release that I had been face to face with one of my captors and my blood seemed to freeze. 'You mentioned Ravensbrück in your talk,' he was saying. 'I was a guard in there.' No, he did not remember me.

'But since that time,' he went on, 'I have become a Christian. I know that God has forgiven me for the cruel things I did there, but I would like to hear it from your lips as well. Fräulein ' – again the hand came out – 'will you forgive me?'

And I stood there – I whose sins had every day to be forgiven – and could not. Betsie had died in that place – could he erase her slow terrible death simply for the asking?

It could not have been many seconds that he stood there, hand held out, but to me it seemed hours as I wrestled with the most difficult thing I had ever had to do. For I had to do it – I knew that. The message that God forgives has a prior condition: that we forgive those who have injured us. 'If you do not forgive men their trespasses,' Jesus says, 'neither will your Father in heaven forgive your trespasses.'

I knew it not only as a commandment of God, but as a daily experience. Since the end of the war I had had a home in Holland for victims of Nazi brutality. Those who were able to forgive their former enemies were able also to return to the outside world and rebuild their lives, no matter what the physical scars. Those who nursed bitterness remained invalids. It was as simple and as horrible as that.

And still I stood there with the coldness clutching my heart. But forgiveness is not an emotion – I knew that too. Forgiveness is an act of the will, and the will can function regardless of the temperature of the heart. 'Jesus, help me!' I prayed silently. 'I can lift my hand. I can do that much. You supply the feeling.'

And so woodenly, mechanically, I thrust my hand into the one stretched out to me. And as I did, an incredible thing took place. The current started in my shoulder, raced down my arm, sprang into our joined hands. And then this healing warmth seemed to flood my whole being, bringing tears to my eyes.

'I forgive you, brother!' I cried. 'With all my heart!' For a long moment we grasped each other's hands, the former guard and the former prisoner. I had never known God's love so intensely as I did then.[12]

How to Understand Sex in the Twenty-First Century

*You have heard that it was said, 'Do not commit adultery.'
But I tell you that anyone who looks at a woman lustfully
has already committed adultery with her in his heart. If
your right eye causes you to sin, gouge it out and throw it
away. It is better for you to lose one part of your body than
for your whole body to be thrown into hell. And if your
right hand causes you to sin, cut it off and throw it away. It
is better for you to lose one part of your body than for your
whole body to go into hell.*
Matthew 5:27–30

Our culture seems to be increasingly obsessed with sex. Sex before
marriage is now regarded as the norm; it is assumed that it is
necessary to test whether you are physically compatible. Thirty or
forty years ago the pressure from parents was not to have sex before
marriage. Now there is substantial pressure in the other direction:
if you are not having sex before marriage people may be worried
for you and you may be made to feel abnormal, or even stupid.

Pornography has now become more mainstream. According to
a survey in the *Sunday Times*, 'using internet porn has been cited by
40 per cent of couples suffering relationship problems.'[1]

The physical act of an adulterous sexual relationship has
become far more acceptable. Celebrities thrive on it and politicians
no longer resign when it has been revealed they have carried on
relationships outside their marriage.

In order to understand Jesus' teaching on this subject, we need
to consider the biblical view of sex which underlies it. I want to

begin by looking at the biblical framework for sex through the themes of creation, fall, redemption and glorification.

Creation: Sex is good

The Bible tells us that sex was created by God, affirming its goodness (Genesis 1:26–31). So, sexual desire is good and healthy; it is God's beautiful gift. C. S. Lewis often used to say that pleasure is God's idea, not the devil's. God is not surprised by sex, he came up

with the idea. He is not looking down at the earth and thinking, 'Oh my goodness, what will they get up to next?!'

Sex brings delight and contentment. In fact, there is a whole book of the Bible, the Song of Songs, devoted to the subject. We are not meant to feel guilty about its enjoyment in its proper context. But what is the proper context?

It is God's design that sex should cement the relationship of marriage. Marriage brings about a union that is not just physical and biological, but emotional, psychological, spiritual and social. Sex not only expresses that union, it also brings it about.

Fall: Sex is complicated

The second great theme that runs through the Bible is that of the fall. All of us have fallen short in every area of our lives, including in the area of sex, and therefore sex is complicated and difficult. For many people it is a very painful subject. This is true for men and women, married and unmarried, Christians and non-Christians.

The American pastor Rob Bell writes:

You are not alone. Whatever you struggle with, whatever you have questions about, you are not alone. It doesn't matter how dark it is or how much shame or weakness or regret it involves; you're not alone... We have cravings and desires and urges and temptations that can easily consume us and make us feel helpless in their presence... Some of the most comforting words in the universe are 'me too.' That moment when you find out that your struggle is also someone else's struggle, that you're not alone, and that others have been down the same road.[2]

For this reason it is important that we are open and honest when addressing this subject. But how do we respond to these difficulties?

Redemption: Sex can be restored

The third great theme that runs through the Bible is that of redemption. Sex can be restored. Jesus died for you and for me, which means that we can make a fresh start. It does not matter how far we have fallen or how much we feel we have messed up; forgiveness is possible. Those who have experienced abuse in the past may find it particularly difficult to forgive. However, the cross and resurrection of Jesus are the source of forgiveness and of our ability to forgive, as well as the healing of wounds and the power to live differently. But how?

Glorification: Sex is not an end in itself

The fourth great theme that runs through the Bible is that of glorification. This earthly life is not the end, and so sex is not an end in itself; it points to something even more amazing. Therefore being single is a valid way to be a Christian today. Everyone is single at some stage in their lives. After all, Jesus himself was single.

Rob Bell, again, said:

> If you are single, and you've been sent messages or it's been hinted at or even said to your face that you are somehow missing something, that you aren't good enough, that you don't fit – that is not true. It's not just that you're fine single. The premise of the Scriptures is that you are able to connect with God and serve God in ways that those who are married can't.[3]

Ultimately, marriage and sex are only a picture, a glimpse, of something even more glorious that is to come.

"Single? Oh dear.. are you ill?"

The introduction to the Anglican wedding service summarises the purposes of marriage. First, there is the joy of companionship, 'that as man and woman grow together in love and trust, they shall be united with one another in heart, body and mind, as Christ is united with his bride, the Church.' Second, marriage is the context for children to be brought up in an atmosphere of security and love. For the children, the relationship between the parents is even more important than the parent/child relationship. Third, there is the joy of physical union: 'The gift of marriage brings husband and wife together in the delight and tenderness of sexual union and joyful commitment to the end of their lives.'[4]

Adultery, which means sexual intercourse with a person who is not one's spouse, is expressly forbidden by the seventh commandment (Exodus 20:14; Deuteronomy 5:18). In the Old

Testament the Mosaic penalty for adultery was stoning. It was taken so seriously because of the damage it does to marriage. It is a form of unfaithfulness, which often wrecks a marriage. It is almost always secret and almost inevitably leads to pain. All the parties involved are hurt in one way or another, especially any children.

So what was Jesus' teaching in this area?

1. Be radical

Being a Christian is not just a nice addition to your life, as though we could say 'I've bought a car', 'I've joined the gym', 'I've become a Christian.' Rather, it is both radical and counter-cultural, and always has been. Jesus intensifies and sharpens the seventh commandment. He says, 'You have heard that it was said, "Do not commit adultery." But *I* tell you that anyone who looks at a woman lustfully has already committed adultery with her in his heart' (vv.27–28, italics mine). In the culture of Jesus' day there were those who were trying to limit the seventh commandment, 'Do not commit adultery' to the physical act of adultery. As before, Jesus is not contradicting the law of Moses; he is saying that this command applies not just to the physical act but to the heart and mind as well. The command not to commit adultery is not just about the letter of the law; it is about the spirit. So it applies to everyone: men and women, married and unmarried.

What Jesus is saying in this passage is radical. In fact, in this respect our culture is moving in completely the opposite direction to the teaching of Jesus. There is an increasing relaxation of all sexual standards, but especially regarding adultery, and the resulting breakdown in family life is unravelling the very fabric of our society.

Jesus calls us to be different. I recently read an interview with a young Film Studies graduate, aged twenty-two, who said that she was still a virgin:

> 'I've decided that when I have sex for the first time I want it to be special and I will wait until my wedding night.'
>
> *Having watched her friends get hurt over the years, she feels vindicated by her decision.*
>
> 'A lot of my friends have casual flings, and I've noticed that the ones who jump into bed with someone too soon are the ones who often get hurt the most when the relationship flounders. People may be surprised that I'm still a virgin in my twenties, because there's such pressure on young women to 'enjoy themselves' and apparently feel liberated by having lots of lovers. Because of my choices, I've never had to worry about sexually transmitted diseases, pregnancy or any of the other troubles which can go hand in hand with casual sex. But it has not been easy.'[5]

It is not easy to be different; one can feel like the odd one out when trying to meet the standards set by Jesus. It takes courage to swim against the tide. For some this will involve enduring ridicule. But Jesus tells us that this radically different way of living is so beautiful and so wonderful that it is something to which everyone can aspire. Even if it is more difficult, it is far more fulfilling and exciting than the alternative.

2. Be romantic

Jesus gives us the context in which the gift of sex is to be enjoyed to the full: 'For this reason a man will leave his father and mother and be united to his wife, and the two will become one flesh. So they are no longer two, but one. Therefore what God has joined together, let no one separate' (Matthew 19:5–6).

Jesus tells us that it is not just love and sex that go together. Sex also goes together with long-term commitment in marriage. Such commitment is shown today in our society by the marriage vows. Marriage is not just a piece of paper, nor is the wedding day simply dressing up and having a party with family and friends; it is a public, responsible expression of lifelong commitment. It is in this context that sex then signifies, seals and brings about an unbreakable, personal unity. Without such a commitment, sex is cheapened; it becomes a life-uniting act without a life-uniting intention. The life-uniting intent is evidenced by marriage alone. To be engaged is not enough because engagements can be broken; this is the whole point of a period of engagement. Irrevocable commitment comes only with the public act of marriage. In this context the act of sex is 'the epicentre of the personal centre of a marriage'.[6]

The Bishop of Kensington and President of St Mellitus College in London, the Right Reverend Dr Graham Tomlin, says, 'Sex is the mysterious, ecstatic union of two created beings who are bound together inextricably in a lifelong, permanent bond. We are on holy ground.'[7] Sex is designed in a way that the association of the pleasure of sex should be with one person only, and in that context it acts like glue. It is so beautiful that it is worth waiting for. John Diamond, the journalist, wrote in *The Times* about those who have waited until their wedding day:

> Those who've waited have something to look forward to. They leave their parents' home on the morning of the wedding as children and climb into bed that night as adults. There's so much to play with and all at the same time: the new house, the giggling joint washing-up sessions, the bed, the joint chequebook. And because it all started with the

wedding, it all becomes part of the same adventure. The rest of us, the over-the-broomstick lot, we get up, we tap our partners on the shoulder, make jokey gulping noises, get a minicab round to the register office, listen to our mates making faux ironic jokes about what we'll be getting up to tonight, ho-ho, and then come back and do last night's washing-up. We try out the new Mr and Mrs names for a day or two, then realise that our joint chequebook and the mortgage are in the old names anyway, and we go back to them. We've done chequebooks a dozen times and decided on the new paint for the hall a hundred. There's nothing new you can tell us about the socks-on-the-bathroom-floor conundrum and whose-turn-is-it-to-do-Waitrose mantra is one we know by heart. Our own marital plans mean we're stuck on the Woolwich ferry arguing about who forgot to bring the packed lunch, while newly-met newlyweds can set sail on their magical voyage of discovery.[8]

Having celebrated dozens of weddings at our church, I have seen that there is a difference with a couple who have not slept together before their wedding day. You can sense it in the atmosphere. There is something thrilling, new and adventurous about it because they have the rest of their life to unpack and enjoy this amazing gift.

An actor well-known for his romantic roles was asked during a television interview, 'What makes a great lover?' He answered: 'A great lover is someone who can satisfy one woman all her life long and who can be satisfied by one woman all his life long. A great lover is not someone who goes from woman to woman; any dog could do that.' Of course, this applies to men and women alike.

This is the most romantic view that there is of sex and marriage and Jesus tells us not to let anything tarnish it.

3. Be repentant

If the standard were merely the Pharisees' standard, many of us would be able to say that we had not broken the command, 'You shall not commit adultery.' However, when Jesus shows us its true meaning, surely all of us become conscious of our failure. Can any of us honestly say that we have never looked at someone else with lust in our hearts? So what can we do when we fail?

We know because of the cross and the resurrection of Jesus that it is never too late to start again; to receive forgiveness. Even one of the great heroes in the Bible, King David, made mistakes in this area and his actions resulted in dire consequences for the history of Israel (2 Samuel:11–12). David committed adultery, had a child by that union and killed the husband of the woman that he wanted to marry. But he came to his senses and recognised that he had sinned. In Psalm 51 we see David's prayer of repentance. He did not try to justify himself or make excuses, but rather accepted responsibility and cried out for mercy.

David did not escape the consequences of his sin, but his guilt was removed. We do not need to go on feeling guilty. David prayed for and recovered much of what he had lost. He recovered a sense of the presence of God, the power of the Spirit, the joy of his salvation, his enthusiasm for God's work, his effectiveness and his intimacy with God.

If we have been sinning in this area, we need to stop. The word repentance is a very positive word in the Bible. It involves turning towards God, and in the process it means turning away from what we know is wrong. So we need to stop any sexual relationship that is outside of marriage. We need to get rid of any pornography. We may need to get rid of magazines and DVDs and perhaps to put our computer in a public area in our home to avoid temptation. If you are struggling in this area, find somebody of the same sex with whom you can pray; someone you can talk to and be accountable to. This is a benefit of the depth of friendship we have in a Christian community: we can be open and honest and know that nobody is going to judge us.

When we have repented we can experience God's love and forgiveness. This is one area amongst many that can rob us of our intimacy with God. Yet the moment we receive forgiveness, Paul tells us that 'there is now no condemnation for those who are in Christ Jesus' (Romans 8:1). We are accepted as sons and daughters of God, righteous in his sight, and we can be free.

"They've put his computer screen on the roof"

4. Be ruthless

Jesus urges us to take extreme action. His teaching applies to all sin. Nowhere does he suggest that sexual sin is the most serious, but this particular teaching is in the context of sexual sin. Jesus says, 'If your right eye causes you to sin, gouge it out and throw it away. It is better for you to lose one part of your body than for your whole body to be thrown into hell. And if your right hand causes you to sin, cut it off and throw it away' (vv.29–30).

Jesus did not mean us to interpret his teaching with crude literalism. One source suggests that the early theologian Origen (c.186–255) castrated himself so that he would not be tempted. Such action was eventually forbidden by the Council of Nicaea in

AD 325. Jesus did not mean 'a literal physical self-maiming, but a ruthless moral self-denial'.[9] We are not to flirt with sin, but to deal drastically with it. Some of us are more prone to temptation in this area than others. We may need to examine our lives honestly and prayerfully in order to recognise where we are vulnerable and then to act ruthlessly.

It is important to note that Jesus does not forbid looking at someone; rather it is looking 'lustfully' at them that constitutes adultery of the heart. Someone asked, 'Well, what's the difference between looking and looking lustfully?' The answer was given, 'About two seconds.' There is nothing wrong with the appreciation of a person's beauty. Nor is Jesus outlawing the natural and normal human desires that are part of our instinct and nature. We are not intended to feel guilty about the longing for personal fulfilment or the feeling of attraction towards someone else.

What Jesus is speaking against is the uncontrolled and consuming sexual passion which leads us first to contemplate adultery, and then to commit it in our mind. It is 'the untamed desire for another's body'.[10] It applies to both men and women, married or unmarried.

This kind of lust is well described in an article which appeared in Leadership Today entitled, ' "The War Within: an Anatomy of Lust" – an anonymous Christian leader recounts his experience.' It began: 'I remember vividly the night I first encountered lust. Real, wilful commitment to lust.'

He describes how he was on a trip away from home and was lured into going to a strip club:

> Ten years have passed since that awakening, ten years never far away from the presence of lust... I learned quickly that lust, like physical sex, points in only one direction. You cannot go back to a lower level and stay satisfied... Lust does not satisfy; it stirs up... where I ended up [would have been]... incomprehensible to me when I started.

Although he never committed the physical act of adultery, it had a subtle effect on his marriage as he began to devalue his wife as a sexual being and focus on her minor flaws. It also had a devastating effect on his spiritual life, with lust becoming the one corner of his life which God could not enter.[11]

We must also bear in mind that Jesus is not saying that all temptation is sin. All of us will be tempted to have immoral thoughts; Jesus himself was tempted. The thoughts themselves are not sinful; rather, the entertaining of them is. The more we give in to these thoughts, the more difficult it gets. Graham Tomlin writes, 'Lust is like eczema: the more we scratch it, the more it itches.'[12] Conversely, the more we resist, the easier it gets. The New Testament writer, James, says, 'Resist the devil, and he will flee from you. Come near to God and he will come near to you' (James 4:7–8).

Jesus is saying that adultery destroys something very precious, and therefore we need to avoid it at all costs. We need to start a long way back; not with the act but with the heart. We can help each other by not laying temptation in someone's path. For example, it is not a good idea to sleep in the same bed with someone if you are trying to resist temptation! Sometimes people ask, 'How far can we go?' The Bible does not lay down rules, and I don't think that we should either. People and circumstances vary. But we should remember that it is hard not to go further the next time. It is also worth considering how you would feel if the relationship did end. It is much easier to retain dignity, respect and friendship when restraint has been shown.

We must exercise self-control with the use of our hands (v.30).

This applies to what we pick up to read and to how we touch other people. Physical contact is healthy but hugging and touching must not be open to misinterpretation. Sexual touching is part of foreplay, which is intended to lead to intercourse, and so it should be reserved for marriage.

Jesus also warns us of the possibility of our feet leading us into sin (Matthew 18:8). We may need to be careful of the places we go to, both physically and online. Certain areas of town, shops and places of 'entertainment' may not be conducive to sexual purity. Jesus is saying that anything which helps seduce us into sin must be ruthlessly rooted out of our lives. It is unwise to wait until we are on the brink of the physical act of adultery before we take action. The time to start is much earlier in the chain of temptation. We need to watch the friendships we make. Of course, all our lives are enriched by friendships with the opposite sex, but it is unwise for a married person to get too close to someone of the opposite sex, whether it be a work colleague, friend or confidante. As a minister, I do not think it is wise for men to counsel women on their own, or vice versa. I try to make it a rule that I will not pray with a woman other than Pippa on my own.

So many Christian men who have had an affair say that it all began because they entered a close pastoral relationship with a woman. My response may seem exaggerated or over-cautious, but my understanding of the teaching of Jesus is that it is worth taking extreme measures. These precautions do not stem from a lack of trust in God or our partners, but from the realisation that many of us are vulnerable in this area.

' A couple of hours of
prayer... and then we talk more ? "

I love the story that one leader shared in a talk:

This is a story about where I fell, where I messed up. It was one
evening. I was going out to speak at a meeting and I knew the
next day I was having some friends over for lunch. I thought,
'What are we going to have for dessert?' I remembered that
there was a double chocolate cake in the freezer. I took it out
of the freezer early that afternoon and put it in the fridge so it
would defrost slowly and be ready for our meal the next day.

I went to the meeting and arrived home late. When you
do ministry or work hard at the office in any way, you come
home and you're tired and you're vulnerable, especially if you
come home on your own. I came home and I thought, 'I'm
going to go straight to bed. I'm not going to eat anything.'
Then I thought, 'I'll just have a glass of water before I go to
bed.' I went into the kitchen, poured myself a glass of water
and I started sipping the water. I suddenly remembered that
I'd put the double chocolate cake in the fridge to defrost. I
was just curious, and wondered, 'Has it defrosted?' I thought
I would just have a look to check if it looked okay.

I opened the fridge door, and you will not believe what

happened next. As I opened that door, the double chocolate cake spoke to me. It said, 'Hello!' And I said, 'Oh, hello, double chocolate cake!' Then the double chocolate cake said, 'How are you?' I said, 'Oh, I'm OK. I'm very tired. I've just come back from a meeting and I'm about to go to bed.' I added, to be polite, 'How are you?' The double chocolate cake said, 'Well, I'm okay. I'm just very bored in this fridge. I only have a lettuce and two tomatoes for company.' Then it said, 'Well, listen. You're tired, I'm bored. Why don't you put me on the kitchen table, sit down and we can have a little chat? Then you could put me back and go to bed.'

I thought, 'That sounds fair enough! It's only a chat while I'm drinking my water.' So I said to the double chocolate cake, 'We'll have a chat. But I'm not going to eat you.' Then the double chocolate cake said, 'Of course not. You've had your evening meal, and I'm for tomorrow.' We'd got that out of the way. So I put the double chocolate cake on the table, and we had the sort of late-night conversation you have with a double chocolate cake. Then after a while I said to the double chocolate cake, 'Listen, Cakie,' because by this stage we were getting intimate, 'I was just wondering: are you defrosted?' And Cakie thought for a moment and said, 'You know, I'm not quite sure. There's only one way to find out: if you just run your finger along my cream and have a little taste.' And I thought, 'Just run my finger through Cakie's cream to have a little taste. I mean, that's not wrong, is it! Technically, that's not going all the way, is it! Is it?'

So I had a little taste of Cakie's cream and said, 'Cakie, your cream is defrosted. But what I want to know is, are you defrosted deep, deep in the heart of you?' And Cakie thought for a moment and said, 'You know, I don't know. The only way we can find out is if you cut just a little slither of me, just a little slither. Then you can just put the cream over and no one will know tomorrow.' And I thought, 'Just a little slither. If I don't, I will not know, will I?' So I had a little taste and said, 'Cakie, you are defrosted deep, deep in the heart of you!' Well, that night one thing led to another, and by the end of the evening that double chocolate cake and I were one flesh.

I wish I could stand here and tell you every mouthful was agony, was horrible; but it was not. It was wonderful; I loved every moment. And, do you know, as I was eating Cakie, I thought, 'This seems so right. What's wrong with this? I'm not hurting anyone. We're not hurting anyone else, are we, Cakie and I? We love each other.' And I loved it. That's the problem with sin: it's nice at the time. If that double chocolate cake had been cold Brussels sprouts, guess what, I would not have opened the fridge door, no problem. I loved eating Cakie until the last mouthful went down my throat. Then, when I finished, I looked at the empty plate; I looked at the spoon with those little chocolate hundreds and thousands things on; the knife with bits of cream and sponge attached and suddenly the plate, knife and spoon all screamed at me, 'Murderer! Murderer! Murderer!' I thought, 'What have I done? I've killed Cakie! I'VE KILLED CAKIE!' Immediately I felt ill. I felt, 'This is horrible, this is horrible! I don't know what to do with myself. I just feel sick. Why did I do that?'

That's the problem with sin. At the time it's nice, but afterwards it's payback time. All that evening I had payback time. Where did I go wrong? I'll tell you where I went wrong: when I opened the fridge door. Do not open the fridge door.

And we all know what I'm talking about, don't we? I'm not just talking about double chocolate cake; I'm talking about strawberry cheesecake, profiteroles and cream, lemon meringue pie; and I'm talking about sex outside of marriage. Do not open the fridge door.

5. Be role models

Jesus says, 'You are the salt of the earth... You are the light of the world' (vv.13–14). We cannot escape temptation. Christian history gives us examples of those who have taken the battle of the Christian life very seriously. St Anthony lived a hermit's life, fasted, went without sleep and beat his body into submission. For thirty-five years he lived in the desert and for thirty-five years he fought a non-stop battle.

It is not enough to be ruthless. Gardening does not only involve plucking out weeds but also planting flowers. We have to be different in a positive way; the Christian community should be a beautiful alternative society. As John Wimber often said, 'It is hard to sit still and be good.' The best way to keep out of trouble is to get involved in Christian service.

Again, Graham Tomlin writes:

I think the church needs to be a place where it becomes possible to live a good and wise and holy life. Out in the world it's very hard to live a life of purity and goodness, because the standards are sometimes set so low and the expectation is that people will often lie, cheat on their partners, sleep together outside marriage, fly off the handle, etc. It's much easier to live a pure life if you're in a community where there are not constant innuendo jokes and sex is not a constant topic of conversation. The reasons we keep to high standards of behaviour in the church is to encourage one another to live

like this. That's why Paul says that there must not be even a
hint of sexual immorality among you.

We are to be a society of deep, intimate friendships. All of us,
whether we're married or single, are to be role models to the world
in this area.

The thing is we're all built for intimacy. At the heart of creation
is the activity of the Trinity, and if we're made in the image of God
we're made for intimacy. We're made for relationships. Human
beings can survive without sex; human beings cannot survive
without relationships, or without intimacy.

Billy Graham is a wonderful role model. As a married man, he
has wisely taken extreme measures as a result of his 'passion to be
pure'. William Martin, writing in *A Prophet with Honour*, says:

> Long clearly understood that his best strategy for avoiding
> sexual temptation was to keep himself out of its path. 'I'm
> sure I have been tempted...especially in my younger years.
> But there has never been anything close to an incident.' How
> had he managed that record? 'I took precautions. From the
> earliest days, I have never had a meal alone with a woman
> other than Ruth, not even in a restaurant. I have never ridden
> in an automobile alone with a woman.' Even past seventy,
> on the rare occasions when only he and his secretary are in
> a room together, he keeps the door open wide so that none
> will suspect him of unseemly behaviour.[13]

We all have a drive within us that is a gift from God. I find it very
interesting that Jesus uses the Greek word *epithumia* for lust in a
negative way in this passage, describing it as a desire for something
forbidden. But this same word can also have a positive sense;
Paul uses it in Philippians 1:23 when he talks about his desire, his
passion, to be with Christ.

Again, Rob Bell says:

> Life is not about toning down and repressing your God-given
> life force. It's about channelling it and focusing it and turning
> it loose on something beautiful, something pure and true and
> good, something that connects you with God, with others,
> with the world.[14]

To do that we need to be filled with the Holy Spirit, and we need to
seek God first. Will power on its own is not enough. We need the
Holy Spirit's power. We are not on our own in this struggle. The
apostle Paul writes, 'Live by the Spirit, and you will not gratify the
desires of the sinful nature' (Galatians 5:16). Someone put it like
this:

> Seek pleasure as a god – in the long run we find emptiness,
> disappointment and addiction. Seek God first and we find,
> amongst many other things, ecstatic pleasure.

How to View Marriage and Divorce

It has been said, 'Anyone who divorces his wife must give her a certificate of divorce.' But I tell you that anyone who divorces his wife, except for marital unfaithfulness, causes her to become an adulteress, and anyone who marries the divorced woman commits adultery.
Matthew 5:31-32

Some Pharisees came to him to test him. They asked, 'Is it lawful for a man to divorce his wife for any and every reason?'

'Haven't you read,' he replied, 'that at the beginning the Creator "made them male and female," and said, "For this reason a man will leave his father and mother and be united to his wife, and the two will become one flesh"? So they are no longer two, but one. Therefore what God has joined together, let no-one separate.'

'Why then,' they asked, 'did Moses command that a man give his wife a certificate of divorce and send her away?'

Jesus replied, 'Moses permitted you to divorce your wives because your hearts were hard. But it was not this way from the beginning. I tell you that anyone who divorces his wife, except for marital unfaithfulness, and marries another woman commits adultery.'

The disciples said to him, 'If this is the situation between a husband and wife, it is better not to marry.'

Jesus replied, 'Not everyone can accept this word,
but only those to whom it has been given. For some are
eunuchs because they were born that way; others have
been made eunuchs; and others have renounced marriage
because of the kingdom of heaven. The one who can accept
this should accept it.'
Matthew 19:3-12

Recently I visited a course that we run at our church for those
recovering from divorce and separation. At the first session of the
course the guests had been asked to write down the feelings they
associated with divorce and separation. Some of the responses
included: 'excruciating pain', 'grief', 'despair', 'hurt', 'anger',
'murder', ' sadness', ' rejection', 'guilt', 'anguish', 'shock, 'betrayal',
'anxiety', 'fear', 'isolation', 'loneliness', 'depression' and feeling
'broken hearted'.

Divorce can be one of the most painful experiences in life,
and the church should bring hope to those who have experienced
this pain. To those who are badly hurt by divorce, the church is a
hospital. To those who acknowledge that they were responsible for
such pain, the church is a community of forgiven sinners. Divorce
is not an unforgivable sin. To those who are experiencing despair,
the church is a community of hope. God loves us and he wants to
bring us restoration and healing.

The issue of divorce and remarriage is complex, controversial,
painful and stressful.[1] Even if it does not affect us directly, we are
almost certain to know someone who is struggling in this area. It is
a vital issue for all of us. One of the leaders of our divorce recovery
course said that, in his case, 'There were at least ten people affected:
two parents, my sister, my brother-in-law, their two kids and, say,
four close friends.' In the last ten years there have been 150,000
divorces each year in the UK, which equates to one and a half

million divorces; three million people. For each of those divorces ten people might have been directly affected.

This issue affects others indirectly; there are those who are struggling in their marriages and who have considered divorce. There are those who are not sure that they want to get married at all because they have seen so many marriages break down. Those who have watched their own parents' marriage break down sometimes ask, 'Is it worth getting married?'

All of us are affected because we belong to a society that is deeply affected by divorce. The institution of marriage is under attack. Official figures revealed on 28 June 2007 show that marriage has slumped to its lowest level since records began more than 150 years ago. Between 1961 and 2005, the divorce rate rose from 27,000 to 155,000 per annum.[2] The social cost of

"I only put them there 'cos they smelt."

this is vast. Increasingly we are living in a fatherless generation. Of the 60,000 children living in care, 98 per cent of cases are due to family breakdown.

Divorce was also a hot issue in the time of Jesus – family life stood in great danger of destruction when Christianity first came into the world. In the Graeco-Roman world – although not in Judaism – relationships outside marriage were considered natural and normal. Written or oral notice in the presence of two witnesses was sufficient for a divorce. It was almost as straightforward as the Pueblo Indians today, where a woman can divorce her husband by leaving his moccasins on the doorstep!

According to Jewish rabbinic law a man had the right to divorce his wife, but the woman had no such right to divorce her husband. All that the husband had to do was to hand the document to the woman in the presence of two witnesses and she was divorced. As for the grounds for divorce there were two different schools of thought, revolving around the interpretation of Deuteronomy 24, which appears to allow divorce when a husband finds out 'something indecent' (v.1) about his wife. According to the strict school led by Rabbi Shammai, this meant a serious sexual offence. According to the liberal school led by Rabbi Hillel, the husband could divorce his wife 'for any and every reason' (hence the question asked by the Pharisees in Matthew 19:3). This was taken to include gossiping in the street, losing her looks, having an unsightly mole or putting too much salt in his soup!

In the Sermon on the Mount Jesus gives his view about divorce and remarriage and expands on this later in the Gospel (Matthew 19:3–12). The Pharisees asked Jesus, in effect, whether he agreed with Hillel's view. It is fascinating to me that when the Pharisees came and asked Jesus about divorce, he replied by talking about marriage. This is the place to begin.

1. Choose wisely

I would like to start by saying that those who are unmarried should not view singleness as a curse, but as a blessing; an opportunity to accomplish much in life without distractions and the inevitable giving of time and energy to a spouse and family. Certainly, it is better to be single than to be unhappily married. Jesus says there are various reasons why people remain single. Some 'have renounced marriage because of the kingdom of heaven' (Matthew 19:12). The decision to get married is a voluntary one.

Marriage is one of God's greatest blessings. It brings some of the highest joys of human life. Singleness may be an even higher calling, but marriage is God's norm. So we should not reject marriage. In reply to the Pharisees' question about divorce, Jesus says:

> Haven't you read... that at the beginning the Creator 'made them male and female', and said, 'For this reason a man will leave his father and mother and be united to his wife, and the two will become one flesh'? So they are no longer two, but one. Therefore what God has joined together, let no one separate.
> Matthew 19:4–6

Single people have a choice; they can choose whom they marry. Some people today believe that there is one person out there for them, Mr Right or Miss Right, their 'soul mate'. Others believe that you can marry anybody; it is just a matter of who you happen to be going out with at the time you want to get married.

" My surname is "Right" but that as far as it goes Godfrey"

There is of course a big difference between the choices open to you before you are married, and those open to you once you are married. Before you are married, you are free to choose anybody. Personally, I do not think it is healthy to search with the attitude that there is a Mr or Miss Right. Rather, we are free to choose. However, as Bishop Sandy Millar has said at many weddings, when you get married the moment for choosing is over! Those who are married are married to Mr Right or Miss Right; they should view their husband or wife as the person that God designed for them.

It is worth stressing, though it may seem obvious, that great care needs to be taken over the choice of a marriage partner (see my *Questions of Life*, chapter 7, and *Ready For Marriage?* by Nicky and Sila Lee). Yet we must also be prepared to take risks. It is not a failure to have a relationship that does not end in marriage. It is not even a failure to have a broken engagement. One date should not commit you to another date. I think we need to develop a culture in the church where an invitation to go out for coffee is not perceived to be the first step on the road to marriage. There needs to be time to get to know each other.

Second, we should allow for trial and error. I know of one church that organises speed-dating. They call it 'The Meet Market'! I believe that it is right to be open to relationships within the boundaries that we looked at in the previous chapter. Third, we should avoid being over-intense in the search for a marriage partner. It is not fair to say to someone, 'God has told me that I'm to marry you!' before being married to that person. The problem with this approach is that if this feeling is not reciprocated, it can be a form of manipulation. The only time to say this to someone is when you are actually married; then they are the person that God has called you to marry.

2. Invest massively

There are many views today about the nature of marriage. The secular world regards it as self-chosen, self-created and self-sustained. It is a voluntary partnership created by the decision of the two parties involved and, like any other civil contract, it can be terminated. It is often seen as a romantic alliance based on erotic attraction. If love dies, there is no reason why the marriage should not be dissolved, leaving the parties free to enter into other partnerships. Some take an increasingly reductionist view of what marriage is about. For example,

John Diamond, writing in *The Times* on the nature of divorce, said:

> Nowadays, for most people at least, marriage is one of those optional things you do if you want to make a particular sort of statement about the life you already share... that I share a bed and a mortgage with somebody is the substance of the relationship: the marriage certificate has turned out to be no more than a mere bureaucratic curlicue ornamenting seven years of my life.[3]

Jesus had the highest view of marriage. When he spoke about marriage (Matthew 19:4–6), he pointed to the creation account and drew four conclusions. First, marriage involves one man and one woman for life. Second, it entails leaving parents. This involves a public act which breaks the links with the former family. This does not mean that the parents are never seen again. Rather, a new family unit has been formed and the husband and wife's primary responsibility and loyalty are to that new unit. Third, there is a uniting and a personal commitment. The word used implies both passion and permanence. The bond is intended to be deep and lasting. Fourth, the 'two will become one flesh'. Whereas leaving and uniting are active ideas, 'becoming one flesh' is something that happens to the couple – they are joined by God. The union takes place at the deepest level of personality; sexual intercourse both facilitates and symbolises this union.

Sociologist Dr Patricia Morgan wrote:

> It is the greatest irony of all: that one of the most common motivations for cohabitation is the desire to prepare safely and responsibly for marriage. It is, it now seems certain, a snare and a delusion. Far from cohabitation strengthening marriage, the evidence is

that those who live together before marrying stand a
higher chance of divorcing, and certainly do where both
partners have had a previous cohabiting relationship with
someone else.[4]

Less than 5 per cent of cohabiting couples stay together for longer
than ten years.[5] And the statistics show that while 8 per cent of
married couples split up within five years of the birth of their
child, 50 per cent of cohabiting couples split up within five years
of the birth of a child.[6]

Jesus' model for marriage is the best and the most beautiful. It
involves an order: you leave, you cleave and, within that context,
sex takes place. The world has messed up the order. So often it
starts with sex, then cohabitation, then a child, then engagement,
and then, further down the road, perhaps, marriage.

Jesus summarised this teaching as meaning that in marriage,
husband and wife are no longer two but one. 'Therefore what God
has joined together, let man not separate' (Matthew 19:6). The
fundamental rule is that marriage is permanent and divorce should
be ruled out, not because marriage cannot be broken, but because
it ought not to be broken. Separation is possible, but it is not right.
As Karl Barth once said, 'To enter marriage is to renounce the
possibility of leaving it.'[7]

In 1991 the Law Society called for legislation that would enable
couples to draw up legally binding marriage contracts setting out who
would get what if they were to divorce. This is totally contrary to the
Christian idea of marriage and it is hard to think of anything more
undermining to this union. The possibility of divorce should be ruled
out from the start. Indeed, it is wise not to let the word 'divorce' enter
the marriage relationship, even as a joke. To rule divorce out right
from the start gives great security and freedom within a marriage.

I do not mean to suggest that avoiding divorce is easy. The

American pastor Rick Warren said this:

> I would be divorced today if it weren't for Kay and my stubborn persistence. We said, 'Divorce is not an option for us.' We locked the escape hatch on our marriage the night we got married, and we threw away the key. On 21st June this year Kay and I will celebrate our twentieth wedding anniversary. We like to say we've had seventeen great years – the first three years were hell on earth!

One couple, who had been married for fifty-three years, when asked what their secret was, the husband replied:

> We waited until we were really sure we were the ones for each other; we made our marriage a priority; we nurtured it, developed it; we fed our marriage. Whenever we got stuck, we didn't stay there long: we were not too proud to get help, and we needed it many times. The last thing is that we really committed ourselves to Jesus Christ in our individual lives. We were committed to Christian causes that made life more exciting. We had a larger vision and not just our little union. Generally, I think that we should welcome criticism.

"My surname is "Right" but that as far as it goes Godfrey"

All of us who are married need to build strong marriages and we need to see this as the highest priority of our lives, after our relationship with God. We must avoid succumbing to the temptation of putting our work or our children before our marriage partner.

Strong marriages are built by regular and intimate communication, which increases friendship, trust and mutual respect. More relationships break down through lack of communication than for any other reason. Communication takes time and this needs to be built into marriage.

We are put under great pressure, both from our society whose values are not those of Jesus Christ, and from the devil whose aim is to steal, kill and destroy. It is sometimes said, 'If the grass is greener on the other side of the fence it is time to start watering your own.' Strong marriages always require attention and are sustained by prayer. We need to put Jesus at the centre of our marriages. Couples must find time to pray together and separately for their relationship.

Rick Warren quotes a survey conducted in the United States that found that one out of every two and a half marriages ends in divorce. However, in a relationship in which the couple are married by a minister, attend church regularly, read the Bible and pray together on a regular basis, the divorce rate is one out of 1,105.[8] That's the difference Jesus makes.

We need to model strong marriages to the world. Many people today are not exposed to any model of a good marriage. The most powerful witness to Christ is the different quality of our lives, our relationships and especially our marriages.

The Holy Spirit has the amazing power to transform marriages. Father Raniero Cantalamessa, the Preacher to the Papal Household, has written this:

> One of the most visible fruits of the coming of the Holy Spirit is the revival of dead or dried-up marriages. The Holy Spirit wants to repeat for every couple the miracle of the wedding of Cana. The Spirit wants to transform the water into wine – the water of routine, of lowered expectations, of coldness, into the heady wine of newness and of joy.[9]

All of us can invest in marriage. We can invest in our parents' marriage, our children's marriages, and our friends' marriages. It is important not only to the individual lives of those who are married but to the whole of society.

3. Concede reluctantly

The Pharisees challenged Jesus' view of marriage by quoting, or rather misquoting, Deuteronomy 24:1 (Matthew 19:7). This appears to have been quite a common misquotation, as Jesus points out, 'It has been said, "Anyone who divorces his wife must give her a certificate of divorce"' (Matthew 5:31). This misquotation readily countenances divorce. The original context of Deuteronomy 24:1 was quite different. Mosaic legislation was designed to protect the wife and restrict remarriage by forbidding a husband to divorce his wife and then remarry her if his next marriage failed. In other words, if he gave his wife a divorce, it was to be permanent.

Jesus points out that the Israelites were never commanded to divorce their wives, even in extreme circumstances. Divorce was allowed only rarely – it was a concession 'because your hearts were hard' (Matthew 19:8). God did not originally intend marriage to end in divorce, and declares, 'I hate divorce' (Malachi 2:16).

Starting with this foundation Jesus goes on to say that divorce is the equivalent of adultery (Matthew 19:9; 5:32). He makes one exception over which there has been great debate. The one exception, appearing only in Matthew's Gospel, is 'marital unfaithfulness' (v.9). What did he mean by this? Those who accept the authority of Scripture are divided in their interpretation. The views that I express in the rest of this chapter are my own tentative conclusions.

Some argue that the Greek word used in this phrase (*porneia*) indicates a marriage contracted within the prohibited degrees of kinship, that is, when both parties are closely related (Leviticus 18:6–18). Such a marriage would have been an illicit union and therefore no marriage at all. They take Jesus as prohibiting all divorce.

Others take *porneia* to mean fornication before marriage, discovered afterwards. More commonly it is taken to include adultery. In both cases the penalty under Old Testament law was death (Deuteronomy 22:20–22), which under Roman law could not be enforced. Nevertheless adultery meant a new union had been formed and therefore divorce was a recognition that the marriage had already been terminated. In effect it 'ratifies the rupture'.[10]

Jesus is affirming the permanence of marriage. Only in the most extreme cases can a marriage be ended. Some have interpreted the teaching of Jesus with Pharisaic literalism. One act of adultery is enough to give the other partner 'biblical grounds' for divorce. That is not consistent with the spirit of Jesus' teaching, nor with the rest of the New Testament. Paul, in 1 Corinthians 7, while affirming the permanence of marriage, mentions another example that ends marriage. If an unbelieving partner leaves and will not be reconciled, the believer may with clear conscience let him go. Paul would not have added a new ground unless he thought it was consistent with the broader context of Jesus' teaching. What Jesus and the rest of the New Testament confirms is that marriage is permanent, and divorce should only be allowed in the most extreme cases, where there is gross misconduct such as undermines the whole marriage relationship. For example, if one party leaves and sets up home with another and has children by that new partner and will not return to their spouse, in effect adultery has ended the first marriage. If an unbelieving partner leaves and will not be reconciled, the believer has to let him or her go. Another extreme case could be if someone is on the receiving end of protracted physical or mental abuse. In these cases there is no other option.

Jesus' teaching, which is more like that of Shammai than that of Hillel, causes a strong reaction in his disciples: 'If this is the situation between a husband and wife, it is better not to marry' (Matthew 19:10). They were surprised by his strictness. But Jesus knew the damage done by divorce. Tearing apart what God has joined together will inevitably cause great damage at least to one of the partners and probably to both. Further, if there are children, they may be seriously affected, perhaps for life.

So, for those who are married, it is essential to do all that we can to avoid divorce. Even if the process of divorce has begun, it is never too late. In Christ, there is no such thing as irretrievable breakdown. If your partner is seeking to divorce you, it is important to explore every possibility of reconciliation. We should believe that reconciliation is always a possibility, even at the very last minute.[11]

If you are in the process of divorcing your partner, think again. Even those who have been at the receiving end of gross misconduct should still be willing to seek reconciliation. How long this process will go on will vary from case to case. Talk to somebody about it and consider whether there is not some way that reconciliation could be possible.

If you are not yet at that stage, but your marriage is experiencing difficulties, get help early. Too often people find it hard to acknowledge that their marriage is under pressure. Don't wait until there is a crisis. Take advantage of courses such as The Marriage Course, which is running all over the world. As Christians we have to do everything in our power to avoid divorce and to bring about reconciliation. But as a last resort, we may have to concede reluctantly.

4. Rebuild carefully

For those who are already divorced, in one sense it is obviously too late, especially if one or both of the former partners have remarried. In this instance, the giving and receiving of forgiveness is the key. Almost invariably, to some degree, both parties are to blame for the divorce. It is vitally important to repent where necessary. This may mean asking a former partner to forgive and not to carry bitterness, anger and resentment. It is likely to be an ongoing process. Even more common is a sense of guilt and failure, in which case it is vital to receive forgiveness. Jesus died to set us free from guilt. It is important to accept that the marriage is over, that in Christ the guilt can be removed, and that there is now a freedom to start again. The Anglican position is that this does not mean that remarriage is necessarily right, but it is not necessarily wrong.

Even if divorce ends a marriage legally and morally, this does not mean that for Christians today remarriage should be taken for granted for everyone. Even if the partners are free to remarry, in some cases it may not be right to do so. It might be that God calls a particular person to witness to the permanence of marriage by not remarrying.

Bearing all this in mind, the question of whether a remarriage should take place in a church is extremely difficult. The church has a dual role. First, it has a prophetic role to witness to the permanence of marriage. Second, it has a pastoral role to witness to the possibility of forgiveness and a new start. The approach we take as an Anglican church is normally to disallow remarriage in church, but in appropriate cases to hold a service of blessing after a civil wedding. Although different views are possible, perhaps this solution, which is allowed by the Anglican Church, is an appropriate way of bearing witness to both these roles.

5. Embrace unconditionally

Whatever we feel about divorce, we need to draw alongside those facing marriage problems with compassion and understanding and without being judgmental.

When I visited our church's divorce recovery course I was struck by the degree of pain that those present were suffering. Christopher Compston, who has written a book called *Breaking Up without Cracking Up*, has lost two sons: one at birth, and the other when he was twenty-five years of age. Yet he has said that the pain of losing his sons was nothing compared to the pain of his divorce.

One of the words written down by those on the divorce recovery course to express their feelings after divorce was 'broken hearted'. A divorce is crushing. Jesus said 'He has sent me to bind up the broken hearted' (Isaiah 61:1, quoted by Jesus in Luke 4:18). Psalm 34:18 says that, 'The Lord is close to the broken hearted and saves those who are crushed in spirit.' The Lord is close to those who are suffering the pain of divorce. Jesus loved to spend his time with people who were broken hearted.

The ministry of Jesus is grace, forgiveness and transformation. On the last night of the course various guests spoke about what had happened to them on the course. One young man said, 'I arrived full of bitterness, anger and resentment. Now, I've forgiven my wife – and the guy she ran off with. Most of all, I've forgiven myself... I even invited my wife to this supper.' Someone else said that he had been responsible for the breakdown of his marriage because of addictions in his life, and that he had ended up divorced and bankrupt. He said, 'Eric [one of the course leaders] took me in. I saw in his marriage a model.' Eric commented, 'But you saw us arguing!' He replied, 'Yes, I saw you arguing, but I saw a model of how to resolve conflict.' Eric had given him hope and helped him share his pain.

The heart of the gospel is reconciliation. God in Christ reconciled the world to himself. Our task is to proclaim this message to the world. We do it by our lives, by our example in our relationships and by our lips, proclaiming Jesus' teaching to the world, seeking to reconcile people to God and to each other. When the church truly starts living out the teaching of Jesus, then the world will take notice and will have a chance to respond.

I recently received a letter from a woman in our congregation, in which she said:

> My experience of my parents' divorce was not only deeply painful, having lifelong effects for me and my sibling, I also felt ashamed and that the church considered us shameful. Yet we were the innocent bystanders. The legacy of divorce for children is massive and cannot be emphasised enough. The secular world is full of horrendous statistics of how much divorce will affect children – they're more likely to fail at school, they're more likely to take drugs, they have failed marriages themselves – which is hard enough to deal with when you're growing up, without feeling ashamed and possibly rejected at church. The church needs to preach freedom from this to the children and that there's another way, and to offer them support, love and to show the way to receiving God's love and grace – which I found really hard to do, in spite of doing Alpha, my experience of the Holy Spirit and experiencing God in an amazing and exciting new way. The legacy of our parents' divorce was extremely hard to shake off. Yet God's amazing grace helps me with this still on a daily basis, and my parents divorced over thirty years ago. It's by this grace that

I chose marriage for myself and have four wonderful children of my own, and nearly sixteen years later have every hope that mine will last a lifetime.

Recommended reading and courses

For details of The Marriage Course, including your nearest course see themarriagecourse.org

- *The Marriage Book* by Nicky and Sila Lee (Alpha International, 2011)
- *Ready for Marriage?* by Nicky and Sila Lee (Alpha International, 2007)
- *Breaking Up without Cracking Up* by Christopher Compston (HarperCollins, 2011)
- For the position held by the Roman Catholic Church, see the *Catechism of the Catholic Church*

How to Live and Act
with Integrity

*Again, you have heard that it was said to the people long
ago, 'Do not break your oath, but keep the oaths you have
made to the Lord.' But I tell you, Do not swear at all:
either by heaven, for it is God's throne; or by the earth,
for it is his footstool; or by Jerusalem, for it is the city of
the Great King. And do not swear by your head, for you
cannot make even one hair white or black. Simply let your
'Yes' be 'Yes', and your 'No', 'No'; anything beyond this
comes from the evil one.*
Matthew 5:33-37

There is a breakdown of trust in our society. A recent MORI poll
researched the degree to which the general public trusts different
professions. The report found that politicians and government are
among the least trusted of all professions in the UK. Over 70 per
cent of those polled did not expect them to tell the truth. Only
journalists are less trusted. In some ways it is a relief to know that
people don't believe what they read in the newspapers. It is not just
politicians and journalists; trust generally is on the decline. Trust in
clergy has fallen 10 per cent in the last twenty-five years!

Our society has a serious problem concerning integrity. I read
recently in *The Sunday Times*:

> Under the old moral code, a lie was a lie. Now it is perfectly
> okay to manipulate the facts in a good cause (getting your

child's place in school, putting a roof over their heads,
extricating yourself from a commitment you no longer feel
able to fulfil). Lying or not telling the truth to keep your job
looks like becoming acceptable.[1]

We need to recapture a vision of an honest society where 'our word is our bond' and trust is restored. Integrity is not about hiding or smothering the weakness and sin we see inside ourselves in order to have a 'perfect' outward life: it begins fundamentally with a oneness and an integrity of the heart, soul, mind and strength (Mark 12:30). King David said, 'I know my God, that you test the heart and are pleased with integrity' (1 Chronicles 29:17). Integrity is something that pleases God at a personal level. But it is also vital for the functioning of wider society. Jethro told his son-in-law Moses how to share the burden's of leadership: 'Keep a sharp eye out for competent men – men who fear God, men of integrity, men who are incorruptible – and appoint them as leaders' (Exodus 18:21, *The Message*).

In fact, integrity is a key to leadership. We read in Proverbs 20:28 that 'Sound leadership is founded on loving integrity' (*The Message*). Dwight D. Eisenhower, former US president (1953–61) and supreme commander of allied forces in Europe during the Second World War, said,

[T]he supreme quality
of leadership is
unquestionably integrity.
Without it, no real
success is possible, no
matter whether it is on...
the football field, in an
army or in an office.

So how do we live lives of integrity? We do so by following Jesus. Having looked at the sixth commandment (vv.21–26) and the seventh commandment (vv.27–32), Jesus reverts to the third commandment (vv.33–37). Once again he gives a practical example of how Christians are to live righteous lives and to be salt and light in society. This time it is by integrity, honesty and truthfulness.

1. Live a consistent life without compartments – integrity of life

When the Titanic set sail in 1912, it was called 'unsinkable' due to the use of a new technology. This involved taking the hull of the ship and dividing it into sixteen watertight compartments. This supposedly meant that even if four of those compartments were ruptured and flooded with water, the ship would not sink. On 15 April 1912, at 2.20 am, the Titanic sank and 1,517 people were drowned. Originally it was thought that it sank after hitting an iceberg that created a gash in the hull, rupturing five of the compartments. However, seventy-three years later, on 1 September 1985, explorers found the intact wreck of the Titanic sitting upright on the ocean floor, without any signs of a gash. Scientists posited that instead of rupturing the side of the ship, the collision's impact had buckled or loosened seams in the adjacent hull plates, causing them to separate. This allowed water to flood in and sink the ship. In other words, an impact to one compartment *had* affected all the others.

Rick Warren speaks of the 'Titanic mistake – when we try to compartmentalise our lives into various segments.'[2] For example, when we say, 'This is my church life, where God is involved; this is my work life, where God cannot be involved; this is my social life, where I don't want God to be involved.' The 'Titanic mistake' is when we try to exclude God, confining him to a segment of our lives, and cutting him off from the rest. Perhaps we should think of life as more like a circle: God should be at the centre, affecting everything that is inside the circle.

At work, it is vital that we are the same person on Monday morning as we are at church on Sunday. Living an integrated life at work is not easy, but it is possible.[3] We need to allow God to enter fully into our social lives and our homes. Confucius said, 'The strength of a nation derives from the integrity of the home.' In today's society there is a common fallacy that we need to make a distinction between people's private and public lives. For example, some believe that what politicians do in their private lives won't affect their public lives. However, if a politician is unfaithful to their spouse in private, inevitably this does relate to what they do and say in public. If someone can deceive their spouse, who should be the most important person in their life, how can we, the general public trust what they say and do?

Another fallacy is that faith must be kept private. We need to know what our politicians believe, because what we believe affects how we live, and therefore the decisions that we make. Matthew Parris, an atheist and journalist, pointed this out in a recent article in *The Times*:

> We non-believers are always puzzled by protests that strong religious conviction could be without huge influence in the way a person lives their public as well as their private lives. We read the Gospels (sometimes with more attention than believers seem to)... and it strikes us that these belief systems make enormous claims on their adherents, with the most profound, practical consequences.[4]

Jody Jonsson, a member of our congregation, is a portfolio manager for one of the biggest mutual funds in the US. She spoke at the church one day about 'Success without Compromise' and commended her company's 'Wall Street Journal Front Page Test': that no one should do anything, say anything or write anything – especially on email – that they wouldn't want to appear on the front page of a newspaper.

We should live our lives as if everything will be disclosed. Our personal and professional lives form a single whole. Life cannot be divided into compartments. God sees the whole of our lives. We are called to live and act with integrity wherever we are, no matter whom we are with and whoever is watching. This is not about being something that we are not, but about allowing God to change us, while experiencing the vulnerability and honesty with ourselves and with one another that is made possible by God's grace.

2. Speak the truth without deception – integrity of word

When we give someone our word we should mean it and keep to it. There is not one language for church and another for the workplace. God is involved in all we do and say. He hears every word we utter, whether it is addressed to him or not. Our words and our lives should be consistent. All promises are sacred since they are all made in the presence of God.

Jesus says, 'Again, you have heard that it was said to the people long ago, "Do not break your oath, but keep the oaths you have made to the Lord"' (v.33). This is not a quote from the Old Testament but it is an accurate summary of the Old Testament teaching on the subject of oath-taking. God allowed people to make vows using his name to reinforce their commitment, but once made, such vows had to be kept. The Old Testament prohibited all false swearing and perjury. The intention was to stop lying, and to prevent the chaos caused when people cannot rely on another's words. The principle was so important that it was enshrined in the third commandment, 'You shall not misuse the name of the Lord your God, for the Lord will not hold anyone guiltless who misuses his name' (Exodus 20:7; Deuteronomy 5:11).

Further teaching on the subject is found in the rest of the Pentateuch (the first five books of the Old Testament): 'Do not steal. Do not lie. Do not deceive one another. Do not swear falsely by my name and so profane the name of your God. I am the Lord' (Leviticus 19:11–12), and, 'When a man makes a vow to the Lord or takes an oath to bind himself by a pledge, he must not break his word but must do everything he said' (Numbers 30:2).

However, on some occasions oaths were commanded to be made (Numbers 5:19). In the rest of the Old Testament there are further references to the need to keep such vows: 'Fulfil your vows to the Most High' (Psalm 50:14) and, 'When you make a vow to God, do not delay in fulfilling it. He has no pleasure in fools; fulfil your vow. It is better not to vow than to make a vow and not fulfil it' (Ecclesiastes 5:4–5).

Behind the whole of God's law is the desire of a loving God to create a society in which it would be a joy to live. If the three commands to which Jesus refers in these verses (vv.21–37) were kept, there would be no wars, no defence budget, no divorce, no adultery, no keys and no burglar alarms. Everyone could trust their husbands, wives, neighbours, business partners, employees, employers and all those around us. It would be a society in which politicians could be trusted and there would hardly be a need for lawyers.

Jesus does not abolish the law, but in his radical teaching on integrity, he goes back to the original purpose behind the law. That purpose was to ensure truthfulness. Since the whole system of oath-taking had become corrupt and was being used to avoid telling the truth, he forbids all oaths. He says, 'Do not swear at all... simply let your "Yes" be "Yes", and your "No", "No"; anything beyond this comes from the evil one' (vv.34, 37).

Honest people do not need to resort to oaths. William Barclay commented:

Clement of Alexandria insisted that Christians must lead such a life and demonstrate such a character that no one will ever dream of asking an oath from them. The ideal society is one in which no man's word will ever need an oath to guarantee its truth, and no man's promise ever need an oath to guarantee its fulfilling.[5]

I remember my father used to say, 'I expect to be believed.' He regarded honesty as the highest possible value and sometimes went to absurd lengths to tell the truth. On one occasion, he and my mother got on the wrong bus, went 200 yards in the wrong direction and got off without paying a fare. My father sent tuppence ha'penny for the fare to the bus company, but they sent it back. This resulted in a long correspondence, which my mother found hard to understand. Later, he conducted a similar exchange with British Rail when, for a different reason, he felt he owed them money. Unfortunately, their accounting system could not cope with the money he had sent. Going through Customs with my father was a nightmare. Most people go through the 'Nothing to Declare' channel, but my father always insisted on going through 'Something to Declare'. He made us write down lists of everything in our luggage, 'Three sweets, one stamp, one banana skin' and so on! These examples may be trivial but, nonetheless, as Christians we should 'expect to be believed'.

Jesus tells his disciples simply to speak the truth on every occasion. We are to cut out all finger crossing: Yes must be Yes and No must be No. To add anything else is unnecessary. Indeed, 'Anything beyond this comes from the evil one' (v.37).

Meaning what we say is another outworking of Jesus' appeal for simple truthfulness (v.37). This applies to the small things as well as larger situations. If you make a pledge, keep it. If you are in debt then please get help and advice on how to get out of it. Don't travel on public transport without paying. If someone undercharges you by mistake, point it out. If you make an arrangement, keep to it, even if you get a better offer. Don't make promises that you cannot keep, or that you have no intention of keeping. If you promise to keep a secret, keep it; don't share it just for prayer or because you are 'concerned', which can all too often be an excuse for gossip.

When Jesus says, 'Simply let your "Yes" be "Yes" and your "No", "No"' (v.37), does this mean that all oaths and vows are prohibited to the Christian? C. H. Spurgeon, writing his commentary on these verses, argued that a Christian should not take an oath, even in court. 'Christians should not yield to an evil custom, however great the pressure put upon them; but they should abide by the plain and unmistakable command of their Lord and King.'[6] The Quakers have traditionally taken the same line.

However, it is not necessary to take the words of Jesus so literally as to exclude an oath in a court of law. Jesus himself responded to the oath of testimony at his trial (Matthew 26:63–64). St Paul used solemn expressions to appeal to God (2 Corinthians 1:23; Galatians 1:20; 1 Thessalonians 5:27). Jesus is not outlawing, for example, the marriage vows. These are solemn vows that invoke God's name to underscore the commitment to the marriage.

We must not be pedantic in our interpretation of the words of Jesus, lest we fall into the same trap as the Pharisees. They took too literal an approach to God's words in the Old Testament and failed to see that what lay behind the commands was the need for honesty, truthfulness and reliability. The same desire lies behind Jesus' words as once again he goes back to the spirit and intention behind the Old Testament law. Jesus said, 'I am the... truth' (John 14:6) and, as his followers, we should be known for our reliability and integrity.

3. Cultivate a pure heart without faking it – integrity of heart

We will never have integrity of life, word and speech without integrity of heart. Jesus said it is '...out of the overflow of the heart that the mouth speaks' (Matthew 12:34).

To us, the heart is a metaphor for the seat of the emotions, but in Bible times it had a broader reference, and was understood to include a person's intellect and their will. In other words, the heart stood for the personality as a whole, the essence of a person, whatever it is that makes us who we are.

The Bible has a great deal to say about the heart. It is with our hearts that we love God, and again and again we are called to love God with all our hearts (Deuteronomy 6:5; 10:12; 11:13; 30:6). We are warned not to 'harden' our hearts against God (Hebrews 3:4–16), but to 'guard' them, as they are the 'wellspring of life' (Proverbs 4:22–24).

The psalmist David examines his own heart deeply in Psalm 51, recognising his sin and his need to be forgiven by God. He turns to God, trusting that he will accept him: 'a broken and a contrite heart, O God, you will not despise' (v.17). He knows that it is only with God's help that he can only change, and prays: 'Create in me a pure heart'.

Only when, with God's help, our hearts are truly surrendered to God, and to God alone, can there be true godly integrity between our thoughts, words and actions.

Jesus was a man of supreme integrity and he treated everybody equally. As the Pharisees said to Jesus, 'We know that you are a man of integrity... you pay no attention to who [people] are' (Matthew 22:16). If you treat the person who serves you in a restaurant in the same way that you would treat royalty, this shows you have integrity.

Living with integrity involves everything we do and say (vv.34–36). God's commands were intended to avoid perjury. The

Pharisees built an entire legalistic system around the Old Testament laws. They made a distinction between vows: some were binding and some were not. Vows that included God's name were binding, but a person did not need to be so careful if his name was not involved. Like children crossing their fingers behind their backs, they managed to find a way to avoid binding commitments.

This system of evading God's law reached its climax in a discussion that can be seen in the Jewish law where one whole section is given over to a discussion about oaths. The idea was that if God's name was used he was a party to the transaction. If not, he had nothing to do with it. Oaths by 'heaven' or 'earth' were not binding on witnesses. According to one rabbi, oaths 'towards Jerusalem' were binding, but oaths 'by Jerusalem' were not. Therefore, evasive swearing became a justification for lying. Instead of inspiring integrity, oaths became a breeding ground for corruption. Instead of reinforcing promises, oaths provided loopholes for people to break their commitment without repercussions.

Jesus is confronting this corrupt system of oath-taking in the Sermon on the Mount. He points out that it is not a question of bringing God in; we cannot keep him out. He is already there. Everything comes back to God in the end. Jesus quotes the Old Testament to show that heaven is God's throne and earth is his footstool (vv.34–35; Isaiah 66:1) and Jerusalem is the city of the Great King (v.35; Psalm 48:2). Even our head, which might be thought to be a person's absolute possession, belongs to God; he decides the colour of our hair (v.36). God is involved in every part of our lives.

True integrity is when our lives, our words and our hearts are all in alignment and there is no great difference between our public and private lives. Integrity is doing the right thing even when nobody is watching. It is a lifelong struggle, and a challenge. Only Jesus lived with 100 per cent integrity, but we can all aspire to it.

I once knew a godly man nicknamed 'Gibbo' who, when he

was young, worked as a clerk at Selfridges, the London department store. One day, when the owner Gordon Selfridge was there, the telephone rang and Gibbo answered it. The caller asked to speak to Gordon Selfridge. Gibbo passed on the message and Selfridge replied, 'Tell him I'm out.' Gibbo held out the receiver to him and said, 'You tell him you're out.' Gordon Selfridge took the call, but was furious with him. Gibbo said afterwards, 'If I can lie for you, I can lie to you.' From that moment onwards Gordon Selfridge had the highest regard for and trust in Gibbo.

Speaking the truth is not always easy and living with integrity does not mean that everybody will speak well of us. We read in the book of Proverbs that people of integrity are often hated by others (Proverbs 29:10). As Rick Warren says, 'You cannot control the lies that people may speak about you. But you can control the truth. Live so that people have to make up stuff in order to accuse us.' In this life, we will be tested and it won't always be easy to live with integrity. However, as Warren goes onto say, 'Christians are like tea bags, you don't know what they're like inside until you put them in hot water.'[7]

Dietrich Bonhoeffer, we have heard, was one of the German Christians who opposed Hitler during the Second World War. His integrity cost him his life: he was murdered by the Nazis shortly before the end of the war. In his commentary on these verses he wrote:

> Only those who follow Jesus and cleave to him are living in complete truthfulness. Such men have nothing to hide from their Lord... Complete truthfulness is only possible where sin has been uncovered, and forgiven by Jesus... The cross is God's truth about us, and therefore it is the only power which can make us truthful. When we know the cross we are no longer afraid of the truth. We need no more oaths to confirm the truth of our utterances, for we live in the perfect truth of God. There is no truth towards Jesus without truth towards man. Untruthfulness destroys fellowship, but truth cuts false fellowship to pieces and establishes genuine brotherhood.[8]

This is the challenge for all of us – as individuals and as a community – to live our whole lives surrendered to the Lordship of Jesus Christ. As John Stott writes, 'When Jesus is Lord of our beliefs, opinions, ambitions, standards, values and lifestyle, then we are integrated Christians. Then integrity marks our life. Only when he is Lord do we become whole.'[9]

How to Respond to Difficult People

You have heard that it was said, 'Eye for eye, and tooth for tooth.' But I tell you, Do not resist an evil person. If someone strikes you on the right cheek, turn the other cheek also. And if someone wants to sue you and take your tunic, hand over your cloak as well. If someone forces you to go one mile, go two miles. Give to the one who asks you, and do not turn away from the one who wants to borrow from you.
Matthew 5:38–42

How do we respond when we are wronged by another person? How do we feel when insulted or when someone is rude to us? What is our response when our property or possessions are stolen or damaged in a burglary or a car crash? Or when someone robs us of our time? What should we do or say when we lose money due to someone else's fraud, theft or negligence?

In this section of the Sermon on the Mount Jesus makes the most extraordinary demands of his disciples. He tells them, 'Do not resist an evil person' (v.39). What does this mean? Does it mean that all Christians should be pacifists? Does it mean that children should not fight back when they are bullied in the playground? Does it mean that we should never go to court if we are wronged? Should we give money to everyone who approaches us in the street?

Some have taken the words of Jesus absolutely literally. Martin Luther describes the eccentric saint 'who let the lice nibble at him and refused to kill any of them on account of this text, maintaining that he had to suffer and could not resist evil.'[1]

Towards the end of his life, Leo Tolstoy, the nineteenth-century novelist, also took this passage absolutely literally. He believed there should not only be no soldiers, but no police, no magistrates and no law courts. He was also opposed to any form of government. Even today many Christians, like the Mennonites, opt out of almost all social control for reasons based largely on the Sermon on the Mount.

At the other extreme there are others who totally reject this passage. Journalist and atheist Christopher Hitchens describes Jesus' teaching as 'deranged, suicidal and immoral.'[2] He is following in the footsteps of the atheist philosopher Friedrich Nietzsche, who also totally rejected this teaching and was notorious for his claim that 'God is dead'. He contended that Jesus' words were proof of the fact that Christianity was for the weak and the cowardly. He regarded it as a slave-like morality where charity, humility and obedience replaced competition, pride and autonomy. His search for a 'superman', perfected in both mental and physical strength and without moral scruples, was later taken up and adapted by Adolf Hitler.

So, just how should this section of the Sermon of the Mount be interpreted? What do these words mean for us today?

1. Expect to encounter difficult people

Bishop Sandy Millar often quotes the *Devil's Beatitudes*. If the devil were to re-write the beatitudes, they would probably look something like this:

> Blessed are those Christians who wait to be asked and
> expect to be thanked – I can use them.
> Blessed are the touchy, with a bit of luck they may stop
> going to church altogether – they are my missionaries.

Blessed are those who are very
religious and get on everyone's
nerves – they are mine forever.
Blessed are the troublemakers –
they shall be called my children.
Blessed are the gossipers –
for they are my secret agents.
Blessed are the complainers –
I am all ears for them.
Blessed are you when you read this
and think it is all about other people
and not yourself – I've got you.

"Could we have the devil's beatitudes at our wedding?"

Jesus used the word 'evil' in varying degrees, of which he gives four examples. First, expect to encounter those who are rude, insulting and even abusive; resulting in a *loss of pride*. Jesus says, 'If someone strikes you on the right cheek, turn the other cheek also' (v.39). According to Jewish rabbinic law a backhanded slap (on the right cheek) was twice as insulting as one with the flat of the hand (on the left). Even today in the Middle East a slap in the face is regarded as a particularly insulting assault, a gesture of extreme abuse, showing the greatest possible contempt for someone. Jesus himself endured such assaults on more than one occasion (Mark 14:65; John 18:22; 19:3). Even without being physically hurt it's still possible for our pride to be injured.

Second, expect to encounter those who persecute or even prosecute you; resulting in a *loss of possessions*. As Jesus says, 'If someone wants to sue you and take your tunic, hand over your cloak as well' (v.40). Losing a tunic, which was the inner garment, would not have been a desperate matter, as even the poorest person would have more than one. A cloak was more valuable and essential (Exodus 22:26; Deuteronomy 24:13). Most people would have had only one and used it as a robe by day and a blanket by night. Thus, Jesus encourages us not only to give up inessentials without opposition but also to add even that which we consider essential.

Ravi Zacharias, a Christian apologist, went to speak at a university in Malaysia. When he was there he met one member of the staff there who was a Christian from a Chinese background. This man had been praying for years that the gospel would be preached in this university. After Ravi had spoken, the man told him about something that had happened to him four years earlier when a famous anti-Christian lecturer had come to speak at the university. In an auditorium of over 2,000 people, this man was the only Christian. The anti-Christian lecturer called him out, as a staff member, in front of all his students and said, 'You're a Christian, I want you to come up on stage.' So he came forward and he stood on the stage. The lecturer then slapped him around the face really hard. Then he said 'I'm waiting. What does your Jesus tell you to do?' So our friend did what Jesus told him to do and turned the other cheek. The lecturer slapped him across the head again. Remember this is in a shame culture; this was the teacher of many of the students and they were totally shocked. The lecturer then went on to say, 'Look at the weakness of Christians. Christianity is founded on weakness.' Then he said, 'Give me your coat.' So the man took off his coat and handed it over. He said, 'I'm waiting, what does your Jesus tell you to do now?' Standing before an audience of thousands, many of them his students, this man said, 'I just want to say to all of you who are my students, I don't want you to be embarrassed because of me, so you may want to close your eyes at this moment.' Then he took off his clothes and he gave them to the man, and he walked out, tears pouring down his face, humiliated.

The next day an amazing thing happened; one after another of his students came into his study and said how ashamed they were about what had happened. They asked him to tell them more about Jesus. As a result he received many letters and was able to talk freely about his faith with hundreds of students.

Third, expect to encounter those who take advantage of us: resulting in a *loss of time*. Jesus says, 'if someone forces you to go one mile, go two miles' (v.41). The Romans, as an occupying power, used to compel citizens to carry baggage for them. If a citizen felt the touch of a Roman spear on his shoulder he knew he was about to be compelled to carry baggage for a Roman mile (about a thousand paces – just less than a mile). It was a form of service that was obviously regarded as unreasonable. It was under this custom that Simon of Cyrene was compelled to carry Jesus' cross (Matthew 27:32). Jesus taught that we were not to respond to such evil with a vengeful attitude, but to offer to do even more.

Fourth, expect to encounter those who are takers; resulting in the *loss of money*. Jesus says 'Give to the one who asks you, and do not turn away from the one who wants to borrow from you' (v.42). In the Old Testament, generosity to the poor was taught:

> If there are poor among your people in any of the towns of the land that the Lord your God is giving you, do not be hard-hearted or tight-fisted towards them. Rather be open handed and freely lend them whatever they need... Give generously to them and do so without a grudging heart; then because of this the Lord your God will bless you in all your work and in everything you put your hand to. There will always be poor people in the land. Therefore I command you to be open-handed towards those of your people who are poor and needy in your land.
>
> Deuteronomy 15:7–8, 10–11

Jesus goes even further than this, teaching us to say 'no' to any kind of tight-fisted, penny-pinching attitudes; to put the needs of others before our own convenience; and to be willing to suffer financial loss in the service of others who will never pay us back.

So how do we respond to Jesus' teaching? At a recent prayer breakfast at our church for people working in the City of London, I asked a friend how I could pray for him. He mentioned one or two things about his work situation and then added, 'Oh, and the usual, difficult people.' I asked him to elaborate and he said, 'Well, people who don't listen and therefore waste your time; people who are rude.' And then he added, 'Money; people who take more than their fair share.' It is interesting that those are exactly the categories that Jesus identifies in this passage; little has changed in 2,000 years.

How do we respond to these difficult people?

2. Rise above taking revenge

A number of years ago on the BBC talk show programme, *Kilroy*, Robert Kilroy Silk asked the studio audience whether we should take revenge. Here are some of the answers: 'I cannot allow him to get away with it'; 'most certainly'; 'you feel a lot better when you've done it'; 'revenge can do you good' and 'if you don't take revenge, you lose your self-respect'.

Each time one of the participants described the steps they had taken to get revenge, there was a round of applause and cheers from all the others. Many of the replies were understandable. One had suffered sexual abuse; another had lost a limb due to a medical error; another's husband had an affair with her sister.

However, in the audience there was one West Indian woman who had a radiant expression. When Robert Kilroy Silk asked her, 'Should we forgive?' she replied, 'Absolutely, my forgiving released me to get on with my life. You forgive and you get the healing and that causes you to be a better person.'

She told the story of how she had been living with a man and expecting his child. One day her partner went off on holiday and met another woman. Shortly afterwards, he came back to her and announced, 'I'm married'. She said it took three weeks for this to sink in and then the rage came. She started to plot. She went into the kitchen and took out a hammer and put it in a plastic bag. 'I wanted to hammer his head in,' she said. 'I wanted to scar him in a way that he would always be reminded when he looked in the mirror. He would think, 'This is because of what I did to Mary.'

Kilroy asked, 'What stopped you?' She replied, 'I became a Christian. I was told I had to forgive.' Mary shone like a beacon of light on that programme. She urged the others to forgive and help others in similar situations rather than harbouring bitterness. One man said to her, 'This world's not the way you preach. There are not too many like you around.' Kilroy replied and ended the programme by saying, 'Perhaps there ought to be more'.

'An eye for an eye and a tooth for a tooth' is the oldest law in the world. It is known as the *lex talionis*, which means essentially the law of 'tit for tat'. It was part of the civil law of Israel and is quoted three times in the Old Testament (Exodus 21:23–25; Leviticus 24:19–20; Deuteronomy 19:21). Even earlier than that it was part of the law code of the Babylonian King Hammurabi. The actual code probably dates from the eighteenth century BC and is one of the earliest known codes of law. The code of Hammurabi made a distinction in the punishments for an offence against a gentleman (eye for eye) and offences against a poor man (monetary penalties). The Old Testament law made no such distinctions. Does Jesus then contradict this? If we look at the Old Testament law, there were four qualifications that we find within the Old Testament itself.

First, in the Old Testament this law was intended to be a

law of mercy; it was restrictive rather than permissive. The legal punishment was not to exceed the gravity of the crime, but was designed to rule out escalating revenge and replace the unlimited excesses of blood feuds. These feuds were characteristic of early society. If one member of a tribe was injured by another member of a tribe, all the members of the offended tribe would take revenge on all the members of the offending tribe. This law was intended to rule out such vendettas. Instead there was to be exact correspondence and compensation. This is still a valid legal principle. It prevents an escalation such as: 'I hit you on the nose. You cut off my hand. I kill you. Your brother kills me and my family.'

Second, the law was clearly created for judges and not for private individuals. 'The judges must make a thorough investigation... You must purge the evil from among you... life for life, eye for eye, tooth for tooth, hand for hand, foot for foot' (Deuteronomy 19:18–21). It was a guide for judges in sentencing. There was to be an exact correspondence in compensation. It was never intended that individuals should exact such revenge.

Third, it was almost certainly never taken literally except in the case of capital offences. Penalties were generally replaced by financial fines and damages. The Jewish Law laid down how the damages were to be assessed. This was in many ways similar to our own legal system – giving damages for injury, pain and suffering, medical expenses and loss of wages.

Fourth, this was not the whole picture, as far as the Old Testament was concerned. Individuals were taught not to seek revenge and not to bear grudges. Rather they were taught, 'Love your neighbour as yourself' (Leviticus 19:18). 'Do not say "I'll do to them as they have done to me; I'll pay them back for what they did"' (Proverbs 24:29). Indeed, they were specifically taught, 'Let them offer their cheek to the one who would strike them' (Lamentations 3:30).

So, from the very beginning it was God's will that no human

being should take revenge. However, by the time of Jesus, this Old Testament law had been manipulated, and used to justify personal vendettas, vengeance, malice and hatred.

As before, Jesus is not contradicting the Old Testament; however, he is repudiating the misinterpretation and the misapplication of the Old Testament. Jesus is therefore forbidding revenge. He gives four concrete examples of non-retaliation. First, we are not to get even, nor are we to stand by passively. There is nothing passive about any of Jesus' illustrations; we are to act in a way that changes the dynamic of the encounter. We are not to reply like for like and not to adopt the style of the opponent. Jesus says, 'Turn the other cheek' (v.39). This is not surrender; it is active engagement to take charge and overcome evil with good. Second, don't just let him sue you but take the initiative; 'Hand over your cloak as well' (v.40). Third, turn the tables and 'Go two miles' (v.41); the oppressor can only force you to go one mile, but go the other one as a volunteer to show that you are not under his orders. Last of all, change the dynamics – this takes courage.

Referring to this passage, John Stott writes that we are not supposed to be 'a doormat... rather a strong [person] whose control of [themselves] and love for others are so powerful that [they] reject absolutely every conceivable form of retaliation.'[3] This is of course what Jesus did when he was abused and assaulted; he showed incredible strength and extraordinary self-control when he was tortured and crucified.

Pete Dobbs was a football hooligan, a member of the National Front, and a violent man. After he became a Christian he spoke about what his life used to be like:

> Once when I was on my bike, a guy cut me up along the Blackwell Tunnel. I got off my bike, walked around to where he was stuck in traffic and I put my fist straight through his window. I punched him several times in the face, then I took

his car keys, jumped back on my bike and rode off with his keys and left him there.

Pete also spoke about an incident that occurred more recently after he had become a Christian:

I was in the house and heard a crunch as someone ran over my motorbike. I went out to the car and this little bloke was shaking. Before becoming a Christian, I'd have dragged him out of the car and battered him. However, this time I said, 'Are you alright, mate? Look, sit down, don't worry about it.' The driver asked whether it was my bike and I replied, "Well it's only a bike; what's a bike? Don't worry about it."'

He rose above taking revenge.

3. Act with an attitude of radical love

The illustrations that Jesus gives are all illustrations of the law of love. We have to interpret Jesus' teaching in the context of everything else that Jesus did and said and also in the context of the rest of the New Testament. Jesus himself, on one occasion, took a whip of cords and drove out the moneychangers from the temple; he overturned their tables and ordered them out (John 2:13–16). He stood up to the hypocrisy of the Scribes and Pharisees, and on one occasion he verbally assaulted them (Matthew 23). He also demanded an explanation when struck by an official of the high priest (John 18:23).

Likewise, Paul refused to allow the authorities at Philippi to get away with beating him and Silas illegally (Acts 16:37). On other occasions he appealed to his right as a Roman citizen not to be flogged without a guilty verdict against him (Acts 22:25).

In his teaching, Paul makes a clear distinction between the dealings of the state and personal morality. Paul emphasises that the governing authorities are established by God. In Romans 13 he says, 'For the one in authority is God's servant to do you good. But if you do wrong, be afraid for they do not bear the sword for nothing. They are God's servants, agents of wrath to bring punishment on the wrong doer' (Romans 13:4).

Paul's teaching does not contradict Jesus'; rather it complements it. Moreover in his attitude to personal morality, Paul's attitude is exactly like that of his Master: 'Do not repay anyone evil for evil... live at peace with everyone... do not take revenge' (Romans 12:17–19). The principle of love lies behind both. The state is concerned with the protection of others. To stand by and allow murder or violence would be unloving and un-Christian.

By analogy, if it is right for the state to use force to protect its citizens from internal threats, is it not equally right to use force to protect its citizens from external threats? As Thomas Aquinas put it,

> Just as they use the sword in lawful defence against domestic disturbance when they punish criminals... so they lawfully use the sword of war to protect them from foreign attacks.[4]

Our duty as citizens may also involve us in the use of force to restrain evil people. A Christian soldier may need to kill in the course of military action. A Christian police officer may be required to use force in performing his duty. A Christian judge may be required to send people to prison. All of us as Christian citizens may be required to use force to restrain evil and to protect others. If we see a child being attacked and abused we are not to stand by idly. The principle of love requires us to interfere with force if necessary.

There is bound to be a tension within all of us. We are all private individuals with a command from Jesus not to retaliate or take revenge. We are citizens of the state with a duty to prevent crime and to bring wrong doers to justice. If we are the victim of a crime, we should forgive the criminal, not seek revenge, and yet we should do all in our power to bring the perpetrator of the crime to justice. It is not easy to hold this tension but the attitude of love requires that we do so.

The same applies to civil wrongs perpetrated against us. It is not wrong to go to court provided that our motive is love and justice, not retaliation or revenge. Likewise, an evil or oppressive employer may need stopping in his tracks, but we must ensure that our motives are right. Similarly, it is not the most loving thing to give money to those who we know will use it to abuse their own bodies with alcohol or drugs. We must ensure we do not refuse to give simply because we are not prepared for the financial loss. The test may be whether we are willing to spare the time to go and buy them food to eat.

We must feel the challenge of the words of Jesus and not allow his words to die the death of a thousand qualifications. We must never allow ourselves to be motivated by revenge or malice. Rather we are to be peaceful, willing, generous and liberal with our time, money and resources. Jesus calls us to disregard our rights and be passionately concerned for the rights of others. We are called to be totally different from the world around us; to be salt and light.

Once again Jesus takes the Old Testament law to an even deeper level. He does not supersede the Old Testament requirements; rather, he shows his disciples the true meaning of the law. He calls his disciples to suffering love in the face of evil. By his own example on the cross he showed how only such an attitude can ultimately triumph over evil. Dietrich Bonhoeffer powerfully makes the point, 'It looked as though evil had triumphed on the cross, but the real victory belonged to Jesus... The cross is the only power in the world which proves that suffering love can avenge and vanquish evil.'[5]

On 12 June 1972, a photo appeared on the front page of the *Washington Post*. It was of a young girl running towards the camera, her arms outstretched, her clothes burnt off and her skin blackened by napalm and screaming in pain. The image was taken by photojournalist Nick Út. The girl's name was Kim Phúc which means 'Golden Happiness'. After fourteen months in hospital and seventeen operations, she returned home worried that her wounds were so ugly that no one would ever want to marry her. Nick Út's photo won the Pulitzer Prize and become an emblem for a nation questioning its reasons for being in Vietnam.

Some years later, Kim read the New Testament for the first time in a local library and became a Christian. She said: 'It was the fire of the bomb that burned my body, and it was the skill of the doctor that mended my skin, but it took the power of God to heal my heart.' As a medical student in 1986 (fourteen years later), her burns still required daily washing and medication. A fellow Vietnamese student named Toan offered to carry buckets of water up to her apartment and it wasn't long before he was touched by the loveliness of Kim's spirit. They married in 1992 and emigrated to Canada.

In 1996, Kim agreed to speak at a Veterans' Day ceremony held in Washington DC. She took her place on the rostrum, flanked by US military dignitaries, before a huge crowd of veterans. As she stood before a sea of uniforms, a sight that brought back terrifying memories of the war, she said, 'I have suffered a lot from both physical and emotional pain. Sometimes I thought I could not live, but God saved my life and gave me faith and hope.' And then she uttered healing words of grace and forgiveness: 'Even if I could talk face-to-face with the pilot who dropped the bomb, I would tell him we cannot change history, but we should try to do good things for the present and for the future to promote peace.' When she had finished her brief but moving remarks, the veterans rose to their feet and broke into an explosion of applause, many of them in tears. 'It's important to us that she's here,' one veteran said. 'For her to forgive us personally means something.'

One man, overcome with emotion, rushed to a patrolman and scribbled out a note, asking him to deliver it to Kim. 'I'm the man you are looking for,' the note read. Intermediaries asked if she was willing to see him. 'Yes', she said; if they could arrange a meeting away from the crush of people. Officials brought the man over to her car. When the reporters cleared away, Kim turned and looked straight into the man's eyes and then held out her arms... the same arms she had held out as she ran along the road, in agony from her burning skin. She hugged the man and he began to sob. 'I am so sorry. I am just so sorry!' he said. 'It is okay. I forgive. I forgive,' said Kim Phúc, echoing her favourite Bible verse, 'Forgive, and you will be forgiven' (Luke 6:37).

That day the famous photo of the terrified little Vietnamese girl fleeing the napalm flames, was replaced in the national consciousness by the image of a young mother embracing an ex-GI. The words of forgiveness Kim extended that Veterans' Day helped heal the consciences of the thousands of veterans gathered there. And as news reports carried the story far and wide, her words and the striking photo helped heal the nation's wounds as well.[6]

How to Handle Conflict

You have heard that it was said, 'Love your neighbour and hate your enemy.' But I tell you: Love your enemies and pray for those who persecute you, that you may be children of your Father in heaven.
He causes his sun to rise on the evil and the good, and sends rain on the righteous and the unrighteous. If you love those who love you, what reward will you get? Are not even the tax collectors doing that? And if you greet only your own people, what are you doing more than others? Do not even pagans do that? Be perfect, therefore, as your heavenly Father is perfect.
Matthew 5:43-48

We live in a world in conflict. There are wars between nations, civil wars, and religious conflicts, such as the ongoing tension in the Middle East. At a local level we see hatred, bitterness and hostility. Even in neighbourhoods we see disputes. G. K. Chesterton said this: 'The Bible tells us to love our neighbours, and also to love our enemies; probably because they are generally the same people.'[1]

Pánfilo de Narváez died in 1528. He was a Spanish explorer and a soldier. The story is told that when Narváez lay dying, his confessor asked him whether he had forgiven all his enemies as it commands in the Bible. Narváez looked astonished and said, 'Father, I have none – I have shot them all!'[2]

God did not make us solitary creatures; he made us with a capacity for friendship. He created us to have a loving relationship with him and with other people. But this is not always easy. There are some people with whom we naturally get on; others can be more difficult. People can be rude, aggressive or even hostile towards us. Sometimes this can even come from our own family and friends, leading to broken relationships, hurt, pain, grudges and misunderstandings.

As life goes on we can find that the number of conflicts we experience increases. Someone said, 'Friends may come and go; enemies accumulate.' Some can be permanent, others just temporary. It is not a sin to have enemies; Jesus himself had enemies. To those who would become his followers, Jesus said, 'People will hate you because of me' (Luke 21:17). St Paul, William Wilberforce and Martin Luther King all had enemies. Even Mother Teresa had enemies; some people opposed what she was doing. If we want to achieve anything for God, we are most likely to arouse enmity. What is the right way to respond?

Jesus said to his followers, 'Love your enemies' (v.44). Canon Paul Oestreicher, who helped to found Amnesty International, said that this is the command of Jesus on which Amnesty is founded. He said, 'This is unique to Jesus. Nobody up until Jesus had ever said it as explicitly as "love your enemies"'.[3]

This is the first time that the word 'love' has been mentioned in the Sermon on the Mount. When Jesus said, 'You have heard that it was said, "Love your neighbour and hate your enemy." But I tell you: love your enemies' (vv.43–44), he was once again dealing with a scribal misinterpretation. The Old Testament taught, 'Love your neighbour' (Leviticus 19:18). Nowhere does it say, 'Hate your enemy.' The command to 'love your neighbour' was interpreted as being limited to other Jews and therefore it was permissible and indeed right to hate (or at least 'love less'[4]) those outside Israel. Similar teaching is found in the writings of the Qumran community – a sort of Jewish monastic sect from the time of Jesus – which we know about from the Dead Sea Scrolls: 'That they (members of the sect) may love all the sons of light, each according to his lot in God's design, and hate all the sons of darkness, each according to his guilt in God's vengeance.'[5] There is no Old Testament warrant for such an attitude. Indeed, even in the Old Testament there are a number of passages suggesting the opposite (Exodus 23:4–5; Proverbs 25:21).

Yet no passage in the Old Testament goes as far as Jesus does here. Indeed, there is no parallel in Jewish literature to the 'sweeping universality'[6] of the teaching of Jesus. We are to love our enemies, regardless of race, colour, creed or background; regardless of what harm they have done us and how much revenge seems to be justified.

This teaching was not purely hypothetical for the disciples. They had no doubt been insulted and derided, mocked for their humility and apparent weakness, and been unjustly accused of being dangerous revolutionaries. In due course they were to suffer far more serious forms of persecution: to be flogged, tortured and many of them executed for their faith. Yet Jesus says to them, 'Love your enemies.'

How do we love our enemies? It takes initiative, strength and courage. It means demonstrating total forgiveness. In these verses Jesus gives us six practical ways to love our enemies.

1. Speak graciously

Jesus says, 'Bless those who curse you' (v.44).[7] The Greek word for bless is *eulogeo*, from which we get the word 'eulogy'. It means to 'bless, speak well of, praise, or extol'. At a funeral there's often a eulogy, when someone offers positive reflections about the person who has died. The writer of Proverbs points out, 'A gentle answer turns away wrath' (Proverbs 15:1). A gracious reply to a rude or aggressive comment can turn a potential enemy into a lifelong friend.

I must admit I'm often tempted to do the opposite. Sometimes I receive letters from people who don't like something I have said, and they can be very rude. I heard of how one US senator used to respond when he got such letters. He would reply by returning the letter with a note attached to the bottom, which said: 'I just thought you'd like to know that some nutcase has been writing to me using your name and address.' Jesus suggests a different approach.

One of the dangers of email is that we can reply so quickly. Remember Jesus' words: 'Bless those who curse you.' Not only in front of someone, which is relatively easy, but also behind their back. Jesus is our supreme example of someone who spoke graciously. Sometimes he was silent; sometimes he spoke firmly; but never maliciously.

2. Respond kindly

Jesus says, 'Do good to those who hate you' (v.44).[7] The Greek word for 'do good' means 'to act beautifully'. This is the opposite of revenge and retaliation where hate multiplies hate, leading to a vicious circle of quarrelling, unkindness and misery. We all know families, relationships, firms and organisations ripped apart by hate. The only way to break the vicious circle is with love. This begins first and foremost with forgiveness, but it also involves positive action. 'If your enemies are hungry; feed them; if they are thirsty, give them something to drink' (Romans 12:20).

Non-retaliation is hard, particularly when we are in the right!

Sometimes I cycle down a narrow road where cars and buses can block my side of the road. I can't get past and it's frustrating because it's my right of way. At this point I have to remember the story of Jonathan Jay:

> This is the story of Jonathan Jay,
> who died defending his right of way.
> He was right, dead right, as he went along,
> But now he's as dead as if he was wrong.

Revenge and retaliation don't just destroy the other person, they destroy us as well. As the Chinese proverb says: 'Whoever opts for revenge should dig two graves.' One clergyman I know makes this recommendation to a couple whose marriage is in trouble: 'Every day do ten kind things for your wife or for your husband. If you want to rekindle love, this is what you should do.'

Love is also the way to transform an enemy into a friend. Abraham Lincoln had an arch-enemy called Edwin Stanton. Stanton hated Lincoln and used every ounce of his energy to degrade him in the public eye, even down to his physical appearance. When Lincoln was elected President, he was looking for someone to fill the vital post of Secretary of War. He chose Stanton, knowing all that he had said and done, and in spite of the advice of those close to him, because he was the best man for the job. When Lincoln was assassinated, many men spoke laudable words about him. But the words of Stanton were the most moving. He used the immortal phrase, 'He now belongs to the Ages', and referred to Lincoln as one of the greatest men that ever lived. The power of Lincoln's grace and kindness had transformed Stanton from an enemy into a friend.

3. Pray positively

Jesus says, 'Pray for those who persecute you' (v.44). Sometimes it's hard not to pray, 'Lord, bring them to a sticky end!' However, Jesus is talking about praying positively and interceding for our enemies. As Bonhoeffer put it, 'Through the medium of prayer we go to our enemy, stand by his side, and plead for him to God... For if we pray for them, we are taking their distress and poverty, their guilt and perdition upon ourselves, and pleading to God for them.'[8] Prayer is the acid test of whether or not we truly have love for someone. Coming into the light of God's presence reveals the true feelings in our hearts, which words can sometimes cover over.

A young member of our congregation told me how two of her colleagues at work had said things to her that deeply offended her. She felt hurt and told me how these words had consumed everything that she did. It made it hard for her to make progress in her job, in her relationship with God and in her relationship with these colleagues. Finally, she realised that she had to forgive. She decided that, before she spoke to them about her hurt, she would pray for them each day for a month. When the month was over, looking back she realised that the only reason she had wanted to speak to them was to let them know how badly upset she was. After a month of prayer she could still remember the words that they had spoken, but they had lost their sting. I asked her, 'How did you pray for them during that month?' She replied, 'I asked for God's blessing on their lives; for their families; for their work; for their relationship with God; and their relationship with others. The only thing I didn't pray about was their relationship with me. I prayed that God would bless them every single day.'

Jesus gave an extraordinary example of this – praying on the cross for those who were torturing him: 'Father, forgive them, for they do not know what they are doing' (Luke 23:34).

4. Act divinely

To love our enemies is to imitate our Father in heaven: 'That you may be children of your Father in heaven' (v.45). Someone has said that 'To return hate for love, that is demonic. To return love for love, that is human. To return love for hate, that is divine.' God's love extends even to those who are hostile towards him. 'He causes his sun to rise on the evil *and* the good, and sends the rain on the righteous *and* the unrighteous' (v.45, italics mine). In other words, God does not discriminate; he sends the rain on everyone. In the Middle East, rain was regarded as a blessing. Rain in England is not always regarded as quite such a blessing!

When we look around us we see that God's blessing is, in a sense, indiscriminate. He pours out his blessings on everyone. All can enjoy the beauty of God's creation. Furthermore, God's grace is available to everyone, however far they have fallen. Jesus died for all of us; his mercy is available to everyone. We are reminded at this point to look at people in the same way that God does. Henry Wadsworth Longfellow, a nineteenth-century American poet, said: 'If we could read the secret history of our enemies, we should find in each [person's] life sorrow and suffering enough to disarm all hostility.'[9]

I once read an article in a Canadian magazine about a man called Dan Evans. He had been asked by a friend who was a prison chaplain to lead an Alpha for people who were in custody for their own protection, for example, paedophiles. He said, 'I tried to think of any excuse I could to get out of going. God would understand. He knew the pain of my past, about the man who had attempted to molest me when I was eleven years old. I prayed, "I don't want to go. I can't stand the thought of even talking to them." But what excuse could I use? It didn't sound very spiritual to say that I hated them!'

Fourteen prisoners turned up. Dan sat with his arms crossed as far away from the group as he could. He hardly spoke to 'them' and said that it was a good thing that his friend Tim was there to help lead. As the weeks passed, the prisoners began to talk about the cycle of abuse that marked their own lives. One evening an inmate looked at Dan and said, 'Is it true? Do you really believe there is hope for us?' He knew the answer he had to give and as he spoke his heart began to soften. 'I said, "Although you are suffering the consequences of what you've done, there's hope for anyone who truly repents and turns to Jesus for forgiveness." It was as though I was saying it to the man who tried to abuse me years earlier. A heavy weight lifted off me that night, and I learnt a little bit more about the grace and forgiveness of God.'

5. Live differently

Jesus says, 'If you love those who love you, what reward will you get? Are not even the tax collectors doing that? And if you greet only your own people, what are you doing more than others? Don't even the pagans do that?' (vv.46–47). It's interesting that when Jesus is trying to think of the worst people possible he goes for the tax collectors! Even the hated tax collectors were capable of loving each other. As the Living Bible puts it, unbelievers are on the whole 'friendly to friends', with the attitude: 'You scratch my back and I'll scratch yours.' But this love is usually limited to our own circle of friends and seldom extends to those who have done us positive harm. If that is our attitude as Christians, what are we doing 'more than others' (v.47)? The Greek word for 'more than' means 'that which is not usually encountered among men'.[10] We are called to be different. We are called to what Bonhoeffer calls the 'extraordinary... the hall-mark of the Christian'.[11]

Our attitude is different from that of the pagans because we believe there is a God who will judge the world. St Paul writes,

'Do not take revenge, my friends, but leave room for God's wrath, for it is written: "It is mine to avenge; I will repay," says the Lord. On the contrary: "If your enemy is hungry, feed him; if he's thirsty, give him something to drink. Doing this, you'll heap burning coals on his head." Do not be overcome by evil, but overcome evil with good' (Romans 12:17–21).

We see this supremely, of course, in the life of Jesus, who trusted in God to deliver him on the cross. We also see it foreshadowed in the Old Testament in the life of Joseph. R. T. Kendall said in his book *God Meant it for Good*:

> Do you yearn for the moment of vengeance, for the moment when everybody will see the truth? Of course you do... The wisest thing one can ever do when mistreated is to be quiet about it... Joseph kept quiet. God wanted him to lose the battle so he might win the war... In this way, also, Joseph was a type of Christ. Jesus was never vindicated by those who sent Him to the cross. When Jesus was raised from the dead, did He go straight to Herod and say, 'What do you think now?' Or did he go to Pontius Pilate? To the chief priests? No. Jesus did not go to anybody to clear His name... Jesus lost the battle to win the war. As for Joseph, vindication on the spot might have done something for him in that moment, but it would not have done anything for the kingdom of God. When we are being mistreated in any way, we must realise that our suffering has profound and vast implications for the greater kingdom of God... Who knows what God will do with your life if you take your mistreatment with dignity? What probably means so much to you – to be cleared right now – could well lose the war should you get your immediate wish. Jesus could have come down from the cross. Thank God he did not. Joseph could have been vindicated, but he was not.

His eleven brothers would later be thankful that everything worked out just as it did... Joseph would later say, "You meant it for evil, but God meant it for good."[12]

6. Be perfect

Jesus concludes this passage, as well as this whole section of the Sermon on the Mount, with an all-embracing demand: 'Be perfect, therefore, as your heavenly Father is perfect' (v.48). The section began with a demand for a righteousness that exceeded that of the scribes and Pharisees (v.20). In the last few chapters we have seen six examples of what this means in terms of anger, lust, marriage, integrity, what we do when wronged and now in terms of loving our enemies. Jesus concludes with what appears to be an impossible demand. Clearly human beings cannot be perfect as God is perfect. The Greek word means 'having attained the intended purpose, complete, full grown, mature, fully developed'.

Jesus requires that his disciples do not settle for second best. We are not to be content with being good as far as anger is concerned, but bad at integrity; or good at love, but bad at lust. We are called to the highest possible standard in all these areas. We are called to a whole-hearted devotion to imitating our Father in heaven. We are to be totally different from the world around us. In short, we are to follow the example of Jesus.

At one level this seems impossible. However, with God's help it is possible. First, through Jesus' death on the cross, we know that we are forgiven. When we know how much we have been forgiven we realise that we can't hold anything against anyone else. Second, we receive power from the God who 'has poured out his love into our hearts by the Holy Spirit' (Romans 5:5). This supernatural love enables us to live differently.

Anthony Walker, an eighteen-year-old boy, was hit by a racist thug called Paul Taylor who was twenty years of age. The two-foot mountaineering axe was swung with such force that it punched a hole in his skull. It was still in place when Gee Walker, his mother, reached the hospital. He died six hours later.

Mrs Walker, a special needs teacher from Liverpool, was leaving the Crown Court room where she had just forced herself to listen to the hideous forensic detail of how her son had been murdered, when Paul Taylor slipped her a note. He said he was sorry. But, she had already forgiven him and his seventeen-year-old accomplice Michael Barton. After they were jailed she said, 'I cannot hate. I have to forgive them. Hate is what killed Anthony'.

The magnanimity of her gesture took people's breath away. There were radio phone-ins, polls, and TV debates asking how she could show humanity to the people who'd killed her son so. She was amazed at the public reaction. To her it was obvious that if she didn't answer racism and hate with forgiveness and love, it would insult the memory of Anthony, who like her, lived by the tenets of Jesus.

Of course, she is still fraught by grief. *The Times* asked, 'Do killers like Taylor and Barton deserve forgiveness?'[13] Mrs Walker doesn't see forgiveness quite like that: 'Unforgiveness is a heavy weight. It's a big load to carry. I've seen what it does to people: they become bitter, angry. I don't want to be like that. I don't want to be a victim twice over.' She prays every day for strength and remembers what Anthony always said to her, 'We can do everything through Christ' (Philippians 4:13).

How to Become a Generous Giver

Be careful not to do your 'acts of righteousness' before others, to be seen by them. If you do, you will have no reward from your Father in heaven.

So when you give to the needy, do not announce it with trumpets, as the hypocrites do in the synagogues and on the streets, to be honoured by others. I tell you the truth, they have received their reward in full. But when you give to the needy, do not let your left hand know what your right hand is doing, so that your giving may be in secret. Then your Father, who sees what is done in secret, will reward you.
Matthew 6:1-4

In the autumn of 1992, Michael Plant, a popular American yachtsman, set out on a solo crossing of the North Atlantic Ocean from the United States to France. He was an expert, who had sailed solo around the world more than once. The sailing community universally acknowledged him as a yachtsman whose sea-faring skills were without equal. His mid-sized sailing boat, the Coyote, was the epitome of modern sailing lore. He had the best expertise, experience and equipment.

Eleven days into the voyage radio contact with Michael Plant was lost. When the Coyote's radio silence persisted for several days a search was launched. The Coyote was found, floating upside down, by the crew of a freighter 450 miles north west of the Azores Islands.

Everyone in the sailing world must have been surprised that

when the Coyote was found it was upside down in the water. Sailing boats will always right themselves, even if a wind or wave were momentarily to push it over on its side or even upside down. In order for a sailing boat to maintain a steady course, and in order not to capsize but to harness the tremendous power of the wind, there must be more weight below the water-line than there is above it. Any violation of this principle of weight distribution means disaster. When the Coyote was built, an 8,000-pound weight was bolted to the keel for this very reason. No one knows why or how, but the weight beneath the water-line broke away from the keel. The four ton weight was simply missing. When that occurred, the boat's stability was compromised. The result was that a very capable, experienced and much-admired sailor was lost at sea.[1]

In this section of the Sermon on the Mount, Jesus examines the part of our Christian life that is below the water-line. The same principle is true. There must be more weight below the water-line than there is above it. So what is the equivalent to the weight below the water-line? It is the part of our Christian life that no one else can see – our secret life with God.

At the beginning of the Sermon on the Mount (Matthew 5:1–16, chapters 1–2 of this book), Jesus spoke about what sort of people we should be as Christians. In the next section (Matthew 5:17–48, chapters 3–9), he spoke about how we should live out the Christian faith in the world. Now, in this section (Matthew 6:1–18, my chapters 10–11), he speaks about our intimate relationship with our Father in heaven.

In one of the most challenging sections of the entire Bible, Jesus looks at the three pillars of contemporary Jewish piety: giving, praying and fasting. Again he contrasts how his followers should act with the actions of the Pharisees and the pagans. The religious people – the Pharisees – he called 'the hypocrites' who liked everyone to see how religious they were. They were ostentatious about their faith. The irreligious – 'the pagans' (v.7) – had no reality about their relationship with God. When they prayed there was a 'mechanical formalism'.[2] Followers of Jesus are to be unlike both of these.

As he looks at giving, praying and fasting in turn, Jesus' teaching follows the same pattern. Each section starts with a command to be unlike the hypocrites (vv.2, 5, 16), because he says in each case 'I tell you the truth, they have received their reward in full.' He teaches how the Christian should be (vv.3, 7ff., 17ff.), because 'Then your Father, who sees what is done in secret, will reward you' (vv.4, 6, 16).

The section is introduced by a general command: 'Be careful not to do your "acts of righteousness" before others, to be seen by them. If you do, you will have no reward from your Father in heaven' (v.1). The rest of the section is a commentary on this verse. Jesus begins by talking about giving. In this passage we find guidance on becoming a generous giver.

1. Be converted

Jesus introduced the first example with the words, 'So *when* you give' (v.2, italics mine). Jesus assumed that his disciples would give. A devout Jew would give in two ways: by the tithe, a tenth of his income (compulsory), and second by giving alms (voluntary). 'To give alms was beyond the letter of the Law', with 'special merit attached'.[3] In total, a devout Jew would give away at least one sixth of his income.

The act of giving is part of what it means to be a Christian; it is one of the things that happens when we come to Christ. Martin Luther said that three conversions take place: the conversion of the mind, the conversion of the heart and the conversion of the wallet.

I had a great friend called Mick Hawkins. He was one of the most generous people I have ever met. I remember him saying that he was not truly converted until he was converted in his wallet. When this happened, he was constantly giving things away. We thought that he must be very rich, but in fact he was just very generous.

To be converted requires a change of heart and a change of attitude. Before we are converted we tend to think that our money is our own and that we have the right to do with it whatever we like. When we are converted we realise that everything we have belongs to God, and that it is he who is sharing it with us.

Sometimes people say, 'I work really hard for the money I've got.' This may be true, but where did the energy, ability and gifts come from? When we come to Christ, we should realise that rather than being the owners of our money, we are the managers; the stewards of God's gifts to us.

A few years ago, while I was in the United States speaking at some Alpha conferences, some friends lent us their house to stay in. They had a sports car in their garage and asked us to drive it regularly, explaining that if we didn't it might not start when they returned. I had not driven a sports car before, and have not done so since, but I really enjoyed it! I didn't for one moment think that I *owned* it; rather I had the responsibility for it for that time. In the same way, we are responsible for the money that God entrusts to us. However, the owner has the right to direct how we use it.

The New Testament says that we should give regularly, proportionally, generously, and cheerfully (1 Corinthians 16:2; 2 Corinthians 8:12; 2 Corinthians 9:6). The apostle Paul says that 'God loves a cheerful giver' and for this reason he urges us to give (2 Corinthians 9:7). That is why Paul urges us to give 'not reluctantly or under compulsion'. Our giving should not be out of sorrow, nor should it be forced out of stern duty or necessity. Giving should be fun. Receiving presents is fun, but giving them is even more enjoyable.

There are no rules about how much we should give, only that it should be a generous proportion of what we have. Oswald Sanders points out that Jacob the swindler gave a tenth. Zacchaeus the despised tax collector gave a half. The poor and unnamed widow gave 'all she had to live on'. The devout Jew gave at least a sixth of his income. Jesus does not discuss what percentage we should give away. If we take this teaching of Jesus on board we will realise that even to argue about percentages is to miss the point. It is not a matter of, 'How much must I give away?' but, 'How much do I need to keep?'

Hudson Taylor, the founder of the China Inland Mission, who determined 'to move man through God, by prayer alone', saw thousands converted through his ministry and is seen by many as having laid the foundations for the present revival in China. At the age of twenty-seven he was preparing to go to China. He was working hard, was ministering on Sundays and was living a very frugal life. One Sunday, after he had had a bowl of gruel the night before, porridge in the morning and nothing for supper, he was asked to go and pray for a poor man and his wife who was dying. He had a half-crown coin in his pocket. He saw their poverty and wanted to give. He said that if he had had two shillings and a sixpence he would have given one shilling. When he saw the poverty of the mother and her five children he felt he would gladly have given her one shilling and sixpence. He then told them about the love of their heavenly Father, but he felt a hypocrite that he was not prepared to trust God without two shillings and sixpence. At this point he would gladly have given two shillings and kept sixpence. Eventually he said, 'Well, you asked me to pray, so let's pray.' He began, 'Our Father....' He struggled through the prayer. The father of the family said, 'If you can help us, for God's sake do.' After a tremendous struggle, he gave them the half-crown. Joy flooded his heart. He sang all the way home and as he ate his gruel, he reminded the Lord that 'he that giveth to the poor, lendeth to the Lord'. He slept peacefully. The following morning, he was surprised to receive a letter – he had not been expecting anything. Inside he found a pair of gloves and half a sovereign. He had received a 400 per cent return in twelve hours. This incident was a turning point, and he came back to it time and again because through it he had learned to trust God in little things. Later, it helped him in the more serious trials of life.[4] Giving is a virtuous circle.

2. Build your secret life with God

Jesus puts giving first in the catalogue of secret activities in our relationship with God. He speaks about it even before he speaks about prayer. To the Jews, giving was the most sacred of all religious duties. In addition to expressing the importance of giving, the rabbis forbade ostentatious giving. It was not the teaching of the rabbis that Jesus denounced; it was the practice of the Pharisees that fell short of this teaching and was hypocritical (v.2). The Greek word for 'hypocrite' was originally used for an actor in a play and came to mean 'someone who is pretending to be something they are not'. Jesus parodies the giving of the

of course, I'd never tell anyone that I give away half my salary."

Pharisees as if, when they gave, they sent the trumpeters on ahead, blowing a fanfare to draw the crowds so that the maximum number

of people would see their
generosity, and so they would
be 'honoured by others' (v.2).
As we would say, they were
'blowing their own trumpets'.

Jesus says that if we give
in order to get 'honour from
others', then that is exactly
what we will get and no
more. He says, 'I tell you the
truth, they have received their
reward in full.' If we give
in order to receive honour

"Here's an enormous cheque –
– keep it quiet, eh."

from other people, we may be able to bask in the warmth of their
gratitude and praise, but that is all we receive. To gain such a
reward from others is to lose it from God. Martyn Lloyd-Jones, in
his commentary on these verses, invites us to examine our lives in
the light of Jesus' words and asks the question, 'How much remains
to come to you from God?' He adds, 'It is a terrifying thought.'[5]

Jesus says that when we give, not only should we not tell
others, but we are not even to tell ourselves. He says, 'Do not let

'Actually, right hand,
It's um, scratching
my back right now..'

your left hand know what your right hand is doing' (v.3). He uses this figurative language to express the need for total secrecy. Our giving should not even be self-conscious. To avoid the danger of self-righteousness, self-congratulation and pride, we ourselves are scarcely to know that we have given. Otherwise, 'altruism has been displaced by a distorted egotism'.[6]

How do we attain this balance? Earlier in the Sermon on the Mount Jesus commanded us to let our 'light shine before others, that they may see your good deeds and praise your Father in heaven' (Matthew 5:16). The distinction, therefore, is in our motive. Whatever we do, whether in secret or in the open, our motive should be the glory of God and not our own glory. Our motive should not be that we may be seen. Our Christian activity might be seen, but it must never be done for the sake of being seen. As A. B. Bruce put it, we should 'show when tempted to hide and hide when tempted to show'.[7]

3. Become more like God

We should become more like our 'Father in Heaven' (v.1). What is God's attitude? Paul says, 'Thanks be to God for his indescribable gift!' (2 Corinthians 9:15). This is the supreme example of giving: 'God so loved the world that he *gave* his one and only Son, that whoever believes in him shall not die but have everlasting life' (John 3:16, italics mine). God's motive for giving is love.

I heard a story about a priest in the United States who was working in a tough area. A man in his parish, who was a member of the Mafia, an extremely violent man, and a notorious criminal, died. The man's brother visited the priest and asked him to perform a Christian burial for his brother. The priest felt a little uncomfortable about this and worried about what it might entail. The brother said to him, 'I will give you $200,000 for your steeple appeal if, at my brother's funeral, you say, "He was a saint." But, if you don't say that he was a saint, I will make your life pretty difficult. And trust me, I've got the ability to do that!'

So the priest had three sleepless nights before the funeral; tossing and turning as he wondered what on earth he was going to say. On the day of the funeral, when the time came for the priest to say some words about the man in the coffin, he said: 'As you all know, the man whose body is in the ground today was a liar, a murderer, an adulterer and a cheat.' There was an intake of breath. He looked across and pointed to the man's brother, and said: 'But compared to his brother, he was a saint!'

The motive for giving should be love. Giving is a way to become like God; it's the path to holiness. Giving prises our characters from the constricting grip of materialism that destroys so many lives. John Wesley said, 'When I have any money I get rid of it as quickly as possible, lest it find a way into my heart.'

4. Benefit from God's reward

Our giving should be the result of an overflowing love and kindness of heart. It should be impossible for us not to give. Our hearts should be so full of thanks to God for all that he has given us that we cannot wait to give in response to his love. When we give with this attitude Jesus says, 'Then your Father, who sees what is done in secret, will reward you' (v.4).

Some manuscripts have the word 'openly', suggesting a contrast between hidden giving and an open reward. But the word 'openly' is not in the most reliable manuscripts. What Jesus is contrasting is not the method of reward, but the source of the reward and therefore its quality. He is contrasting the wonderful reward that comes from a heavenly Father with the relatively miserly reward of human approval.

Many find the concept of reward distasteful and inappropriate in a Christian context. Surely, they say, we should give without expecting any reward at all. Isn't the idea of a reward worldly and materialistic? However, we must be careful not to try to be more spiritual than Jesus. Jesus spoke a lot about rewards. True, this teaching has often been misunderstood and misrepresented. Neither Jesus nor the other New Testament writers ever promised us material prosperity in this life, but nevertheless they did speak in terms of rewards.

C. S. Lewis drew a very helpful distinction between different types of reward. He wrote:

> We must not be troubled by unbelievers when they say that this promise of reward makes the Christian life a mercenary affair. There are different kinds of rewards. There is the reward which has no natural connection with the things you do to earn it and is quite foreign to the desires that ought to accompany those things. Money is not the natural reward of love; that is why we call a man mercenary if he marries a woman for the sake of her money. But marriage is the proper reward for a real lover, and he is not mercenary for desiring it. A general who fights well in order to get a peerage is mercenary; a general who fights for victory is not, victory being the proper reward of battle as marriage is the proper

reward of love. The proper rewards are not simply tacked on to the activity for which they are given, but are the activity itself in consummation.[8]

St Paul sees giving as the best investment we can make: 'Whoever sows sparingly will also reap sparingly, and whoever sows generously will also reap generously' (2 Corinthians 9:6). This is the principle of the harvest. Giving is planting seed. It is investing for the future. Whatever we give to the Lord he multiplies, whether it is our spiritual gifts or our material possessions and money. If we lay up for ourselves treasures here on earth, then moth and rust consume them. It is only treasures in heaven that are permanent. If we want treasure in heaven, we have to send it on in advance. What we hold onto we lose, but what we give we keep for ever.

Giving does not mean handing over financial responsibility to God, but it does mean handing over the burden and the worry of the responsibility.

The people I know who are generous seem to be so much happier, freer, and lighter in their souls. 'The world of the generous gets larger and larger; the world of the stingy gets smaller and smaller' (Proverbs 11:24, *The Message*).

Mother Teresa was asked whether it is only the affluent who give. 'No', she replied, 'Even the poorest of the poor give. The other day a very poor beggar came up to me and said, "Everyone gives to you and I also want to give to you" (it was the equivalent of two pence). I thought to myself, "What do I do? If I take it, he won't have anything to eat. But if I don't take it, I'd hurt him so much." So I took it. And he was so happy, because he'd given to Mother Teresa of Calcutta to help the poor'.

5. Begin to change the world around you

Jesus said '...when you give to the needy' (v.2). Meeting people's needs changes lives. The local church can be an agent of change; it is the hope for the world. The church is best placed to do something about global poverty, preventable diseases, and AIDS. It is also the hope for the world in terms of healthcare, crime and education.

We should give generously to local churches and to Christian organisations that are seeking to bring change in our society. William Wilberforce was able to play his part in bringing an end to slavery because there was a group of bankers who got together to fund what he was trying to do. One of them, Henry Thornton, gave six-sevenths of his income. Some of us are called to be the Henry Thorntons of the twenty-first century; to give to the church so that it is able to carry out its God-given mission to be the hope for the world.

Jesus was rich, yet for you and for me he became poor, so that we might become rich. We are now co-heirs with him (2 Corinthians 8:9, Romans 8:17). We will inherit all that he has. In the meantime, he asks us to follow in his steps and give generously.

Six-year-old Hattie May Wiatt was a Sunday school pupil at Grace Baptist Church in Philadelphia. But the school was so crowded that not everyone could get in. Russell H. Conwell, the pastor, told her that one day they would have buildings big enough to allow everyone to attend. She said, 'I hope you will. It is so crowded I am afraid to go there alone.' He replied, 'When we get the money we will construct one large enough to get all the children in.'

Two years later, in 1886, Hattie May died at the age of eight. After the funeral Hattie's mother gave the minister a little bag they had found under their daughter's pillow containing 57 cents in change that she had saved up. Alongside it was a note in her handwriting, 'To help build the little temple bigger so that more children can go to Sunday school.'

The pastor took the coins and changed all the money into pennies and offered each one for sale. He received $250 – and 54 of the cents were given back. The $250 was itself changed into pennies and sold by the newly formed Wiatt Mite Society. A local business man offered them a house, taking 54 cents as the first payment and giving a mortgage for the rest at 5 per cent.

Twenty years later the minister of what was by now a thriving church preached a sermon, in which he said:

> Think how her life was used. Think of this large church, membership over 5,600 since that time.
>
> Think of the influence of its membership going out and spreading over the world. Think of the institutions that this church has founded. Think of the Samaritan Hospital and the thousands of sick people that have been cured there and the thousands of poor that are ministered to every year – over 30,000 people go to the dispensary of the one hospital every year... Think of the influence of that 57 cents just for a moment. Almost 80,000 young people have gone through the classes of the Temple University. In addition, 2,000 people preach the gospel because Hattie May Wiatt invested her 57 cents, because she laid the foundations and gave her life for it... Being dead, she yet speaks.[9]

How to Pray (and Fast) Like Jesus

And when you pray, do not be like the hypocrites, for they love to pray standing in the synagogues and on the street corners to be seen by others. I tell you the truth, they have received their reward in full. But when you pray, go into your room, close the door and pray to your Father, who is unseen. Then your Father, who sees what is done in secret, will reward you.

And when you pray, do not keep on babbling like pagans, for they think they will be heard because of their many words. Do not be like them, for your Father knows what you need before you ask him.

This, then, is how you should pray:
'Our Father in heaven,
hallowed be your name,
  your kingdom come,
your will be done
on earth as it is in heaven.

  Give us today our daily bread.
  Forgive us our debts,
as we also have forgiven our debtors.

  And lead us not into temptation,
but deliver us from the evil one.'

For if you forgive others when they sin against you, your heavenly Father will also forgive you.

But if you do not forgive others their sins, your Father will not forgive your sins.

When you fast, do not look sombre as the hypocrites do, for they disfigure their faces to show others they are fasting.

I tell you the truth, they have received their reward in full.
But when you fast, put oil on your head and wash your
face, so that it will not be obvious to others that you are
fasting, but only to your Father, who is unseen; and your
Father, who sees what is done in secret, will reward you.
Matthew 6:5–18

Martin Luther, the sixteenth-century reformer, once gave a talk called, *A Simple Way to Pray*. He said this: 'I will tell you as best I can what I do personally when I pray. May our dear Lord grant to you and to everybody to do it better than I! Amen.'[1]

I don't find communicating very easy. Thankfully, I'm married to a very good communicator. Recently, Pippa and I were going to be interviewed at an event at Westminster Central Hall in London. We spent the first part of the morning planning together, preparing what we were going to say. Then we got on our bikes and cycled to Westminster Central Hall, talking along the way. We both spoke at the event and then chatted over lunch. We cycled back home, discussing how it went. Over supper and watching a film that night we continued to talk. Then Pippa said to me, 'Nicky, you haven't communicated with me all day!' I said, 'We've done nothing but communicate all day! We were talking this morning, we were talking on our bikes, what do you mean, I haven't communicated all day?' Her response was, 'Yes we've been talking, but you haven't said what's really going on. You haven't said what you're really thinking, what you're really feeling.' She was right; communicating properly involves expressing what is really going on inside.

As prayer is talking with God it should be the most important activity of our lives. Mother Teresa of Calcutta said,

Prayer is simply talking to God.
He speaks to us: we listen.

We speak to him: he listens.

A two-way process: speaking and listening.[2]

According to surveys 90 per cent of people pray each day. But are they really *communicating* with God? Jonathan Aitken, the former Cabinet minister who spent time in prison, came on Alpha at our church. He said that before his conversion to Christianity he had treated God a bit like how he treated his bank manager:

I spoke to him politely, visited his premises intermittently, occasionally asked him for a small favour, or overdraft, to get myself out of difficulty, thanked him condescendingly for his assistance, kept up the appearance of being one of his reasonably reliable customers, and maintained superficial contact with him on the grounds that one of these days he might come in use.[3]

For other people, prayer is like a first aid kit or fire extinguisher, a last resort for use only in emergencies. Rather like the vicar who said, 'I guess all we can do is pray,' to which the churchwarden said, 'Has it come to *that*?'

In the sixteenth-century St Teresa of Avila (1515–82) wrote that 'prayer is nothing else, in my opinion, than being on terms of friendship with God .'[4] If we want to learn how to pray, we need to receive instruction from the greatest expert of all – Jesus Christ. So, how can we pray like Jesus?

1. Examine your priorities

Jesus taught his disciples to pray and assumed they would do so. He didn't say to them, 'If you pray'. Three times he says, 'When you pray' (vv.5–7). The Jewish people prayed regularly. Twice a day they recited a prayer called the *Shema* and three times a day they prayed the *Tephillah*, a complex series of blessings upon God's people. Jesus' clear expectation was that his disciples would pray daily (v.11). In the Gospels there are many descriptions of Jesus withdrawing from the busyness of life to pray, sometimes getting up while it was still dark to go to a quiet place to pray. For Jesus, prayer was his top priority.

Stephen Covey, author of the book *The Seven Habits of Highly Effective People,* says that the key is not to prioritise what is on our schedules, but to schedule our priorities. He illustrates this in his seminars by taking a glass jar with some sand in it. He invites people to come up on stage to try to add some big stones and some small pebbles. No one can fit the stones and pebbles into the jar.

Then he shows them how to do it. The only way is to empty the sand out of the jar first. You need to put the big stones in first, those things that are priorities in your life. Next come the small pebbles, the secondary things. Finally, you put the sand on top. When you do that, the stones, pebbles and sand fit into the jar. In other words, when we get our main priorities right, we find we have room for everything else.

I make prayer my first activity in the morning. Of course there are challenges to this as well as many distractions. C. S. Lewis describes how '... the very moment you wake up each morning... All your wishes and hopes for the day rush at you like wild animals. And the first job each morning consists simply in shoving them all back, in listening to that other voice, taking that other point of view, letting that other larger, stronger, quieter life come rushing in.'[5]

Some people have good reasons why they can't pray in the morning, but if we can prioritise prayer first thing, it makes a huge difference to the day ahead. Martin Luther wrote about the distractions 500 years ago, before newspapers, television, and mobile internet:

It's a good thing to let prayer be the first business of the morning... Guard yourself carefully against those false, deluding ideas which tell you, 'Wait a little while. I'll pray in an hour. First I must attend to this or that.' Such thoughts get you away from prayer into other affairs, which so hold your attention and involve you that nothing comes of prayer for that day.[6]

Then Jesus says, 'When you fast... ' (v.16). We read of Jesus fasting on at least one occasion and there are many more references to prayer than fasting in the Bible. Certainly in my own life I would have to say that fasting is pretty rare, particularly in recent years! For some people it really isn't wise; for example, if you're pregnant, breastfeeding, diabetic, ill, stressed, depressed, bereaved, or liable to eating disorders.

On the other hand there can be spiritual benefits to fasting, including:
- Strengthening and reinforcing prayer (Matthew 4:2)
- Sign of repentance and humility before God (Daniel 9)
- Seeking God's guidance (Acts 13:2)
- Self-discipline (1 Corinthians 9:24–27)
- Sharing food with the hungry (Isaiah 58:6–10)

Bishop Sandy Millar often advises people, when they are facing a major decision, for example about marriage or a career choice, to go away for a weekend to fast and pray. Fasting enables us to concentrate solely on one thing, and to give ourselves to praying for it.

In the New Testament, fasting means going without food for spiritual reasons, as opposed to any kind of dieting. We can also be more imaginative about fasting, giving up, for example, magazines, TV, the internet, or even buying clothes. I remember one young woman in our congregation went on a clothes 'fast' for a year. She wanted to break the hold of the habit of buying clothes. For the first two weeks she found it very difficult but after that she found the desire was broken. It also saved her a great deal of money! I think I can honestly say that would be the easiest fast I could go on. In fact, some might think I have been on a clothes fast for rather a long time! However, there are other things that I would find much more difficult to give up.

2. Enjoy the privilege

As with giving, Jesus promises that when we fast and pray, we will receive a reward from God. He says, 'your Father, who sees what is done in secret, will reward you' (vv.6, 18). God chiefly rewards those who fast with answered prayer. The rewards of prayer include experiencing the joy of God's presence (Psalm 16:11) and receiving God's peace (Philippians 4:6–7). As we unload our burdens, guilt, fears, and worries, we discover a peace that is beyond understanding. We are able to receive a new perspective on our problems and God's guidance.

Jesus gives us three invaluable guidelines to help us enjoy the privilege of prayer.

Keep it real

Jesus says, 'When you pray, do not be like the hypocrites. They love to pray standing in the synagogues and on the street corners to be seen by others. I tell you the truth, they have received their reward in full' (v.5).

Jesus is not criticising public worship, coming to church, praying out loud or corporate prayer. In fact, there are more references to corporate prayer in the New Testament than to personal prayer. He is simply warning against doing these things for the wrong motives, hoping that others will be impressed by our spirituality. If we go to a prayer meeting in order simply to be seen by others, then that is the only reward we will get. We are hypocrites because we are pretending to be spiritual when we are not. We are insincere. The right motive for prayer is a desire to encounter our Father in heaven.

We are called to be genuine in our relationship with God. C. S. Lewis said, 'The prayer preceding all prayers is, "May it be the real I who speaks. May it be the real Thou that I speak to." '[7] There should be no pretence. Our relationship with God is to be real, honest and authentic. This is the opposite of hypocrisy.

Keep it quiet

Jesus says, 'When you pray, go into your room, close the door and pray to your Father, who is unseen. Then your Father, who sees what is done in secret, will reward you' (v.6).

Jesus went to the mountains to pray. I have a corner of a room that I use regularly for prayer. But it can be hard to find a quiet place to pray. Susannah Wesley, mother of John Wesley (the eighteenth-century preacher and founder of Methodism), had nineteen children. When she wanted to spend time with God she had a unique way of finding her 'quiet place'. She would sit down in her kitchen and pull her apron up over her head. She would spend time in prayer and her children knew not to disturb her at that moment! It's important to find a place where you can pray without being distracted.

Jesus encourages his followers to find time to be alone with God in a secret place. No doubt part of the reason for this is that when we are alone there will be no distractions. But Jesus is speaking more about ostentation than of distractions. To 'go to your room' is a metaphorical way of denoting privacy and the absence of admirers.

The Greek word for 'room' means 'inner room', which was also a store room where treasures might be kept. It is here that 'your Father who sees what is done in secret, will reward you' (v.6). What we seek is what we get. If we seek the admiration of others, then that is all we get. If we seek to encounter God, then that will be our reward. We will experience his love for us and be filled with love for others. He will make his presence known to us. 'You will fill me with joy in your presence,' writes the psalmist (Psalm 16:11).

We will be able to off-load our guilt, our problems and our burdens in prayer to God and find a peace that passes understanding. We will gain a new perspective on life as we begin to see things from God's perspective. We will hear his voice and receive his guidance for our lives. We will have the joy of seeing our prayers answered. We will receive power for living as he fills us with his Spirit. In comparison to this and the countless other blessings God gives us, the rewards of being seen by others pale into insignificance.

Keep it simple

Jesus also admonishes us to keep our prayers simple. He says that the pagans pray in a wrong manner: 'And when you pray, do not keep on babbling like pagans, for they think they will be heard because of their many words. Do not be like them, for your Father knows what you need before you ask him' (vv.7–8).

The pagans did not pray to the one true God but to a panoply of gods. In order to be sure that they were addressing the right god by the right name, they sometimes addressed all the gods with all their various titles. What mattered, they thought, was the correct repetition rather than the worshipper's attitude and intention. Jesus denounced such formal invocation and magical incantations as 'babbling'.

Moreover, the pagans had a mathematical notion of prayer. They believed that the longer they prayed the more likely they were to be heard. Jesus said that it is not the length of prayer that counts but its sincerity. He was about to teach them a prayer with only fifty-seven Greek words, which can be prayed in less than thirty seconds.

Jesus was not against repetition in prayer, but he was against *mindless* repetition. Indeed he taught his disciples to be persistent in prayer, to go on asking, to go on seeking, to go on knocking. He taught them two parables to this effect. One went like this: suppose you get a surprise visit from a friend who has been abroad for some time. It is late at night and the fridge is completely empty, so you pop round to see a friend, whom you know always has lots of food in his house. You ring the doorbell and find that he is already asleep. He wakes up and tells you to go away and come back in the morning. However, you persist and say, 'I really need that food now.' Because you insist, he gets the food for you (see Luke 11:5–8).

The second parable was to show his disciples that they should always pray and never give up. He told them a story about a terrible old judge who was not remotely interested in justice. He was totally godless. A woman who had lost her husband was in a dispute with her neighbour and so she took legal action. The judge was not interested, but she kept coming back. Eventually the judge decided that it was easier to give her justice than to have to put up with her coming to court all the time (see Luke 18:1–8).

Jesus himself in the Garden of Gethsemane repeated the same prayer three times. But neither the prayer of Jesus, nor that which he taught his disciples, was mindless repetition intended to impress by its length. Jesus cried out to his Father from the agony of his situation. Likewise, when we are weighed down, we cannot help but cry out constantly to God to answer our prayers.

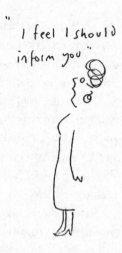

Jesus points out that we do not pray like this in order to inform God of something he does not know about, 'for your Father knows what you need before you ask him' (v.8). Rather, God gives us the privilege of being involved in his plans. In that sense prayer is for our benefit, not for his.

3. Establish a pattern

Jesus says, 'This, then, is how you should pray' (v.9). He goes on to give his disciples a model for prayer. It is not intended to be the only model, but it is the simplest and yet the most refined. It is comprehensive and universal in that it covers in principle everything that we could ask of God. Essentially, it is supplication (asking). Adoration, praise and thanksgiving are very important, but we are not to look down on asking as the lowest form of prayer. Supplication is at the very heart of the prayer that Jesus taught his disciples. Sadly, it has often been prayed mechanically, which is exactly what Jesus has just been teaching us not to do. However, many have found it to be a helpful and inspirational structure for prayer.

Begin with thanksgiving, praise and worship (v.9)

The prayer begins with a recollection of who we are approaching. Almost certainly, Jesus originally prayed and taught his disciples to pray in Aramaic. The word he used for Father was 'Abba', a word which conveys intimacy, like the English word 'Daddy' or 'Dad', but without the childish connotations. It is also quite extraordinary that Jesus tells us to go into a secret room, shut the door and then pray, 'Our Father...' and not, 'My Father... ' Here is a clear sense of being part of God's family, praying with many others.

As we begin to pray it is crucial that we appreciate what we are doing. We are speaking to God. The realisation of this fact transforms our prayers. We are not talking to ourselves or meditating. We are speaking to a person who is as real as we are, if not more so. Moreover, he is a loving Father with heavenly power. This realisation should lift our hearts to thanksgiving, praise and worship as we begin to pray.

Worship is expressing our love for God. My father was a barrister and one of his contemporaries was a judge called Henry Ruttle. When I started practising at the bar he was the senior county court judge in the country. He was a wonderful man and it was quite awe-inspiring to appear in front of him, which I did on a couple of occasions. I was friends with his son Steve who once asked me to a prayer meeting at his house, which was being led by his father. I was surprised when Judge Ruttle told us that he prayed each day and that he began by saying, 'I love you Lord!' He then stood up and began the prayer meeting. He raised his hands in the air and said, 'I love you Lord! I love you Jesus!' This awe-inspiring judge was standing in front of me worshipping Jesus from his heart with total abandonment.

This is also the appropriate moment to thank God for all his blessings, such as health, family, friends and answered prayers.

Focus on God's honour (v.9)

The name of God means the revelation of who he is. Our first concern should be for God's name to be honoured. According to the US Centre for World Missions, the Christian church is growing at a rate three times faster than the world population. However, in the United Kingdom this is not the case. God's name is seldom honoured in the media, in culture, in politics or in schools. The supreme cry of our hearts should be to see his name honoured. I try to pray every day that I will bring honour to God's name. As we look around our nation, we want to see God's name honoured again.

Pray for God's rule and reign (v.10)

God's kingdom is God's rule and reign. What would God's kingdom look like? It would mean knife crime coming to an end. It would be safe to walk on the streets of this country. It would mean that people wouldn't be worried about which school they sent their children to, because all schools would be good schools. It would mean that family life was strong and children were brought up in secure homes. It would mean that we were living in a peaceful and harmonious society.

Globally it would mean an end to extreme poverty, whereby a child dies every three seconds. It would mean an end to preventable diseases. It would mean that something was done about AIDS, and universal primary education. This is God's kingdom coming! That's what we're praying for when we pray 'your kingdom come'.

Commit your decisions (v.10)

This is not a prayer of resignation, but a desire to know God's will and to see God's will done in our lives. God's will for us is 'good, pleasing and perfect' (Romans 12:2). We need to know God's will for our lives, whether for the big issues like marriage and career, or for the details of our lives as we go through each day.

Ask his help with daily needs (v.11)

Jesus teaches us that our most basic material needs should be included in our prayers. Nothing is too small to pray about. It can be good to go through the day in our prayers, asking God for what we need, whether it be housing, food, paying the bills or catching a train.

Make a clean start each day (v.12)

Jesus expands on these words in the Sermon on the Mount: 'For if you forgive others when they sin against you, your heavenly Father will also forgive you. But if you do not forgive others their sins, your Father will not forgive your sins' (vv.14–15).

Later in Matthew's Gospel Jesus tells the story about a foreign king who was owed the equivalent of £10 million by a civil servant (Matthew 18:23–35). The man could not pay and so the king ordered that everything he had be sold. Bankruptcy proceedings were begun against him and his wife and children were to be sold into slavery. The man begged for mercy and asked for time to pay. The king, in an extraordinary act, forgave him the entire debt.

The civil servant himself was owed £2,000 by another man. He grabbed this man and demanded instant payment. This man begged for mercy, but the civil servant took court proceedings and eventually the man was jailed for nonpayment of the debt. The king got to hear about this and was furious. He had the civil servant arrested and said to him, 'You evil man. I let you off a debt of £10 million just because you asked me – shouldn't you have done the same to others?' He ordered the man to be sent to the torturers until he had paid the last penny.

Forgive anyone you need to forgive (v.12)

Jesus said, 'This is how my heavenly Father will treat each of you unless you forgive one another from your heart.' There is a connection between forgiving and receiving forgiveness. We do not earn forgiveness by forgiving others, but it is the evidence that we have received forgiveness. Daily we need to receive forgiveness and daily we need to forgive.

Philip Yancey writes:

> Consider again the act of repentance. Confessing my sins before God communicates something God already knows, yet somehow the act of confession binds the relationship and allows a closeness that could not otherwise exist. I make myself vulnerable and dependent, bringing God and me together. The same kind of intimacy happens when, all too rarely, I apologise to my wife for something we both know about. I do not bring her information; I bring her my heart, my humbled self.[8]

Ask for his protection and power (v.13)

The word used for temptation can mean either 'temptation' or 'testing'. God does not tempt us with evil (James 1:13) but he does allow us to be tested (see for example, the story of Job). Here we are praying, in effect, 'Grant that we will not fail the test.' We are all tempted and we need God's protection and his power. This is a good moment to pray that God would fill us with his Spirit and equip us for the day ahead.

Prayer is not always easy. Some prayers are not answered.[9] Furthermore, we may experience periods when it seems God is miles away. Anyone who has been a Christian for more than a few years is likely to have experienced what is sometimes referred to as 'the dark night of the soul'.[10] These are seasons, sometimes accompanied by tragedy, when we would expect to experience God's closeness but instead it can seem that a door has been 'slammed in your face'.[11] It is important to remember that this, though very hard, is temporary.

I have been attempting to pray for over forty years, and I'm certainly not an expert. I keep prayer diaries, but I really hope that no one ever reads them, because they are so pathetic! However, prayer is never a waste of time. Looking back, so many prayers *have* been answered. Some of them are quite mundane. Some could appear to be coincidences. Yet, as William Temple said, 'When I pray, coincidences happen. When I don't, they don't.' I really believe that prayer makes a difference, not only in our lives; it also changes events. It changes the world. That is why as a follower of Jesus I try to make prayer the top priority in my life.

How to Handle Money

'Do not store up for yourselves treasures on earth, where moth and rust destroy, and where thieves break in and steal. But store up for yourselves treasures in heaven, where moth and rust do not destroy, and where thieves do not break in and steal. For where your treasure is, there your heart will be also.

The eye is the lamp of the body. If your eyes are good, your whole body will be full of light. But if your eyes are bad, your whole body will be full of darkness. If then the light within you is darkness, how great is that darkness! No one can be a slave to two masters. Either you will hate the one and love the other, or you will be devoted to the one and despise the other. You cannot be a slave to both God and Money.'

Matthew 6:19-24

If we grasp Jesus' teaching in this section of the Sermon on the Mount, it will transform our lives. It will affect our security, our vision and ultimately our relationship with God. Yet few people seem to have caught hold of what Jesus is saying.

When we look around us at the idols of the twenty-first century, there are many to follow. First, there is money divorced from reality. Actor and former Governor of California Arnold Schwarzenegger said: 'Money doesn't make you happy. I now have $50million, but I was just as happy when I had $48million.'[1] While we may know that money does not make us happy, somehow it is a powerful force, and all of us can feel the pull. Money, especially money divorced from reality, is something we treasure, a kind of twenty-first century idol. It carries with it a danger of materialism, consumerism, and 'affluenza'. Psychologist Oliver James describes 'affluenza' as 'an obsessive, envious, keeping-up-with-the-Joneses. Buying things we don't need, with money that we haven't got, to satisfy needs that can't be satisfied by material things.'[2]

Another twenty-first century idol is sex divorced from commitment. Indeed, sex is now sometimes divorced from love as well. David Baddiel, writing in *Esquire* recently under the heading 'Sex without Love', said this: 'Love is something that's been invented purely to suppress us. It's time love and sex got divorced. Have sex without pressure whatever you do. Don't think you have to be in love.'[3]

Third, there is fame: fame for its own sake, divorced from any kind of achievement. People now want to be famous without doing anything. They just want to be famous for being famous. I read in *The Week* about a new school that has opened in New York for aspiring reality TV stars to 'train and develop non-actors' to be 'exciting, confident members of reality TV casts'.[4] People want to be famous and if they can't be famous, the second best thing is to know someone who's famous, and if we can't do that, at least to know about famous people. Kate Muir wrote in *The Times* recently, 'Now, our drug of choice is fame, available to everyone... Now more than ever, as we enter the long, dark tunnel of repossession, recession and bloated, busted banks, we will be turning to the comforting world of idol worship.'[5]

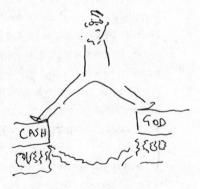

So how can we avoid this kind of idolatry? How can we be ambitious in the right way? How can we handle money well? Most of us have to deal with money every day, but we prefer not to talk about it in church. Jesus talked about it a great deal, however, and in this passage he puts before us a blunt choice between two options. In doing so, he echoes Elijah in the Old Testament, who asked the people: 'How long will you waver between two opinions? If the Lord is God, follow him; but if Baal is God, follow him' (1 Kings 18:21). Jesus puts before us two securities and then calls us to have an undivided heart.

1. Invest your life for a high return

'Do not store up for yourselves treasures on earth where moth and rust destroy, where thieves break in and steal' (v.19). What does Jesus mean when he says we are not to store up treasures on earth? His teaching has often been misunderstood and misinterpreted. First, he does not mean that Christians are required to give away all the money they have. In only one recorded case did he tell someone to give everything away (Mark 10:21). It seems that Joseph of Arimathea continued to be wealthy (Matthew 27:57) after he become a disciple of Jesus and the same is likely to be true of Nicodemus. During his ministry, Jesus was supported by various wealthy women (Luke 8:1–3).

Second, it does not mean that it is wrong to make or invest money. The parable of the talents, in spite of some ingenious attempts to interpret it otherwise, speaks approvingly about making money. Talents were money, which we now interpret as gifts, but originally the reference is to money. Some, it would seem, are called to make money, perhaps even large sums of money, for the glory of God and for the purposes of his use in his kingdom.

I can remember a young man from our congregation telling me

in the 1980s that he felt called to work in finance and to make money for the purposes of investing it in the kingdom of God. As I've watched him over the last twenty years he has been absolutely faithful to that calling, living relatively modestly compared to how he could live, but giving increasingly large sums.

Third, it is not wrong to save. The New Testament encourages us to provide for our relatives and especially for our own immediate family. Indeed, we have a duty to do so. Anyone who does not do so is 'worse than an unbeliever' (1 Timothy 5:8). Jesus chided those who excused the fact that they were not looking after their parents financially on the basis that they had set aside for God the money they would have used to look after them (Mark 7:9–12). Saving enables us to provide for the needs of others.

Fourth, it is not wrong to enjoy the good things of life. God has provided us with all things richly to enjoy (1 Timothy 6:17). Jesus ate with the rich and privileged (Luke 11:37) and went to a lavish wedding (John 2:1–11) and helped to make it even more lavish. Wealth, at least in the Old Testament, was often seen as a sign of God's blessing. God blessed Abraham with cattle, silver and gold, and Solomon's wealth was seen as evidence of God's favour. Under the new covenant, God's blessing is not material but spiritual, but material gifts can still be gratefully enjoyed as undeserved gifts from God.

So what does Jesus mean? He is concerned not so much with our wealth, but with our hearts and affections; that is, what we think about when our minds are in neutral. He is concerned not so much with money as the love of money that the apostle Paul describes as 'a root of all kinds of evil' (1 Timothy 6:10). Jesus forbids the selfish accumulation of money and egocentric covetousness. In other words, he condemns materialism and the unhealthy obsession with and trust in possessions. But he does so without despising material things themselves.

Jesus explains this teaching in two ways. First, he says, the problem with 'storing up treasures on earth' is that they promise security, but actually lead to perpetual insecurity, because 'moth and rust destroy, and... thieves break in and steal.' Life may be different in the modern world, but the principle is the same. George Harrison, despite all the money he had made as one of the Beatles, said, 'For every hundred pounds you earn you get a hundred pounds' worth of problems.' As Seneca put it centuries before, 'Money has never yet made anyone rich.' Jesus is reminding us that treasures here on earth are never going to be totally secure.

Second, materialism leads us away from God. Jesus says, 'For where your treasure is, there your hearts will be also' (v.21). As John Stott puts it, materialism 'tethers our hearts to the earth'.[6] For these reasons, Jesus says that it is a bad investment. Instead of investing in storing up treasures on earth we should invest in storing up 'treasures in heaven' (v.20). This is not describing a way of earning our salvation, but speaks of investing in the kingdom of heaven – God's rule and reign on earth. Investing in this kingdom will primarily mean putting our time, energy and money into people. It will mean, among other things, investing in the evangelisation of our cities, our country and the world. It will also include parents who are bringing up children as followers of Christ and caring for ex-offenders, the homeless and the poor. In AD 250, during the days of the Decian persecution in Rome, the Roman prefect burst into a church service and demanded, 'Show me your treasures.' They had come to take away everything of value. A deacon of the church called Lorencius showed him the adjoining room, threw open the door and replied, 'These are the treasures of our church.' Inside was a group of widows, orphans, sick people and paupers, all being cared for by members of the church.

Why should we invest in storing up for ourselves 'treasures in heaven'? Again, Jesus gives us two reasons. First, this investment is totally secure and it will last forever – 'where moth and rust do not destroy, and where thieves do not break in and steal'. It is a good bargain to exchange the transitory for the eternal. God has given us an inheritance that can never 'perish, spoil or fade' and that is 'kept in heaven' for us (1 Peter 1:4). What we can see is temporary, 'but what is unseen is eternal' (2 Corinthians 4:18).

Second, Jesus says that our hearts will follow our treasure (v.21). Giving is one of the secret disciplines Jesus spoke about in Matthew 6:1–4. People who give to the church are usually the ones who are most committed. As we give generously to the kingdom of God our hearts will follow our money. Sometimes we see people looking at their share prices in the *Financial Times*. Why? Because they've invested money in that company and they really care about how well it does. If we invest money in God's kingdom then Jesus says our heart will be passionate about it as well.

2. Fix your eyes in the right direction

Jesus puts before us two possible visions for our life and calls us to be single-minded. 'The eye is the lamp of the body. If your eyes are good, your whole body will be full of light. But if your eyes are bad,

your whole body will be full of darkness. If then the light within you is darkness, how great is that darkness!' (vv.22–23). Jesus is using here the analogy of physical eyes. If our eyes are working properly we will have light inside. If our eyes are bad and we are blind, we have darkness.

At the spiritual level, it is true that the eyes are the windows of the soul, and so it matters a great deal where we set our spiritual sights. Do we set our spiritual sights on God or greed? What do we spend our time planning? What do we dream about? Where does our effort go? Jesus warns us that if our eyes are bad our whole bodies will be full of great darkness (v.23). The word for 'bad' literally means 'evil'. An evil eye is fixed not on Jesus but on selfish gain and materialism. It is set on obtaining more for ourselves. This eye is full of lust, greed, avarice and resentment. Such an eye inevitably harbours jealousy, which Shakespeare described as 'the green-ey'd monster which doth mock the meat it feeds on'.[7] Once again there is often a physical manifestation – a darkness in people's eyes which reflects the darkness in their souls.

The 'good eye', on the other hand, is translated from the Greek word for 'single'. It means to have a single vision, to be looking in the right direction. And if we've got our eyes fixed in the right direction, everything else falls into place. When mowing the lawn the way to mow in a straight line is not to look down. If you look down and watch what you're doing the mower goes all over the place. The only way to mow in a straight line is to fix your eyes on an object at the other end of the garden. So it is in the spiritual realm: our hearts will follow our eyes. That is why the writer to the Hebrews encourages us to 'fix our eyes on Jesus' (Hebrews 12:2).

Those eyes fixed on Jesus will have their bodies full of the light of the Spirit. A little boy was asked to define a 'saint'. At first he could not think of an appropriate definition, but then he thought of all the saints represented on stained-glass windows. He observed that a saint 'is someone through whom the light shines'. Sometimes this has an almost physical manifestation. On one occasion Jesus' face is described as shining 'like the sun' (Matthew 17:2). There are some people who have 'shining faces' and seem to radiate the love and light of God. They light up a room whenever they enter it. One such person is Jackie Pullinger, who has worked in Hong Kong for the last forty years among drug addicts, the poor and homeless. She says that God gave her 'resurrection eyes'; that is, eyes that see the living Christ.[8]

3. Spend your time working for a liberating boss

Jesus says, 'No one can be a slave to two masters. Either you will hate the one and love the other, or you'll be devoted to the one and despise the other. You cannot be a slave to both God and money' (v.24). He places before us two possible gods and calls us to a surrendered will.

Money is not a neutral, impersonal medium of exchange. The word used in the original is not money but 'Mammon'. 'Mammon' was the god of wealth in Carthage. And money is a kind of god. Money has all the characteristics of a pagan god. It seems to offer security, freedom, power, influence, status and prestige. Simon Cowell, described as 'TV's rudest talent show judge', is clearly extremely good at his job. He was interviewed by Lynn Barber for *The Observer*: 'Why is he so obsessed with adding to his already vast fortune? He has said many times that money is what drives him, that it is his god.'[9]

Money is capable of inspiring this kind of devotion and it requires a single-minded preoccupation. It demands sacrifice and, ultimately, human sacrifice. Many sacrifice their health for money, through stress, long hours and no exercise or relaxation. Worse still, some sacrifice the lives of others as human relationships are destroyed. No time is reserved for a spouse, children, friends or God. 'Drive! Push! Hustle! Scheme! Invest! Prepare! Anticipate! Work! Fourteen hour days... followed by weekends at the office, forfeited holidays and midnight oil.'[10] The result is often broken marriages and single-parent families – the latter created not only through divorce, but because one of the parents is always out at work.

Jesus warns that we cannot serve two gods. Dietrich Bonhoeffer put it like this: 'Our hearts have room only for one all embracing devotion, and we can only cleave to one Lord.'[11] Money is a good servant, but it is a bad master; if we serve it we will become a slave to it. Like seawater, the more you have the more you thirst for. John D. Rockefeller, founder of Standard Oil Company, was once asked, 'How much money does it take to make someone happy?' He answered, 'Just a little bit more than he has.' Barry Humphries (whose best-known character is Dame Edna Everage) entitled his autobiography *More Please*. He wrote:

> I always wanted more. I never had enough milk, or money, or socks, or sex, or holidays, or first editions, or solitude, or gramophone records, or free meals, or real friends, or guiltless pleasure, or neckties, or applause, or unquestioning love, or persimmons. Of course, I have had more than my share of most of these commodities but it always left me with a vague feeling of unfulfilment: where was the rest?[12]

The problem with money is that we think we own it but, if we are not careful, it ends up owning us. Henry Fielding pithily observed: 'If you make money your god it will plague you like the devil.' In the ancient Roman port of Pompeii in the year AD 79, among those who fled from the torrents of lava erupting from Mount Vesuvius was a woman who sought to save not only her life, but also her valuable jewels. With her hands full of rings, bracelets, necklaces, chains and other treasures she was overwhelmed by the rain of ashes from the volcano, and died. In the course of modern building operations outside the area of the buried city her petrified body was unearthed in a sea of jewels. She lost her life to save her treasure.

Jesus warns that if money is our God we will 'despise' the only true God (v.24). The word for 'despise' means 'to be indifferent to or unconcerned about something'. This is exactly what is happening to the church in the West today. As materialism has flourished, people have started to serve the god Mammon and have become apathetic and unconcerned about God. One of the thorns and thistles that Jesus describes in the parable of the sower is 'the delight in riches'. As this grows, it squeezes out life and the seed proves unfruitful.

Ultimately, materialism is atheism; it is to be without God. A friend recently said to me, 'Look what happened to communism. It was a form of atheism and it collapsed. Materialism is a kind of atheism and now it's collapsing.'

We should hold onto everything loosely. We break the power of materialism by generous and cheerful giving. Again, this is an act of the will, saying 'no' to Mammon and 'yes' to God. We cannot serve them both. Generous giving is an affront to Mammon and it destroys the demon greed. That demon will scream out, 'You can't do this to me!' We should reply, 'Yes I can, and I will!' and in doing so we kill it. Sometimes like a weed it re-emerges and we have to kill it again by continuing to give generously. Generous giving celebrates 'the fact that Jesus is Lord and Mammon isn't'.[13]

13

How to Stop Worrying
and Start Living[1]

*Therefore I tell you, do not worry about your life, what
you will eat or drink; or about your body, what you will
wear. Is not life more important than food, and the body
more important than clothes? Look at the birds of the air;
they do not sow or reap or store away in barns, and yet
your heavenly Father feeds them. Are you not much more
valuable than they? Who of you by worrying can add a
single hour to your life?*

*And why do you worry about clothes? See how the lilies
of the field grow. They do not labour or spin. Yet I tell you
that not even Solomon in all his splendour was dressed
like one of these. If that is how God clothes the grass of
the field, which is here today and tomorrow is thrown into
the fire, will he not much more clothe you, O you of little
faith? So do not worry, saying, 'What shall we eat?' or
'What shall we drink?' or 'What shall we wear?' For the
pagans run after all these things, and your heavenly Father
knows that you need them. But seek first his kingdom
and his righteousness, and all these things will be given to
you as well. Therefore do not worry about tomorrow, for
tomorrow will worry about itself. Each day has enough
trouble of its own.*
Matthew 6:25–34

Some people are more prone to worry than others. Two
cardiologists, Dr Meyer Friedman and Dr Ray Rosenman, after

conducting research into the effects of stress upon the heart, divided people into two groups: Type A and Type B. Type A people were more prone to worry than Type B and were three times more likely to have a stroke or a heart attack than those in the Type B category, even if they were doing the same sort of work and living in similar conditions. Rob Parsons, Chairman and Chief Executive of Care for the Family, has identified some of the characteristics of Type A personalities:

We are very competitive. We compete over everything and find to our embarrassment that when playing board games with small children we are desperately trying to win.

We cannot resist a telephone ringing. The worst thing in life that can happen to us is to get to the telephone just as it stops ringing. If that happens we begin to ring people, asking, 'Was that you trying to get me a moment ago?'

We swap lanes in traffic jams – even though we know that there is an eternal law that the lane we have just joined will now move more slowly than the lane we have just left.

When driving down motorways we are constantly working out complicated mathematical sums: 'Stoke-on-Trent is 90 miles. If I drive at 90mph it will take me an hour. If I drive at 180mph it will take me half an hour. If I drive at 70mph... no, that's too difficult.'...

We hate stopping for petrol. Why do we hate it so much? It's because when we pull in at the service station we look out over the road and see all the cars and lorries we had overtaken going past.[2]

Worry is one of the most pervasive phenomena of our time. What causes us to worry?

The main worry Jesus is speaking about is material worry – that is, 'what you will eat or drink... what you will wear' (v.25). Yet Jesus' teaching also has wider application. He says, 'do not worry about your life.'

People are rarely without some kind of worry. There are the day-to-day anxieties of exams, jobs, money or houses. Times of financial crisis often lead to various anxieties: unemployment, bankruptcy, repossessions, redundancy, the harsh reality of bills, debts, mortgages, and the threat of small businesses going under.

Difficult or broken relationships can be a significant cause of anxiety. There is also the stress of singleness and loneliness. People worry about their health, the approach of old age, and death. Catherine Deneuve, once dubbed 'the most beautiful woman in the world', said of growing old, 'It worries me and it bores me. It's very painful to look in the mirror every day and watch yourself ageing.'

Worry can affect our physical and mental health, and can even take years off a person's life. The Middle English word *wyrgan* [from which we get the word 'worry'] means 'to strangle'. Worries often seize us by the throat until we can't think about anything else.[3]

Jesus never promised us a stress-free life; neither will we ever get rid of all the causes for worry. As soon as we get rid of one problem, others will move in to replace it. If anyone had cause for worry, Jesus did. He faced the pressures of day-to-day living and had no regular source of income. He knew what it felt like when a close friend died, he experienced the pressure of being misunderstood, threatened with death and unfairly tried. He knew the pressure of powerful temptations, of suffering and living his life under the shadow of the cross. He knew he was to die on the cross for the sins of the world. The whole human race depended on him. He is supremely qualified to say, 'Do not worry', and to tell us why not.

1. Understand life's purpose

To worry is to miss the point of life. Jesus says, 'Therefore I tell you, do not worry about your life, what you will eat or drink; or about your body, what you will wear. Is not life more important than food, and the body more important than clothes?' (v.25). Life is far more important than material things. So often our worries are about relatively unimportant matters, such as food, drink, clothing, houses and cars.

Magazines today may often contain advice on how to combat stress while also being devoted to the very things Jesus told us not to worry about – clothes, food and drink. They include many articles and advertisements about the body: how to feed it; 'Eat Yourself Beautiful in 30 Days!', how to shape it, how to 'take four-and-a-half inches off without moving an inch', and how to make it attractive.

Jesus says that if we simply seek external things, we are missing the whole point of life. The point of life is to have a relationship with God through Jesus Christ. He asks: 'For what profit is it to a man if he gains the whole world, and loses his own soul?' (Matthew 16:26, NKJV). Understanding life's purpose protects us from unnecessary worry.

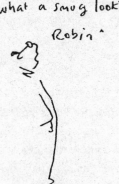

" what a smug looking Robin "

2. Keep perspective

Worry is illogical. Jesus says, 'Look at the birds of the air; they do not sow or reap or store away in barns, and yet your heavenly Father feeds them. Are you not much more valuable than they?' (v.26). Jesus tells us that worry is a slander on God's character, suggesting that he is more interested in his pets than in his children. Birds are kept alive by food provided by nature, such as worms and insects. They have to spend a lot of time hunting and searching for the food, but it is there to be found. We should not simply sit back and say, 'God will provide.' The birds of the air work extremely hard, but they are free from worry. Jesus encourages us to look at them and to think about these facts.

He reminds us that we have a 'heavenly Father' (v.26) who loves us. Since we know that he cares about us so much that he sent his only Son to die for us we can feel secure. The psalmist said:

> The Lord is my shepherd, I shall not be in want...
> Even though I walk
> Through the valley of the shadow of death,
> I will fear no evil
> Psalm 23:1, 4

We must keep perspective, remembering that God is ultimately in control; he is the Sovereign Lord. The apostle Paul also writes, 'We know that in all things God works for the good of those who love him, who have been called according to his purpose' (Romans 8:28).

3. Be practical

Worry is a complete waste of time. Jesus says, 'Who of you by worrying can add a single hour to your life?' (v.27). Worry is futile, unproductive and pointless. There is detailed discussion by biblical historians about whether Jesus meant that he could not add a 'single cubit to his height' or 'a single hour to his life', but it does not really matter which is right. The point Jesus is making is that we cannot add anything. In fact, worry can only subtract from our lives by causing things like stomach ulcers or heart problems.

It is better to be practical; to take practical steps to look after ourselves. If we watch what we eat and drink, make sure we get sufficient sleep and take regular exercise, we will perform better at work and are less likely to get ill. Our spiritual health is, of course, also important. As Paul says, 'For physical training is of some value, but godliness has value for all things, holding promise for both the present life and the life to come' (1 Timothy 4:8).

It is also well known that physical exercise will actually help relieve stress and anxiety, and certainly for me it is an important way of dealing with worry. Similarly we need to find ways to replenish our emotional 'tanks', through spending time with family and friends, listening to music or going for a walk in the countryside. Rick Warren often says that we should 'divert daily' (don't work sixteen-hour days), 'withdraw weekly' (take a day off) and 'abandon annually' (take holidays).

So many of the things that we worry about never happen. Sir Winston Churchill said, 'When I look back on all these worries, I remember the story of the old man who said on his death bed that he had had a lot of trouble in his life, most of which never happened.'[4] Mark Twain similarly reflected: 'Most of my disasters never happened to me.' William Barclay recalls the story of a London doctor who:

Was paralysed and bedridden, but almost outrageously cheerful, and his smile so brave and radiant that everyone forgot to be sorry for him. His children adored him, and when one of his boys was leaving the nest and setting forth on life's adventure, Dr. Greatheart gave him good advice: 'Johnny,' he said, 'the thing to do, my lad, is to hold your own end up, and to do it like a gentleman, and please remember the biggest troubles you have got to face are those that never come.'[5]

4. Trust God's provision

Worry is incompatible with faith. Jesus says (vv.28–32),

And why do you worry about clothes? See how the lilies of the field grow. They do not labour or spin. Yet I tell you that not even Solomon in all his splendour was dressed like one of these. If that is how God clothes the grass of the field, which is here today and tomorrow is thrown into the fire, will he not much more clothe you, O you of little faith? So do not worry, saying, 'What shall we eat?' or 'What shall we drink?' or 'What shall we wear?' For the pagans run after all these things, and your heavenly Father knows that you need them.

Faith and anxiety are like fire and water. Faith involves trust in God's care and provision. I once saw a poster outside a church, which asked, 'Why pray when you can worry and take tranquillizers?' To be a Christian is to walk in a trusting relationship with God, but sin interferes with that relationship and often leads to worry.

Jesus says that 'the pagans run after all these things, and your heavenly Father knows that you need them' (v.32). A primary concern with material needs is a characteristic of those who do not have faith in God, but we, through our trust in God, are called to be different. We have a 'heavenly Father'. We should not run away, rather we should tell God what we are feeling and draw near to him in times of anxiety. St Peter said, 'Cast all your anxiety on him because he cares for you' (1 Peter 5:7). Paul says: 'Do not be anxious about anything, but in everything, by prayer and petition, with thanksgiving, present your requests to God. And the peace of God, which transcends all understanding, will guard your hearts and your minds in Christ Jesus' (Philippians 4:6–7).

I have found it extremely helpful to write down my prayers in a prayer journal. When I have prayed about something that I am anxious about, and asked for God's help, I know then that I can leave it with him. We can trust in God's provision.

Not only do we have a heavenly Father; we also have brothers and sisters in Christ. We do not have to cope with these things on our own. Paul advised the Galatians to 'carry each other's burdens' (Galatians 6:2). Of course, this applies to marriages, families, parents, and children; but also to our small groups. If we have people around us that we can talk to, we will not become isolated.

5. Focus on the present

Worry is incompatible with common sense. Jesus says, 'Therefore do not worry about tomorrow, for tomorrow will worry about itself. Each day has enough trouble of its own' (v.34). We will have enough to worry about each day. God has given us our lives in units of twenty-four hours and we should take it a day at a time.

Jesus does not say that we should not think about the future. The Authorised Version's translation, 'take no thought for the morrow', is misleading. The Greek word means 'to take no anxious thought' about tomorrow. It is not an excuse for a happy-go-lucky, irresponsible attitude to life. The book of Proverbs often makes it clear that planning is vital and we need to make prudent provision for the future. Indeed, one of the ways to avoid stress is to look ahead and plan.

However, Jesus reminds us to focus on present. Corrie ten Boom said, 'Worry does not empty tomorrow of sorrow; it empties today of strength.'[6] We should live in 'day-tight compartments'.[7] This is an area of life about which we can learn from the attitude of young children. They are naturally inclined to live in the present, rather than worrying about last week or next year.

6. Sort out your priorities

Worry is unnecessary. Jesus said, 'But seek first his kingdom and his righteousness, and all these things will be given to you as well' (v.33). This will entail getting our ambitions and priorities right. Some of these are modest, such as food, drink and clothing. Others are more grandiose: a bigger house, a new car, a better salary, reputation, fame or power. But all these are self-centred and ultimately meaningless.

Jesus says we need to change our priorities and our ambitions. It is not that we are to opt out, but quite the reverse. We are to take on a different set of responsibilities which are far more exciting and challenging. Jesus calls us to a nobler ambition – to seek his kingdom. We are to seek his rule and reign in our lives, our marriages, our home, family and lifestyle. We are also to seek it in the lives of others – our friends, relations, neighbours, work colleagues and in the community. We are to make the most of every opportunity.

One man who seems to have made the most of every opportunity in his life is Billy Graham, now almost a hundred. He has considered leaving his final sermon on tape, giving mourners a chance to respond to the gospel at his graveside. His message would start: 'I'm not here in person today, I'm in heaven. But I want to tell you, this is a wonderful place to be and if you want to come here you need to repent of your sins and come to Christ.'[8]

Further, we are to seek God's 'righteousness' in our lives and in society. We should seek to see his standards universally accepted, and invest our time, energy and money in this pursuit. There are many men and women who, in God's strength, have made a great impact on the society around them. For example, William Wilberforce, as a Christian Member of Parliament, devoted his life to seeing God's standards in our society, campaigning for forty-five years for the abolition of slavery. The necessary Act of Parliament was passed in July 1833, three days before he died.

As Christians today, we need to face up to poverty, the spread of AIDS, the breakdown of marriage and the abuse of children, and determine to do something about them. Jesus promises that if we get our priorities and our ambitions right, then 'all these things will be given to you as well' (that is to say, all the little worries will be dealt with). Lesser ambitions are good, provided they are in second place. It is alright to want to be chairman of a major public company or to own a bank or to win Wimbledon, provided that these lesser ambitions serve greater, God-centred ambition.

Jesus says that if we take on his priorities and make them our greater ambition, then he will provide us with everything else we need.

The wealthy Baron Fitzgerald had only one son and heir, who died after leaving home. This was a tragedy from which the father never recovered. As his wealth increased, the Baron continued to invest in paintings by great masters, and when he died his will was found to call for all his paintings to be sold. Because of their quality and artistic value, messages were sent out to museums and collectors, advertising the sale.

When the day of the auction came, a large crowd assembled, and the lawyer read from Fitzgerald's will. It instructed that the first painting to be sold was that 'of my beloved son'. The portrait was by an unknown artist and it was of poor quality. The only bidder was an old servant who had known and loved the boy. For a small sum of money he bought it for its sentimental value and the memories it held for him. The attorney again read from the will, 'Whoever buys my son gets all. The auction is over.'⁹

Jesus said, 'Seek first his kingdom and his righteousness, and all these things will be given to you as well' (v.33). That is how to stop worrying and start living.

14
How to Deal with Criticism

Do not judge, or you too will be judged. For in the same way as you judge others, you will be judged, and with the measure you use, it will be measured to you.

Why do you look at the speck of sawdust in someone else's eye and pay no attention to the plank in your own eye? How can you say, 'Let me take the speck out of your eye,' when all the time there is a plank in your own eye? You hypocrite, first take the plank out of your own eye, and then you will see clearly to remove the speck from the other person's eye.

Do not give dogs what is sacred; do not throw your pearls to pigs. If you do, they may trample them under their feet, and then turn and tear you to pieces.
Matthew 7:1-6

All of us can be on the receiving end of criticism from time to time. At work criticism can come from a boss or a colleague; at home it can come from parents or children; at school or university it can come from a teacher; even our friends can be very critical at times. People may be negative about our work, marriage, or how we bring up our children. It can be very hard to receive criticism and sometimes we can be deeply scarred by it.

Twenty years ago a review of our church appeared in the *Daily Telegraph*. This wasn't something we were used to. The paper sent a journalist along one Sunday morning, when I happened to be preaching. Later, I read the review and was devastated; he tore my talk apart. Looking back, if I'm honest, I don't think it was a very good talk either. However, at the time I felt humiliated. Imagine people reading this about me! I felt defensive and wanted revenge. So we analysed the article and found eighteen inaccuracies in it. We wrote a letter to the editor complaining about the inaccuracies. We thought about going to the Press Complaints Commission. I even thought of suing for li██ I wanted this journalist fired. As I sat in judgment over him I found him guilty and worthy of punishment!

Since then, as Alpha has grown, many more articles have been written. Many have been very supportive; some have been critical. Looking back, the article in the *Telegraph* was actually quite mild. Sometimes when I read one of these articles or I receive a rude letter I am tempted to respond as the German composer Max Reger did to one of his critics. He wrote a reply, saying: 'Dear Sir, I am sitting in the smallest room of my house. I have your review before me. In a moment it will be behind me.'[1] Over the years since that first article was written, I have discovered that criticism can actually be a blessing, because if there is some truth in it we have an opportunity to learn.

"I'm indebted to you for your criticism"

(cartoons are fictional)

Today, we live in a highly critical society – you only have to read the newspapers or watch talent contents like *The X Factor* to see how critical we are. We quickly make judgments about performance, style, clothing, image and appearance.

How should we respond when we are criticised? What is the difference between constructive criticism and destructive criticism? Is it ever right to criticise other people? What does Jesus have to say on this subject?

So far, Jesus has taught us about who we are (character), how we live (conduct), who we are when no one is looking (secret life) and what our desires are (ambitions). Now he moves on to how we respond to other people (relationships). We are not Christians on our own – we belong to a Christian community.

1. Distinguish good judgment from judgmentalism

Jesus begins by saying to his disciples, 'Do not judge, or you too will be judged' (v.1). Some have taken this as a blanket command that prevents Christians from ever making any kind of judgment. However, Jesus' words must not be taken out of context. We have to look at the immediate setting of the Sermon on the Mount (see, for example, v.6 and vv.15–20), Jesus' teaching as a whole (e.g. Matthew 10:14–15; 18:15–17) and the rest of the Bible.

First, we must look at what Jesus does *not* mean. He is not talking here about the authority of the state. Jesus recognised that even Pilate had a God-given right to judge. Pilate's power was given to him 'from above' (John 19:11). In a fallen world we need judges. The apostle Paul describes a judge as 'God's servant to do you good. But if you do wrong, be afraid, for he does not bear the sword for nothing. He is God's servant, an agent of wrath to bring punishment on the wrongdoer' (Romans 13:4).

"I'm afraid I cannot comment on the weather"

Nor is Jesus talking about the exercise of authority in the home or in the church. The book of Proverbs is full of exhortations to parents to exercise authority in the home. This is a kind of judgment, but it is a right kind of judgment. Discipline is also necessary in the church. One definition of the church, at the time of the Reformation, was 'a place in which the word is preached, the sacraments are administered, and discipline is exercised'. This is in line with New Testament teaching. In the 'Pastoral Epistles', Timothy, as a church leader, is told to 'correct, rebuke and encourage – with great patience and careful instruction' (2 Timothy 4:2). Paul himself was not afraid of making judgments when it came to false teaching (Galatians 1:8–9; 2:11; 5:12) or serious sin (1 Corinthians 5).

Furthermore, as individual Christians we need to exercise judgment and should not suspend our critical faculties. If we are not to throw our 'pearls to pigs' (v.6) we need to discern who the pigs are. Jesus also warns us to watch out for false prophets (vv.15–20). We are required to distinguish the false from the true and use the test Jesus lays down: 'By their fruit you will recognise them' (vv.16, 20). There is indeed a right kind of judgment. After healing a man on the sabbath, Jesus said to the Jews: 'Stop judging by mere appearances, and make a right judgment' (John 7:24). We are encouraged to 'test the spirits' (1 John 4:1) and even to 'test everything' (1 Thessalonians 5:21). Most of us will be required at times to make value judgments, to choose between different policies and plans of action. None of these judgments by the courts, parents, church leaders or individual Christians is forbidden by Jesus.

We have looked at what Jesus does *not* mean. But what *does* he mean? Surely what Jesus is attacking here is a judgmental attitude towards other people. The Greek word used in this context means 'to criticise, to find fault, to condemn'. We are not to set ourselves up as God, and judge our fellow men and women when we are in no position to do so. Judgmentalism is a danger for all of us, even in the church. I love the episode of *The Simpsons* in which Homer Simpson asks his church-going neighbours, the Flanders, where they've been, and Maude replies, 'I was at Bible Camp. We were learning about how to be more judgmental!'

We should exercise good judgment rather than being judgmental. We are not to magnify the errors and weaknesses of others and make the worst of them. We are not to be fault-finders who are negative and destructive towards other people and enjoy actively seeking out their failures. As Martyn Lloyd-Jones put it: 'If we ever know the feeling of being rather pleased when we hear something unpleasant about another, that is the wrong spirit.'[2]

2. Avoid faultfinding like the plague

Jesus says, 'Why do you look at the speck of sawdust in someone else's eye and pay no attention to the plank in your own eye?... you hypocrite' (vv.3–5). Jesus often referred to the Pharisees as 'blind guides'. A man with a plank of wood in his eye is totally blind, yet he is trying to take a tiny splinter of wood from someone else's eye.

Much criticism is blinded by ignorance. Harold Macmillan, the former British prime minister, said, 'I never found in a long experience of politics that criticism is ever inhibited by ignorance.'[3] Or, he might have added, by a lack of understanding. The Roman philosopher Cicero said, 'They condemn what they do not understand.' Dale Carnegie said, 'Any fool can criticise, condemn and

" I spy a speccypoo Deirdre "

complain – and most fools do.'[4]

Hypocrisy is the gap between what we show on the outside and what we know is true on the inside. Indeed, the things we criticise in other people are often the things we see in ourselves. By criticism, we build ourselves up. Speaking ill of others is a way of dishonestly speaking well of ourselves. It makes us feel better to gloat over the sins and errors of others – hence our love of scandals. We lap up all the sordid details and every speck we collect helps us ignore the logjam in our own eye.

This applies not only to the moral faults of others, but also to doctrinal ones as well. Some doctrinal critics may agree with 99 per cent of their opponent's view. We may agree on the Trinity, the person and work of Jesus Christ, the nature of the atonement, the authority of Scripture and issues of morality, but we find what is objectively a minor area of disagreement and latch onto it. We feel that we are not 'sound' unless we are constantly denouncing and condemning. So we write with poisoned pens. Could it be that we are blinded by the log in our own eye? Unless we first remove the plank of judgmentalism from our own eyes, we will not see clearly to remove the splinter from the eyes of others. As John Stott put it, 'We need to be as critical of ourselves as we often are of others, and as generous to others as we always are to ourselves.'[5]

D. L. Moody, perhaps the greatest evangelist of the nineteenth century, said this:

> You may find hundreds of faultfinders among professed Christians, but all their criticism will not lead one solitary soul to Christ. I have never preached a sermon yet that I could not pick to pieces and find fault with. I feel that Jesus Christ ought to have a far better representative than I am. But I have lived long enough to discover that there is nothing perfect in this world. If you wait until you find a perfect preacher or perfect meetings, I'm afraid you'll have to wait a long time. Let's be done with faultfinding.[6]

3. Learn to give and receive constructive criticism

Not all criticism is bad of itself. Again, it is important to see what Jesus is not saying. He is not ruling out constructive criticism. True criticism of literature, art and music involves a high exercise of the human mind. It should never be merely destructive, but constructive and appreciative. In a similar way all training involves constructive criticism. A teacher needs to criticise his or her pupils constructively if they are to learn. The teacher too will have received constructive criticism during their training. We cannot object to the criticism of a teacher or coach, as it improves our skills and builds us up. Without it, any kind of learning would be impossible. As someone said, 'The largest room in the world is the room for improvement.' Jesus is saying here that we all need help to get the planks out of our eyes so that we can see clearly.

Personally, I don't find it easy receiving constructive criticism. On the rare occasions that I do the washing-up, often there are little bits of food left on the pans as I put them into the drainer – partly because I'm impatient, partly because of my eyesight. If Pippa picks them up and points out that they're not entirely clean, however gentle she is, I don't say, 'Oh, thank you so much, that was really helpful criticism!' I am afraid that I am more inclined to say, 'If you're not happy with the way I do the washing-up, do it yourself!'

But criticism can actually be extremely positive, helpful, and necessary if we're to grow in any area of life. After all, in sport people pay for criticism: they pay someone to help them with their golf swing. Children thrive when they receive loving criticism from their parents. The book of Proverbs says, 'A fool spurns a parent's discipline' (Proverbs 15:5), and, 'Those who heed correction gain understanding' (Proverbs 15:32).

In church, the pastoral care we receive from our leaders and other Christians may be how God offers constructive criticism to us. The writer of Proverbs says, 'Wounds from a friend can be trusted' (Proverbs 27:6). I am so grateful for the many people who have persevered with me. When I am at my best, I try to invite people to offer constructive criticism; this is how we learn and grow.

Jesus says that if we make the effort to get the plank out of our own eyes, we will see clearly to help others (v.5). It is no accident that Jesus uses the analogy of an eye. 'There is no organ that is more sensitive than the eye. The moment the finger touches it, it closes up.'[7] Criticism of others is a delicate operation. If we are to criticise another person, we should do so not in a condemning way, but with humility, understanding, sympathy and generosity. We should be like a mother who notices a speck in her child's eye and very carefully and delicately takes it out. Confrontation should be combined with affirmation. As Paul writes to Timothy: 'Correct, rebuke and encourage – with great patience and careful instruction' (2 Timothy 4:2).

On another occasion Paul writes that we will need to 'speak the truth in love' (Ephesians 4:19). Speaking the truth in love does not mean always saying exactly what you are thinking. There is a time to speak and a time to be silent. Nor does it mean being blunt and rude. Good manners and being gracious with our words are important. However, confrontation at some point is inevitable, particularly for those in

"But, Deirdre it's tiny"

positions of leadership. Bishop Sandy Millar, the former vicar of HTB, who was my boss for twenty years, was very good at speaking the truth in love, especially when giving feedback. He used the analogy of a sandwich: at first he would be positive, encouraging and build you up; then he offered his criticism; and then he would finish with more encouraging words. This meant that I finished the conversation with him feeling encouraged, but also remembering what he'd said. There is an old Arab proverb that says: 'When you shoot an arrow, dip it in honey first.'

We see how Jesus sets out the procedure for confrontation

of sin in Matthew 18:15–17. It starts with a person-to-person encounter (v.15). We should always try to meet face-to-face, and avoid criticising someone publicly or behind their back. There should be no sense of superior attitude or degradation of the other person. If the first step fails, the second step is to get certain other people involved. In this situation, the community as a group has a right to pronounce judgment. The purpose is not to destroy, but to bring someone back to repentance and restoration. We should never criticise unless we can do so in genuine love for our brother or sister. Abraham Lincoln said: 'He hath the right to criticise who hath the heart to help.'

4. Try to find a kernel of truth in every critic's attack

What happens when we receive criticism that is not of the constructive variety? If we want to achieve anything in life, we are bound to receive criticism. Someone once said: 'To avoid criticism, do nothing, say nothing, be nothing.' Jesus himself was inundated by criticism, and he told his followers to expect the same (John 15:20).

If criticism is wholly malevolent or destructive, then it's usually best to ignore it. Someone recommended taking a lesson from the weather: 'However rude we are about it, the weather pays no attention to criticism.' Occasionally we may need to stand up to the critic. Nancy Astor once said to Winston Churchill, 'If I were your wife, I'd put poison in your coffee'; to which Churchill replied, 'If I were your husband, I'd drink it.'

Phillip Brooks was a great nineteenth-century preacher. One day he received a letter in the mail, and opening it he found a clean sheet of paper on which there was written only one word: 'Fool.' So the next Sunday Brooks carried the letter with him into his pulpit in Boston and, holding it up, he announced: 'I have received many letters from people who wrote the letter but forgot to sign their name. However, this is the first time I've received a letter from someone who signed their name but forgot to write the letter.'[8]

Sometimes when we receive criticism, we simply need to communicate with the person concerned, preferably in person. This can often be enough to clear the air. In the book of Judges, the Ephraimites criticised Gideon because he had not involved them in his battle against the Midianites. Gideon went to see them and with great charm and tact he said, 'What was I able to do compared with you?' We are told that, 'At this, their resentment against him subsided' (Judges 8:3). If one meets with a critic, often their resentment subsides.

Generally, I think that we should welcome criticism. The evangelist Dawson Trotman encourages us to look for the kernel of truth: 'There is a kernel of truth in every criticism. Look at it, when you find it, rejoice in its value.'[9]

5. Sow mercy, kindness and love

Jesus said, 'For in the same way as you judge others, you will be judged, and with the measure you use, it will be measured to you' (v.2). Jesus is saying that we should treat others as God treats us. God is so generous to us! He is not in the condemning business. Jesus didn't come into the world to condemn it, but to save it (John 3:17). St Paul writes, 'There is no condemnation for those who are in Christ Jesus (Romans 8:1). God forgives us. Jesus died for you so that you need not be judged, so that you need not be condemned, so that you could receive total forgiveness. He has been merciful to us. In light of all this grace, we should be merciful to others. Martin Luther King said: 'Forgiveness is not an occasional act; it's a permanent attitude.'[10]

In courtroom language, if we attempt to occupy the bench we will end up in the dock. If we judge, we will be judged with equal harshness by others. Those who judge must expect similar treatment. In the end we will create an environment of judgmentalism. It is a tragedy when this occurs in the church. It can be the leader who is judgmental of others, or the congregation who have 'roast preacher for Sunday lunch'. Nothing empties churches faster than this kind of atmosphere. We try to avoid critical people because, deep down, we suspect that if they are critical of others then they are probably equally critical of us when our backs are turned. Eventually, a self-appointed judge finds that the only person with whom he can associate is himself. If we object to others sitting in judgment on us, we should not sit in judgment on them.

Yet when Jesus says, 'Do not judge or you too will be judged,' he is probably thinking not so much of our own judgment, or the judgment of others, as he is of the judgment of God. (Although the first two may be an outworking of the third.) The passive tense of the Greek verb suggests that God is the agent of this judgment, as we have also seen in Matthew 6:14–15. Only God is qualified to judge.

The rabbis used to teach that God has two measures: he has a measure of justice and he has a measure of mercy, and we get to choose . Jesus is advising us here to 'choose mercy.' And if we choose mercy, we'll receive God's mercy. As Christians we have experienced this amazing mercy of God. God has not judged us as we deserve, he has not condemned us; he has died for us and set us free! He's forgiven us. The Holy Spirit gives us an experience of God's love and mercy deep in our hearts.

The book of Lamentations tells us that God's mercies are new every morning. If God treats us so wonderfully, we should do the same to others. We should be kind to people; we should walk in their shoes. I once sat next to a man at a dinner party whom I'd often admired from afar but whom I had never really spent any time with. I was rather disappointed, because I tried to engage him in conversation but he didn't seem very interested. I found him a little bit unfriendly and I made a rather unkind judgment about him. I discovered afterwards that just a few weeks earlier his wife had died, and he himself had just been diagnosed with cancer. I felt terrible; how could I have rushed to such a poor judgment? The Greek philosopher Plato said this: 'Be kind, because everyone you meet is fighting a hard battle.'

In conclusion, Jesus is urging us to act with love towards our fellow human beings. St Paul writes, 'Love is kind... love is not rude... love is not easily angered' (1 Corinthians 13:4–5). We need to choose not to get upset, to forgive quickly and to let go of anger. The American preacher Joel Osteen says, 'Don't pitch your tent in the land of self-pity.'

'Love keeps no record of wrongs' (1 Corinthians 13:5). When speaking at a wedding, Nicky Lee, founder of The Marriage Course, often uses a spiral notebook as a visual aid, explaining: 'Each page represents a day of your life. At the end of the day there are ways in which we may have offended one another. Don't just turn over the page – by doing so you are accumulating all those wrongs. But at the end of each day pull off each page and throw it away.'

'Love always protects' (1 Corinthians 13:6). When we love we make allowances and cover over faults. St Peter writes that 'love covers a multitude of sins' (1 Peter 4:8). We all thrive in an atmosphere of encouragement and love.

We should be aware too that words are very powerful. The book of Proverbs says that 'the tongue that brings healing is a tree of life' (Proverbs 15:4). Jesus tells us that our words have the power to affect the course of a person's life.

In Luke's Gospel, Jesus' teaching in this section of the Sermon on the Mount is expanded:

> Give and it will be given to you. A good measure, pressed down, shaken together and running over, will be poured into your lap. For with the measure you use, it will be measured to you.
>
> Luke 6:38

Whatever we sow, we will reap. We will reap later than we sow, but we will reap far more than we sow. This teaching refers not just to money; but also to loyalty, love and encouragement. We may feel that we are only a little seed. However, Jesus tells us that when a seed is planted, despite being surrounded by heavy earth, it grows into something big. So too, we can all have a significant impact on our place of work, our family, our church, our denomination. What we sow will grow, and it will change the environment around us. Ultimately it can change the world.

We need to follow the words of Jesus and cut out our petty squabbles and our judgmentalism. We need to stop criticising other denominations and other traditions within our own denominations. We need to forget the past, drop the labels and unite around the person of Jesus Christ. We need to get on with the task that he has given us until he comes again. Then he will do the judging and his judgment will be perfect.

How to Respond to the Most Challenging Words Ever Spoken

*Ask and it will be given to you; seek and you will find;
knock and the door will be opened to you. For everyone
who asks receives; everyone who seeks finds; and to
everyone who knocks, the door will be opened.*

*Which of you, if your children ask for bread, will give
them a stone? Or if they ask for a fish, will give them a
snake? If you, then, though you are evil, know how to
give good gifts to your children, how much more will your
Father in heaven give good gifts to those who ask him! So
in everything, do to others what you would have them do
to you, for this sums up the Law and the Prophets.*
Matthew 7:7–12

Lee began his life with a whole host of disadvantages. His mother
was a powerfully built, domineering woman who found it difficult
to love anyone. She had been married three times and her second
husband divorced her because she beat him up regularly. Lee's
father was her third husband; he died of a heart attack two months
before Lee was born. As a consequence, his mother had to work
long hours from his earliest childhood.

She gave him no affection, love, discipline or training during
those early years. She even forbade him to call her at work. Other
children had little to do with him, so he was alone most of the time.
He was absolutely rejected from his earliest childhood. When he
was thirteen years old, a school psychologist commented that he
probably didn't even know the meaning of the word 'love'. During

adolescence, the girls would have nothing to do with him and he fought with the boys.

Despite having a high IQ, he failed academically and finally dropped out during his third year of high school. He thought he might find acceptance in the Marine Corps; they reportedly built 'men', and he wanted to be one. But his problems went with him. The other marines ridiculed him and he fought back. He continually resisted authority, was court-martialled and thrown out with a dishonorable discharge. So there he was, a young man in his early twenties, absolutely friendless and shipwrecked. He was small and scrawny in stature and had an adolescent squeak in his voice. He had no talent, no skills and no sense of self-worth.

Again he decided to run from his problems, and left America to live abroad. There he married a woman who had herself been an illegitimate child, and he brought her back to America. Soon she began to display the same contempt for him that everyone else had. Although they had two children, he never enjoyed the status and respect of being a father. His marriage began to crumble as his wife demanded things that he could not provide. Instead of being his ally against a bitter world, as he had hoped, she became his most vicious opponent. She could outfight him and she learned to bully him, on one occasion even locking him in the bathroom as a punishment. Finally, she threw him out.

He then tried to make it on his own, but he was terribly lonely. After days of solitude, he went home and begged her to take him back. He surrendered any vestige of pride; he crawled, he accepted humiliation, he came back on her terms. Despite his meagre salary, he presented her with $78, asking her to take it and spend it any way she wished. But she laughed at him and belittled his feeble attempts to supply the family's needs. She ridiculed his failure. She made fun of his sexual impotency in front of a friend. At one point, when the darkness of his private nightmare threatened to envelop him, he fell on his knees and wept bitterly.

Finally, in silence, he pleaded no more. No one wanted him. No one had ever wanted him. His ego lay shattered in fragments. The next day, he was a strangely different man. He got up, went to the garage and took a rifle he had hidden there. He carried it with him to his newly acquired job at a book storage building. And, from a window on the third floor of that building, shortly after noon on 22 November 1963, he sent two shells crashing into the head of President John Fitzgerald Kennedy.

Lee Harvey Oswald, who was both rejected and unloved, killed the man who, more than any other man on earth, embodied all the success, beauty, wealth and family affection that he lacked.[1]

Lee Harvey Oswald was a classic case of a casualty caused by a breakdown in relationships, which is so prevalent in our society. So much unhappiness and suffering in the world is due to relationships that are not right – the breakdown of relationships between nations, races, religions, neighbours, friends, work colleagues, fellow students, husbands and wives, parents and children.

The Children's Society recently released an independent report entitled, 'The Good Childhood Inquiry'. *BBC News* summed the report up in the following way:

> The aggressive pursuit of personal success by adults is now the greatest threat to British children... According to the panel, 'excessive individualism' is to blame for many of the problems children face and needs to be replaced by a value system where people seek satisfaction more from helping others rather than pursuing private advantage.[2]

Frankie, a fourteen-year-old from Manchester, gave evidence to the inquiry:

> I think all kids should have the right to live in a happy place where they feel safe and loved. I haven't felt like that in some time but I know my parents don't mean it. It's just they argue and take it out on me.

This is an issue not just in Britain but around the globe. Relationships are a vital aspect of our lives. We can learn a lot about relationships from Jesus' teaching. As he comes towards the end of the ethical teaching in the Sermon on the Mount, before the call to commitment, he summarises all that he has been saying: 'So in everything, do to others what you would have them do to you, for this sums up the Law and the Prophets' (v.12). This section of the Sermon on the Mount sums up not only the sermon itself, but also the Ten Commandments, the law of Moses and all the ethical teaching of the Bible.

On another occasion, one of the Pharisees asks Jesus this question, 'Teacher, which is the greatest commandment in the Law?' Jesus replies: '"Love the Lord your God with all your heart and with all your soul and with all your mind." This is the first and greatest commandment. And the second is like it: "Love your neighbour as yourself." All the Law and the Prophets hang on these two commandments' (Matthew 22:36–40).

In verse 12, the Sermon on the Mount reaches its summit. The saying, 'Do to others what you would have them do to you' is the climax of all Jesus' ethical teaching and is the most universally famous thing Jesus ever said. It is the peak of social ethics. It is said that Emperor Alexander Severus had it written in gold on the walls of public buildings and it has become known as 'the golden rule'.

Many people have taught the negative version of this rule. Confucius said, 'What you do not want done to yourself, do not do to others.' The Stoics taught, 'What you do not wish to be done to you, do not do to anyone else.' One in particular, called Epictetus, said, 'What you avoid suffering yourself, seek not to inflict on others.' The Old Testament Apocrypha said, 'And what you hate, do not do to anyone' (Tobit 4:15, RSV). Rabbi Hillel (c. 20 BC) was challenged by a heathen who said that he was prepared to convert to Judaism if Rabbi Hillel was able to teach the whole law while standing on one leg. Hillel replied, 'What is hateful to yourself, do to no other; that is the whole law and the rest is commentary. Go and learn.'

Jesus was the first to formulate this rule positively. The negative says, 'I won't do anyone any harm', which allows us to be inactive. This is often the philosophy of the world. Many feel they are not 'sinners' because they do not kill or rob or deliberately harm others. This is how I used to think before I became a Christian. But Jesus redefined goodness: followers of Jesus Christ are called to something far higher. We are called to say not only, 'I won't do anyone any harm,' but also, 'I will go out of my way to help them.' We cannot do this without being part of a community. There is no permission to withdraw into a world where we offend no one but do not accomplish any positive good. For example, it is not enough that we do not break up marriages; we must also help to put them back together. It is not enough not to steal; we must give generously. It is not enough not to harm our neighbours; we must also positively help them.

Jesus recognises that self-love is a powerful force in our lives. We are self-centred, self-protective and self-concerned. Jesus challenges us to love others as much as we love ourselves. We are to ask the question: 'How would I like to be treated in that situation?' Properly understood, these are the most challenging words ever spoken.

How can we even begin to live like this? Verse 12 is the conclusion to verses 7–11, in which Jesus offers practical help in how to rise to the challenge.

1. Reach out for God

I recently read an interview with Jeremy Paxman, the former presenter of *Newsnight*:

> 'Is that something I don't want to talk about?' he ponders, when I ask where he stands on God today. 'Yeah, it probably is.' For a moment it is as if he is talking to himself. Then, suddenly earnest, 'I mean, it is the only important question really. Is there a purpose? And I've not got an answer to that.'[3]

Jesus tells us that there is a purpose: to live in a relationship with God, and that this will affect all our other relationships. He says that we are to 'ask... seek... knock' (v.7). The Greek verbs are in the present imperative tense. Literally, this verse means 'to keep on asking, to keep on seeking and to keep on knocking'. We need to realise our need for God and then seek him with persistence and perseverance. We are not to be like those who make a New Year's resolution and within a few weeks have failed to keep it. Nor are we to be like the small boys who knock on a door and then run away. We need to pursue God with a whole-hearted passion. God promises, 'You will seek me and find me when you seek me with all your heart. I will be found by you' (Jeremiah 29:13–14). As we 'ask... seek... knock' Jesus promises that 'the door will be opened' (v.8).

God loves us, and love never forces itself. Knowledge of God is promised to those who seek him with all their heart. This is the relationship for which he created us, and until we find that relationship, there remains a sense that something is missing, as if there were a void deep inside. President Barack Obama expressed the sense of emptiness experienced by many in his book *The Audacity of Hope*:

> Each day, it seems, thousands of Americans are going about their daily rounds – dropping off the kids at school, driving to the office, flying to a business meeting, shopping at the mall, trying to stay on their diets – and coming to the realisation that something is missing. They are deciding that their work, their possessions, their diversions, their sheer busyness are not enough. They want a sense of purpose, a narrative arc to their lives, something that will relieve a chronic loneliness or lift them above the exhausting, relentless toll of daily life. They need an assurance that somebody out there cares about them, is listening to them – that they are not just destined to travel down a long highway toward nothingness.[4]

He goes on to describe how he embraced the Christian faith:

> I was finally able to walk down the aisle of Trinity United Church of Christ one day and be baptised. It came about as a choice and not an epiphany; the questions I had did not magically disappear. But kneeling beneath that cross on the South Side of Chicago, I felt God's spirit beckoning me. I submitted myself to His will, and dedicated myself to discovering His truth.'[5]

At his first National Prayer Breakfast as President, Barack Obama gave the reason why he became a Christian:

> I spent month after month working with church folks who simply wanted to help neighbors who were down on their luck – no matter what they looked like, or where they came from, or who they prayed to. It was on those streets, in those neighborhoods, that I first heard God's spirit beckon me. It was there that I felt called to a higher purpose – His purpose.[6]

He saw in those people that their love for their neighbour came from their love for God.

2. Relate to your Father

Jesus describes God as our 'Father in heaven' (v.11). He is the one whom Jesus taught us to address as 'Abba'. After examining the extensive prayer literature of ancient Judaism, Professor Joachim Jeremias wrote that 'in no place in this immense literature is this invocation of God as *Abba* to be found... *Abba* was an everyday word, a homely family-word. No Jew would have dared to address God in this manner. Jesus did it always... and authorizes his disciples to repeat the word *Abba* after him.'[7]

Jonathan Cavan became a Christian on Alpha at our church and his life changed dramatically. As a young and successful businessman, working for Microsoft, he travelled around the world. On one particular journey he decided to write to his father for the first time in a long while, but never finished the letter because he started to talk to his neighbour about Jesus.

Later on he was explaining to Helena, his fiancée, how he communicated with his business associates via email (this was in the very early days of email). He wanted to show her how he was able to communicate with different people all over the world at the same time. So he created an email on his laptop, which he addressed to all the general managers at Microsoft, all the sales managers at Microsoft worldwide, all the sales people who look after banks worldwide and to the chairman of the organisation. Then he demonstrated how he could embed documents into an email. As an example, he attached the unfinished letter he had been writing to his father on the plane. He thought no more of it until one month later a woman in his group at work borrowed his laptop, plugged it into the corporate network and received the message: 'You have an unsent message. Would you like to send it?' She clicked 'Yes' and that message hit the inboxes of over 500 senior managers and executives in the corporation. Jonathan did not realise this until he got a phone call later. At first he was very worried about it, but then he reread the letter. It went like this:

Dear Dad,

At last I am writing to you. I have thought about you almost daily. I have not written because I have known that I could not write without saying something that would challenge your thinking and tug at your heart. However, my words aim to be an encouragement.

I am playing soccer weekly and play in a team which is doing well; we won our last game 9–1. I have a vitality for life that makes me feel fitter, stronger, happier and more peaceful than ever before. God is restoring the lost years. Many people at Microsoft really do not have a life outside work. The organisation plays an unhealthily central role to their existence. By worldly standards this may appear not a bad option... but it is absolutely no comparison to having Jesus Christ as central to one's existence as he is to mine. He lives inside me and he is able to guide every one of my thoughts, words and deeds if I am obedient to his will.

Do you know how much I craved to speak to you, soft heart to soft heart, even during my most rebellious years? For so many years we have communicated mask to mask...

He received some interesting responses, including two from Microsoft's Chairman, Bill Gates. He also received a message from a director in Canada, saying his father had died one month previously and that he had never known a son to speak so lovingly to his father and that he had cried there in his office. A message of encouragement and support came from the president of Microsoft Europe, and one of his colleagues came into the office, confessing that he had left the Lord and now wanted to return as a result of reading the letter.

This incident shows how powerful the relationship between a human father and son can be. How much more important and loving is our relationship with our Father in heaven?

3. Rely on God's goodness

Jesus says, 'Which of you, if your children ask for bread, will give them a stone? Or if they ask for a fish, will give them a snake?' (vv.9–10). So often we fear that if we pursue God whole-heartedly we will miss out on something good and get a raw deal. But God loves us. Therefore, we can be sure we will receive 'good gifts'. Jesus, using an *a fortiori* argument ('how much more' v.11), assures us that God will never give us anything harmful.

Bread and fish were the two most common foods around the Sea of Galilee. It is possible that a round limestone might look like a loaf of bread. They have the same shape and colour. The eel-like catfish of the Sea of Galilee might look like a snake, but no earthly father would be so cruel to his children as to give them stones instead of bread or snakes instead of fish. It is even more absurd to imagine that God would give us anything harmful. We can be confident in seeking God, because God will *only* give us good things.

It would be a terrible thing if God always gave us what we

asked for, as we would never be able to pray with confidence. We would always be afraid of making an awful mistake. The Greeks had their stories about the gods who answered people's prayers, but the answer always came with a barb in it; it was a double-edged gift. Aurora, the goddess of the dawn, fell in love with Tithonus, a mortal youth, so the Greek story ran. Zeus, the king of the gods, offered her any gift that she might choose for her mortal lover. Aurora very naturally chose that Tithonus might live forever; but she had forgotten to ask that Tithonus might remain forever young; and so Tithonus grew older and older and older and could never die – the gift became a curse.[8]

How different is our heavenly Father from other gods. Good fathers always correct their children's mistakes. C.H. Spurgeon once said: 'Our prayers go to heaven in a revised version.' That is why Martyn Lloyd-Jones wrote:

> I thank God that He is not prepared to do anything that I may chance to ask Him, and I say that as the result of my own past experience. In my past life I, like all others, have often asked God for things, and have asked God to do things, which at that time I wanted very much and which I believed were the very best things for me. But now, standing at this particular juncture in my life and looking back, I say that I am profoundly grateful to God that He did not grant me certain things for which I asked, and that He shut certain doors in my face. At the time I did not understand, but I know now, and am grateful to God for it. So I thank God that this is not a universal promise, and that God is not going to grant me my every desire and request. God has a much better way for us...[9]

God will not give us things which are not good for us or for others, directly or indirectly, immediately or ultimately. Jesus promises here that God will answer when we ask for good gifts.

Jesus says: 'If you, then, though you are evil, know how to give good gifts to your children, how much more will your Father in heaven give good gifts to those who ask him!' (v.11) All human fathers are intrinsically 'evil'. This is a comparative statement. Compared with God, all of us, even kind parents, are evil. Yet even evil people do good things sometimes. Odette Hallowes, a wartime heroine made famous through the film *Odette*, died aged eighty-two in March 1995. *The Times* obituary, after detailing some of her extraordinary acts of courage, added that there was also publicity of a more light-hearted kind.

On one occasion her mother's house in Kensington was burgled, the thief making off with some silver spoons and Odette's George Cross and Légion d'Honneur. Distraught at the loss of her daughter's treasures, Madame Brailly appealed through the press for their return. The thief, evidently a humane soul, obliged. His letter accompanying the decorations read: 'You, Madame, appear to be a dear old lady. God bless you and your children. I thank you for having faith in me. I am not all that bad – it's just circumstances. Your little dog really loves me. I gave him a nice pat and left him a piece of meat – out of fridge. Sincerely yours, A Bad Egg.'[10]

If even bad eggs do good things, how much more will our Father in heaven do good things?

4. Rise to the challenge

W. H. Auden was fond of the phrase: 'We're here on earth to do good to others. What the others are here for, I don't know.' But Jesus said: 'So in everything, do to others what you would have them do to you, for this sums up the Law and the Prophets' (v.12).

Love is something that we can control and that we can choose to do. Rick Warren said:

> Even the language we use implies the uncontrollability of
> love. We say, 'I fell in love,' as if love is some kind of ditch.
> It's like, 'I'm walking along one day and bam! – I fell in love. I
> couldn't help myself'… There's no doubt about it, attraction
> is uncontrollable and arousal is uncontrollable. But attraction
> and arousal are not love. They can lead to love, but they are
> not love. Love involves a choice.

If we love as Jesus tells us to – doing to others what we would
have them do to us – it will transform all our relationships. Jesus
says that 'this sums up the Law and the Prophets' (v.12). He does
not say that it replaces or abolishes them. We need details to keep
us from sentimentalism, but we need general principles to keep
us from legalism lest we forget the spirit of the rules. We are not
to be obsessed by the rules and regulations, nor to obey them
mechanically. The rules are not detached, impersonal or negative,
but their whole purpose is so that we may love our neighbour as
ourselves. Every detailed regulation is simply an illustration of the
great central principle that Jesus teaches here.

J. C. Ryle, the nineteenth-century bishop, once commented:

> This is a golden rule indeed! It does not merely forbid all petty
> malice and revenge, all cheating and overreaching: it does
> much more. It settles a hundred difficult points, which in a
> world like this are continually arising between man and man;
> it prevents the necessity of laying down endless little rules for
> our conduct in specific cases, it sweeps the whole debatable
> ground with one mighty principle; it shows us a balance and
> measure, by which everyone may see at once what is his duty.
> Is there a thing we would not like our neighbour to do to us?
> Then let us always remember that this is the thing we ought
> not to do to him. Is there a thing we would like him to do
> to us? Then this is the very thing we ought to do to him – How

many intricate questions would be decided at once if this rule were honestly used![11]

If everyone acted on this rule, there would be no slavery, war, robbery or lying – only justice and love. It would lead to the transformation of society, of marriages, relationships between parents and children, and communities. As Rabbi Lord Jonathan Sacks sums it up: 'The more law is inscribed upon our hearts, the less it needs to be policed in the streets.'[12]

Such love is only possible as God pours out his love on us. 'We love because he first loved us' (1 John 4:19). As we experience his love, we are enabled through him to love others as ourselves. If the church lived like this then the world would believe.

How to Make the Big Decision

*Enter through the narrow gate. For wide is the gate and
broad is the road that leads to destruction, and many enter
through it. But small is the gate and narrow the road that
leads to life, and only a few
find it.*
Matthew 7:13–14

There comes a point in all our lives when we have to reach a
decision. I practised as a barrister for a number of years. One of the
first cases in which I was involved was a long and complicated fraud
case, involving commodity options. The four defendants had taken
large quantities of money from people and were unable to repay
them. After six months the jury retired to consider their verdict.
They deliberated for a week and when they returned to court they
were asked, in the usual way, this question: 'Have you reached a
verdict on which you are all agreed?' Throughout the Sermon on
the Mount, Jesus spent some time explaining to the people what
it means to follow him – the kind of character, lifestyle, secret life,
relationships and attitudes we need to have. Now, as he comes to
the end of the sermon, he says that it is decision time. It is time to
reach a verdict.

One of the biggest decisions many of us face in our lives is
who we are going to marry. A great deal hangs on the decision.
In September 1977, at the age of twenty-two, I was having dinner
with Pippa in a farmhouse in the Dordogne in central France. It
was a beautiful evening with a stunning sunset. I had planned to
ask her to marry me, but I was worried that she would say 'no'. So
I did not ask her straight out. Instead I asked first: 'Would you ever

like to get married?' She did not have too much trouble with the first question. She said, 'Yes.' So I embarked on the second: 'Whom would you most like to marry?' Quick as a flash she replied, 'Prince Charles.' A bit dejected, I finally plucked up the courage and asked, 'Would you marry me?' At that moment she made a decision that was going to affect the whole course of the rest of our lives. Thankfully, she said, 'Yes.'

Jesus, in this passage, is asking us to make an even bigger decision. It is more important than whom we marry or what job we choose to do. As British church leader Michael Green has said, the Sermon on the Mount is not just 'a collection of ethical maxims such as might have been devised by any cultivated humanist'.[1] There is a call to decide about the person of Jesus Christ. We have to reach a verdict. The decision we make, Jesus tells us, will affect not only the rest of our lives, but the whole of eternity. Jesus says that ultimately there are only two alternatives – to follow him or not to follow him.

1. Choose to live a radical life

Jesus lays before us two possible lifestyles and answers the question: 'Is it going to be easy?' He says there are two roads, one is 'broad' (v.13) and one is 'narrow' (v.14).

The Greek word for the former means 'broad, spacious, roomy'. There are no boundaries and you can do what you like. You don't have to give up anything; permissiveness is the order of the day. You can live a life of ease, without having to keep to the standards Jesus has just set out in the Sermon on the Mount. You can be proud, dishonest, and angry, you can hate your enemy, have sex with whoever you like, and be full of lust. You need not forgive and you need never pray or give. You can abuse your body with drugs or alcohol. You can hold on to all your money and you can be ambitious for yourself. If someone does you wrong, you can retaliate as much as you like and criticise others to your heart's content.

The problem with this road, of course, is that where there are no boundaries people get hurt. We all recognise that children need boundaries or else they end up as spoilt brats, but what we sometimes forget is that adults can be spoilt brats too, and that is even more obnoxious. Further, the result of life on the broad road is that other people get hurt. My freedom to 'drive dangerously' means that someone else may get injured or killed. If I feel at liberty to steal, then someone else gets burgled. My freedom to get divorced means that my children will come from a broken home.

The other road is 'narrow' (v.14). This word means 'restricted, confined, compressed'. This is the pressurised road and there are boundaries. Humility is the order of the day. It is a road where there is no unrighteous anger allowed, no sex outside of marriage, no retaliation and no hatred. You have to give, to pray, to exercise self-control, and to seek first the kingdom of God. You have to say no to drugs and drunkenness. It is a road of purity, integrity, honesty and forgiveness. It is a road where we are required to 'do to others what you would have them do to you' (Matthew 7:12). Life is much more difficult, especially as you can expect that people will 'falsely say all kinds of evil against you because of me [Jesus]' (Matthew 5:11).

Magdeline Makola, aged thirty-eight, was abducted from her home by an illegal immigrant on 16 December 2008. Magdeline, a cardiology nurse, had recently finished a shift at Edinburgh Royal Infirmary, when the man forced his way into her home, threatened to kill her, beat her, and made her tell him the PIN number of her bank cards. He then bound and gagged her, and dumped her in the boot of her red Vauxhall Astra with a rope around her neck. She was eventually found, ten days later, on Boxing Day in a car park.

She had been left starving and thirsty in sub-zero temperatures. She was found by police after she managed to make a small gap in the tape across her mouth and shout for help. She was suffering from hypothermia and dehydration, which had affected her kidneys and circulation. She survived by squeezing her own urine from out of the blanket that was in the boot and drinking it. Magdeline was within hours of death when she was discovered by police officers.

On 25 April 2009, Magdeline's kidnapper admitted fourteen charges, including kidnap, theft and fraud. Magdeline said:

> I feel no anger towards him, only pity. I wish him well in the future and I'll pray for him… I spent a lot of time praying that someone would find me. Praying gave me a lot of strength and when the policeman opened the boot, I was so happy that my prayers had been answered.

She decided not to sell her red Vauxhall Astra, saying, 'I feel we went through a lot together.'[2]

Forgiveness, non-retaliation, and praying for our enemies are countercultural; to live in this way is liberating, exciting, attractive, and radical. But this is not easy; not only is it a more difficult road, it is virtually impossible to keep Jesus' standards. It is certainly impossible to keep them without him. But on this road Jesus goes with us and that is what makes it a much more exciting path. We do not walk alone.

When I first started as a curate at HTB we were offered the chance to do a two-week chaplaincy in a ski resort. On one occasion we were joined by Emmy Wilson, who had been a representative of the Ski Club of Great Britain, a qualified ski guide and hence is a brilliant and graceful skier. I had been skiing on nice flat broad blue runs, but suddenly she was taking us down narrow, steep black runs, full of moguls and in blizzard conditions. It was by far the best skiing of my life and it was exhilarating, challenging and exciting.

If I had got to the top of one of these black runs without Emmy, I would have gone straight back down on the chairlift! I would have hated it on my own, but somehow I felt safe skiing with Emmy, as she knew what she was doing. In the same way, the narrow road is much more exciting, much more fun, and much more challenging.

2. Take the long view

Jesus sets before us two possible destinations and answers the question: 'Where do they lead?' The broad road with its wide entrance, he warns us, leads ultimately to 'destruction' (v.13), whereas the narrow road with its narrow gate 'leads to life' (v.14). I remember reading years ago of an incident in the Italian Riviera. A young man was driving his sports car along a road near the sea. All along the road were warning signs that the road was not yet completed and that no one should be on that road, but he continued at great speed, went over the cliff and killed himself.

Jesus never threatened people, but he did warn them. There is a big difference between a threat and a warning: we threaten people we don't like; we warn people we love. Jesus warns us here that the life on the broad road, which might seem quite harmless, actually leads to destruction. Pride, anger, lust, hatred, greed, unforgiveness, revenge, a self-centred life, destructive relationships, and all the other things which Jesus has been speaking about will eventually destroy us, as well as others.

Jesus warns us that the broad road lifestyle will destroy us. As an image of this Jesus sometimes used the word *Gehenna*, which was the rubbish dump in the valley of Hinnem outside Jerusalem, where the slow fire burned ceaselessly and the worms steadily consumed the rotting rubbish. This is not a threat, but rather it is a warning.

Jesus warns us about where the broad road leads. God loves us and in his love he puts up warning sign after warning sign. He has given us consciences and he has put a hunger in our hearts, which can only be satisfied by a relationship with God through Jesus Christ. He might challenge us through other Christians. Anyone reading this chapter in the Bible is reading a warning sign.

On the other hand, Jesus tells us that the narrow road, with its narrow gate, leads to life. There are two Greek words for life. One means 'earthly, biological life'. The other, which is used here, means both 'life in the physical sense' and 'the supernatural life belonging to God and Christ, which the believers will receive in the future, but which they also enjoy here and now'.[3] This eternal life is only made possible because Jesus died on the cross for us so that we might know God. Jesus defines eternal life like this: 'Now this is eternal life: that they may know you, the only true God, and Jesus Christ, whom you have sent' (John 17:3).

If we simply compared the two roads, we might easily make the wrong decision. The psalmist speaks of how he looked at those who, in effect, were on the broad road and became envious of them. They appeared to have no struggles, they were prosperous, and they had strong, healthy bodies. They seemed free from the usual burdens of life. He thought: 'In vain have I kept my heart pure... till I entered the sanctuary of God; then I understood their final destiny' (Psalm 73:13, 17).

Mother Teresa started an order that now has 537 houses throughout the world in 137 countries. They help house children, people with tuberculosis, the mentally ill, the sick, and particularly the dying. Before she died, she gave an interview to *Hello!* magazine and the final questions went like this:

> *When you think of how much you have achieved in the last fifty years, Mother, you must surely feel just a little bit pleased with yourself?*
> It is not my achievement. I am not important, it is the work that's important. God has helped us and the money has kept coming. I don't think in terms of achievement, I just think

about what needs to be done for the sick and the poor. I really don't have any time to be pleased with myself.

And how is your health these days? Reportedly you've had a chesty cough for several weeks which you can't shake off.
I don't have any time to think about my health either. This cough I have is a gift from God, a birthday present!

When Pope John Paul II visited you here, you said it was the happiest day of your life. What moved you so much about that occasion?
When he arrived in Calcutta he didn't come here but went straight to the Home for the Dying. That was his priority. After that, whenever we met in Rome I would say to him, 'You have so much space in front of the Vatican, Holy Father. Why don't you give me a house for all these people in your city who need help?' I think it was on my third visit that he handed me a set of keys. It was for a home in Rome. Here we give shelter to eighty-five women who were forced into prostitution as their only means of survival.

You've recently celebrated your eighty-fourth birthday. Are you at all afraid of dying?
How can I be, when I have watched and been with so many who have died? Dying is going home to God. You come from there and you go back there. I've never been afraid. No, on the contrary, I look forward to it.[4]

This is the road that leads to life.

3. Aspire to be a good role model
Jesus sets before us two groups of people and answers the question: 'Who will go with me?' There are 'many' (v.13) on the broad road,

with its wide entrance, although it leads to destruction. However, on the narrow road, although it leads to life, there are only a few people.

The large crowd on the broad road can give people a false sense of security. 'Everybody else on the road can't be wrong', we think. But they can. As G. K. Chesterton put it: 'Right is right, even if nobody does it. Wrong is wrong, even if everybody is wrong about it .'[5]

Jesus contrasts the 'many' on the broad road with the 'few' on the narrow road. The few are not as few as all that. John speaks in Revelation of 'a great multitude that no-one could count, from every nation, tribe, people and language...' (Revelation 7:9). There are estimated to be more than 2,000 million Christians in the world today.

The church is growing rapidly; for example in India and China. On a recent trip to the Far East, I came across a magazine from the *South China Morning Post,* a secular newspaper. The front cover of the magazine proclaimed, 'Christ is risen: Jesus of Nazareth now has more followers on the mainland [of China] than the Communist Party.' The article was entitled, 'In God They Trust'.

With as many as 125 million believers, Christianity has more adherents on the mainland than the Communist Party... 'The future of Christianity in China is very different from in the West. In the West, Christianity is in retreat, especially in Europe, but in China it's growing by leaps and bounds.'[6]

The church is growing in many parts of the world and in the UK, too, there are signs of new life. An article in *Fabulous,* formerly the *News of the World* magazine, said:

> Church attendance is on the up, with 7.3 million adults going
> at least once a month... So it seems church is the place to be
> these days.[7]

The article included an interview with Andy Tilsley, who, at that time, was running Alpha at Christ Church, Piccadilly, and a woman called Sthefania, who was invited to church by some friends. The first time she went to church she noticed that it was full of people 'who looked genuinely happy and not "fake happy" ', like she was:

> I looked at them and wanted to feel like they did... Now I don't feel the need to follow the crowd to fit in; I've got an inner peace that makes me feel I'm all right as I am – and it's so much less stressful!

She goes on,

> I was out recently and this guy started chatting me up. When I explained about my faith, he pulled a face which said he knew he wasn't going to get me into bed. He was gorgeous, but I wasn't tempted because my beliefs have made me respect my body and what I do with it. I've realised that, in the past, I used sex as a way of boosting my confidence – I'd feel wanted for half an hour and that made me feel good. But I don't feel I need that now. Having God in my life makes me feel like I'm on Ecstasy. I feel complete and content – I just want to hug the world!

Nevertheless, Christians are the minority and we can often feel alone. We may be the only Christian in our work place or the only Christian among our family, or in our neighbourhood. This can be difficult because of peer pressure and the desire we have to be in with the crowd. That is not a reason to stay on the broad road; rather, it is a reason to get off quickly. In doing so we may encourage others to follow.

When US lawyer and evangelist Charles Finney was preaching at Rochester, New York, in the 1830s, a great many lawyers came to hear him. One night, way up in the gallery sat the Chief Justice of the Court of Appeals for the State of New York. As he listened to Finney's proclamation of the gospel he became convinced of the truth of it. Then the question came to him: 'Will you go forward like the other ordinary men and women?' Something in him said that it would never do, because of his prestigious social position (he was at the top of the legal hierarchy of New York State). He sat there thinking for a while, then he said to himself, 'Why not? I am convinced of the truth… I know my duty; why should I not do it like any other person?' He got up from his place in the gallery, went down the stairway, and came up the stairs at the back where Finney was preaching. Finney, in the middle of his sermon, felt someone tugging at his jacket. He turned around and saw the Chief Justice. He asked, 'What is it?'

The Chief Justice replied, 'Mr Finney, if you will call people forward I will come.'

Finney stopped his sermon and said, 'The Chief Justice says that if I call people forward he will come. I ask you to come forward now.' The Chief Justice went forward and almost every lawyer in Rochester was converted. It is said that, in twelve months, 100,000 people were converted in twelve months in that area.

We may not be able to have quite that effect, but we may be able to help someone on to the right road. We can all have an impact.

4. Embark on a life of adventure

The Christian life is an exciting adventure. G. K. Chesterton described it as the 'whirling adventure'.[8] Jesus lays before us two entrances and answers the question: 'How do I get in?' One entrance is 'wide' (v.13); the other is 'small' (v.14).

On the broad road there is easy access through a wide gate. There are many ways in which you can enter. You could be an atheist or an agnostic; you can be into the New Age or read horoscopes, or you can pick and mix all of these. On the other hand, the entrance to the narrow road is itself a narrow one. There is only one way in, and that is by repentance and faith in Jesus Christ. It's small because you cannot take the rubbish with you. You cannot take sin in with you and you have to turn your back on everything you know to be wrong. That is not at all easy. The longer you have been on the wrong road, the harder it is to admit, and to change, although it is never too late to do so.

A. N. Wilson, an author and journalist, who was well known for being 'anti-religious', recently wrote:

> For much of my life, I... have been one of those who did not believe... I began to rail against Christianity and wrote a book entitled *Jesus*, which endeavoured to establish that he had been no more than a messianic prophet who had well and truly failed and died... Like most educated people in Britain and Northern Europe... I have grown up in a culture that is overwhelmingly secular and anti-religious. The universities, broadcasters and media generally are not merely non-religious; they are positively anti... It felt so uncool to be religious. With the mentality of a child in the playground, I felt at some visceral level that being religious was unsexy, like having spots or wearing specs.... The vast majority of media pundits and intelligentsia in Britain are unbelievers, many of them quite fervent in their hatred of religion itself.
>
> My belief has come about in large measure because of the lives and examples of the people I have known... friends and relations that have lived, and faced death, in the light of the Resurrection story, or in the quiet acceptance that they have a future after they die. The Easter story answers their questions about the spiritual aspects of humanity. It changes people's lives... That... is why I now believe in it. The Resurrection... is the ultimate key to who we are... But

an even stronger argument is the way that Christian faith
transforms individual lives.[9]

On the narrow road access is hard because the gate is 'small'.
We can only enter by faith in Jesus Christ. We live in an age of
pluralism, and the suggestion that there is only one way to God is
not popular to the modern ear, but that is the claim of Jesus Christ.
We have to decide what to make of it, and reach a verdict.

At the beginning of this chapter, I mentioned a court case in
which I was involved and that the jury were asked the question:
'Have you reached a verdict on which you are all agreed?' They
had to reply that they were not agreed and could not decide. That
is not an option open to us. Everyone is on one of the two roads.
We can't have one foot on each road; it is an uncomfortable fact
that there is no middle road, no third gate, no neutral group. If we
are on the broad road we do not need to do anything in order to
stay on it. But if we want to get off it we need to enter the narrow
gate through repenting and putting our faith in Jesus Christ. We
need his forgiveness and we need his Spirit to help us. As we enter
through the narrow gate, we find that although there may not be
huge numbers on the road, we are not alone. Jesus Christ himself
goes with us.

How to Spot False Prophets

Watch out for false prophets. They come to you in sheep's clothing, but inwardly they are ferocious wolves. By their fruit you will recognise them. Do people pick grapes from thornbushes, or figs from thistles? Likewise every good tree bears good fruit, but a bad tree bears bad fruit. A good tree cannot bear bad fruit, and a bad tree cannot bear good fruit. Every tree that does not bear good fruit is cut down and thrown into the fire. Thus, by their fruit you will recognise them.

Not everyone who says to me, 'Lord, Lord,' will enter the kingdom of heaven, but only he who does the will of my Father who is in heaven. Many will say to me on that day, 'Lord, Lord, did we not prophesy in your name, and in your name drive out demons and perform many miracles?' Then I will tell them plainly, 'I never knew you. Away from me, you evildoers!'
Matthew 7:15-23

A recent article in the *Sunday Times Magazine*, entitled 'The Cult of Indecency', told the story of Wayne Bent. Bent was a pastor of a church before leaving to set up his own denomination in 1980, which he called The Lord Our Righteousness (LOR). In December 2008 he was sentenced to eighteen years in prison. The 68-year-old leader of the LOR cult claimed to be the Messiah. There were accusations of brainwashing, planned mass suicide and, most recently, child molestation. News reports like this spectacularly highlight the disastrous results of the false teaching of a cult.

In November 1978, 913 people died in a mass suicide in Jonestown, Guyana. Of these, 200 were children and another

200 were over the age of sixty-five. Babies had cyanide squirted into their mouths, while adults queued up to drink theirs. More recently, in Waco, Texas, eighty-seven deaths followed an assault by the FBI on the Branch Davidian sect led by David Koresh. In 1982, the FBI estimated there were over 3,000 cults in the US. Before her death in 2003, Dr Margaret Singer, an expert in sects, reckoned the number had risen to about 5,000.[1] There are many more all around the world.

In the earlier part of the Sermon on the Mount, Jesus warned against attacks from outside the church in the form of persecution. Now he adds a solemn warning about attacks that come from the inside. He tells us that we are to 'watch out for false prophets' (v.15). This kind of language is foreign to modern thinking, so it is helpful to be more specific. There are those kinds of false prophets, as in the examples above, who are clearly outside the community of orthodox Christian belief, but who claim nonetheless to be the true (and the only) people of God. However, there are others who speak from within the church, and who appear to be saying godly things, but in reality are leading people away from God. Some in the church may say: 'Surely all spiritual teachers are good?' or, 'Surely, if a person talks about God and heals people, it must be all right?' But Jesus tells us that this is not the case. There is a need to discern. In spite of the contemporary love of choosing to hold incompatible beliefs together, there is a distinction between true and false, and we need to discern the difference.

The word 'prophet' here includes anyone who speaks 'in the

name of the Lord'. False prophets include not only those who claim to have a prophetic ministry in the narrow sense, but also anyone who claims to speak from God, such as pastors, vicars, Christian teachers, evangelists and preachers. In all these cases, we need to distinguish the true from the false.

Jesus gives us a very serious warning about false prophets. He says that they are 'ferocious wolves' (v.15). The wolf is the natural enemy of the sheep. The same description is used elsewhere in the Bible to describe officials, rulers, governors and false teachers who are enemies of God's people (Ezekiel 22:27; Zephaniah 3:3; Matthew 10:16; John 10:12; Acts 20:29). It is a very serious matter to harm God's people and Jesus warns that such people will be like trees that are 'cut down and thrown into the fire' (v.19). On the day of judgment he will say to them, 'Away from me, you evildoers!' (v.23). John Wesley emphasises the seriousness of the matter by declaring that such people 'murder the souls of men'.[2]

How are we to spot these false teachers? How do we distinguish cults from the church? How do we distinguish true prophets from false prophets? How do we know that *we* are on the right track? How do we know that the whole Anglican Church isn't a fundamentalist sect (as one national newspaper recently suggested)? Practically every Christian leader has at some point been accused of being a false prophet, including the Pope, the Archbishop of Canterbury, Billy Graham, Rick Warren, John Wimber and Mother Teresa among others. How do we know that they're not?

There is only one true test which Jesus gives, and he repeats it: 'By their fruit you will recognise them' (vv.16, 20). Jesus does not say that you will know them by their roots. Some have suggested that a work of God should be tested by its roots – by who has been involved at an earlier stage. This is not the test Jesus gives and it would be an impossible one to apply. The whole point about roots is that they are underground. It would often take years to investigate a person's roots. Fruit, on the other hand, is visible and is relatively easy to test. Jesus explains the test more fully: 'Do people pick grapes from thornbushes, or figs from thistles? Likewise every good tree bears good fruit, but a bad tree bears bad fruit. A good tree cannot bear bad fruit, and a bad tree cannot bear good fruit. Every tree that does not bear good fruit is cut down and thrown into the fire' (vv.16–19).

In the Middle East there was a thornbush, which at a distance looked much like a vine. It had little black berries which closely resembled grapes. There was also a thistle that produced a flower which could be mistaken for a fig. On closer inspection, it was revealed that the thornbush did not produce grapes and the thistle did not produce figs. As John Stott put it, 'Noxious weeds like thorns and thistles cannot produce edible fruit like grapes and figs.'[3] Nor can a diseased tree produce good fruit, whereas a tree that is in good condition *will* produce good fruit.

One result of this is that although we are to be wise and discerning, we are not to be suspicious of everyone. Nor are we to become heresy hunters, for false prophets will reveal themselves by their fruit. We need not worry.

What kind of fruit should we be looking for? It will involve at least six aspects.

1. The fruit of character

The wrong test is a superficial one. It looks only at the outward clothing. This does not work because 'ferocious wolves' can appear 'in sheep's clothing' (v.15). 'Sheep's clothing' could include an outward profession of faith. Jesus says, 'Not everyone who says to me, "Lord, Lord," will enter the kingdom of heaven, but only he who does the will of my Father who is in heaven' (v.21). Verbal profession is not enough. It is not sufficient to know all the

Christian jargon and recite the Christian creeds.

The 'sheep's clothing' could also include supernatural activity. Jesus warns that 'many will say to me on that day, "Lord, Lord, did we not prophesy in your name, and in your name drive out demons and perform many miracles?" Then I will tell them plainly, "I never knew you. Away from me, you evildoers!"' (vv.22–23). It is interesting to note in passing that Jesus is not speaking against the activities themselves. He clearly expected that his people would 'prophesy', 'drive out demons' and 'perform miracles'. Indeed, Matthew's inclusion of this passage suggests that these activities were continuing in the church.[4] Yet in themselves they are not sufficient to prove that a prophet is genuine.

Rather, we need to look for the fruit of their character. The image of fruit is picked up by Paul in his classic description of Christian character: 'The fruit of the Spirit is love, joy, peace, patience, kindness, goodness, faithfulness, gentleness and self control. Against such things there is no law' (Galatians 5:22–23). These are the characteristics we expect to see growing in a person who is a true Christian and has the Holy Spirit of God living within. We have already seen that Jesus started the Sermon on the Mount with precisely this issue of character. A true follower of Jesus Christ will begin to develop the kind of character described in Matthew 5:1–16. There should be humility, a thirst for righteousness, a merciful attitude, meekness, purity and all the other characteristics described in that passage.

We need especially to look at Christian leaders and ask questions about their character. Of course we will never find perfection, as all leaders are still human beings, subject to the same temptations and weaknesses as the rest of us. But we need to ask whether there are fundamental flaws in their characters.

For example, with many cult leaders there is a disturbing arrogance, which should put us on our guard. We should always be suspicious of those who, in their arrogance, exclude all others. Many cults regard themselves as the only real Christians in the world. I remember asking a member of a cult that used to operate very strongly in Central London, 'How many Christians are there in Spain?' The answer was 'none' because that particular cult did not operate in Spain. It did not matter as far as they were concerned whether they were Roman Catholic, Anglican, Methodist, Baptist, Pentecostal, or any other denomination, as his cult considered none of them to be genuine.

A doctor writing about the cults in *The Big Issue* wrote:

> I myself met David Icke, and others of the many prophets claiming to be on a mission from God, on a TV programme... and was asked to diagnose his mental illness... he was entirely sane in the medical sense. Such people do not hear voices or genuinely believe they are God. What they suffer from is megalomania, self-centredness and a sophisticated ability to manipulate the vulnerable.[5]

2. The fruit of conduct

Jesus says that those who enter the kingdom of heaven will be those who do the will of his Father (v.21). To the wolves he says, 'Away from me, you evildoers!' (v.23). What we believe will affect how we live. Our creed determines our conduct.

In the Sermon on the Mount, Jesus sets out how we should live in terms of love, faithfulness, integrity, forgiveness, and loving our enemies. Of course, we all make mistakes from time to time. Over the years I have met people with amazing prophetic ministries; quite often they've had difficult upbringings, and sometimes they make mistakes. God is gracious and forgiving; enabling us to pick ourselves up and start again. However, there is a significant difference between the person who is seeking to live a consistent Christian life and what Jesus is describing here; wolves who set out to deceive, disguising themselves as sheep for their own gain.

The 'Lord's Resistance Army' is a sectarian guerrilla army based in Northern Uganda. It has been responsible for widespread human rights violations: murder, abduction, mutilation, sexual enslavement of women and children; forcing children as young as five years old to fight. They claim to be fighting in the name of God and for the Ten Commandments. However, despite taking the Lord's name, it is a cult.

Often we also see great sexual immorality. Both Jim Jones (Jonestown) and David Koresh (Waco) plucked sexual partners at will from their flocks. Koresh even persuaded his followers that because his seed was divine, only he had the right to procreate.

As sheep, we may sometimes stray from the right path and make mistakes. When this happens we need to repent and be forgiven. We then try again to do the will of God and so to live a consistent life. This is very different from the deliberate deception and ongoing abuse undertaken by cult leaders.

3. The fruit of teaching

What we teach has an impact on people's lives. Later on in Matthew's Gospel, Jesus uses a similar image of fruitfulness in relation to what people say:

> Make a tree good and its fruit will be good, or make a tree bad and its fruit will be bad, for a tree is recognised by its fruit. You brood of vipers, how can you who are evil say anything good? For out of the overflow of the heart the mouth speaks. Good people bring good things out of the good stored up in them, and evil people bring evil things out of the evil stored

> up in them. But I tell you that people will have to give account
> on the day of judgment for every careless word they have
> spoken. For by your words you will be acquitted, and by your
> words you will be condemned.
> Matthew 12:33–37

One of the Old Testament tests of the true prophet came in
Deuteronomy 13. Even if a prophet performed signs and wonders,
if he said, 'Let us follow other gods,' the people were warned,
'You must not listen to the words of that prophet' (Deuteronomy
13:1–3). In other words, the people were to test the prophet by his
teaching – whether he led people towards God or away from him.

We need to weigh the words of anyone who claims to speak
on behalf of God against what we *know* to be the word of God.
How do the words of the prophet stand up against the teaching
of Scripture? We need to follow the example of the Bereans who
'received the message with great eagerness and examined the
Scriptures every day to see if what Paul said was true' (Acts 17:11).

Cults and sects often claim that the authority of the Bible is not
enough for us, and rely on some other source of authority. The
Church of the Latter Day Saints invoke as their authority the Bible
and the Book of Mormon; Christian Scientists look to the Bible and
Mary Baker Eddy; Jehovah's Witnesses have their own version of
the Bible. In addition, they always depart from at least one major
historic doctrine of the Christian faith, such as the Trinity, or the
divinity of Christ. How do we assess this?

Caryl Matrisciana uses a helpful analogy in her book about the
New Age:

> 'Mum's been working at the bank for over a year,' my friend
> Chris told me. 'And she's getting the most *amazing* education.'
> 'What do you mean?'...

'I mean she's *really* learning about money. They are teaching her to know the colour of each bill, the size of it, even the way it's water marked. They are showing her the details of the inks and papers.'

'How do they teach her?'

'Well, they just keep having her handle it. They point out all the various things they want her to remember. But they figure the more she works with money, feels it, counts it, stacks it, the more familiar it'll be to her.'

'That makes sense, I suppose. But what's the point?'

'Here's the point. Yesterday they blindfolded her. They slipped a couple of counterfeit bills in her stack of money. She picked them out by touch!'

'So she's studying counterfeit money too, then?'

'No... that's just it. The people at the bank know that a person doesn't need to study the counterfeits... The banks know the counterfeits are getting better and better, more and more sophisticated. And it's been proved a thousand times over that *if a bank teller knows the real money extremely well, they can't be fooled by the counterfeits.*'[6]

We don't need to spend our time studying the counterfeits – the heresies and the false prophets. In order to know the truth, we need to soak ourselves in it.

4. The fruit of love

Love for other Christians is the command of Jesus. If we obey this command, we will remain in the vine and bear fruit. Love and fruitfulness go hand in hand:

> If you obey my commands, you will remain in my love, just as
> I have obeyed my Father's commands and remain in his love.
> I have told you this so that my joy may be in you and that your
> joy may be complete. My command is this: love each other as
> I have loved you.
> John 15:10–12

Indeed, as we have seen, love is the first fruit of the Spirit that Paul mentions in Galatians 5:22, and in one sense it encompasses all the others.

Jesus' warning to watch out for 'false prophets' needs to be set alongside his admonition in the previous section: 'Do not judge, or you too will be judged' (Matthew 7:1). There is a delicate balance. We need to beware of judging and condemning other Christians and other churches – of spotting the speck of sawdust in their eyes and missing the major blind spot in our own. Some are far too quick to write off other Christians.

Harsh judgmentalism combined with exclusiveness is one of the marks of cults. Sadly, it is also sometimes seen within the Christian church where believers can be too quick to judge and condemn other genuine Christians. Love, however, embraces; loving other parts of the church not just its own.

Judgmentalism and exclusiveness lead to a kind of isolation, which is a mark of the cults. Love is not isolationist. Yet the cults often take people away from their family and their friends. We need a community to protect us from going off the rails.

Love submits to authority. The cults tend to be highly authoritarian but they do not come under any authority. It is very important to be under authority. There are different kinds of authority in different churches; in the Anglican Church we are under the authority of our bishops, which is a very important safeguard.

Love allows freedom. Paul writes, 'Where the Spirit of the Lord is, there is freedom' (2 Corinthians 3:17). Again, a feature of the cults is manipulation and control. If you join a cult, it's very hard to leave it. Love, on the other hand, allows people to come and go as they choose. Love may sometimes mean protecting the sheep from the false prophets, but we should always act in love.

5. The fruit of relationship

In John 15, Jesus uses the image of the vine. Jesus is the vine and we are the branches. If we stay close to Jesus we will bear much fruit, but without him we can do nothing. The way to produce fruit is to be personally and vitally related to Jesus. Unless we are in this relationship we will bear no fruit. Jesus says, 'Apart from me you can do nothing' (John 15:5). Hence, Jesus will say to the false prophets on the last day, 'I never knew you' (v.23). They were not living in a relationship with Jesus Christ, and the unseen roots of secret giving, private prayer and private fasting had not been built up.

Jeremiah warns against the false prophets who have visions from their own mind, and not from the mouth of the Lord. This is one of the Old Testament tests of a true prophet. He asks, 'But which of them has stood in the council of the Lord to see or to hear his word?... if they had stood in my council, they would have proclaimed my words to my people' (Jeremiah 23:18, 22). The true prophet knows Jesus Christ, listens to him and speaks his word.

6. The fruit of influence

We need to ask what the fruit of the ministry is, in terms of the effect it has on the lives of the congregation. Is it producing a congregation united in love, full of joy, living at peace, full of kindness to others, doing good, and showing themselves to be faithful, gentle and self-controlled?

Is it producing the sort of people and lifestyle Jesus has commanded through this sermon?

The test of preaching is what influence it has on people's lives. Of course, we cannot judge by a single, possibly unrepresentative, member of the congregation. But if we look at the congregation as a whole we will get some feel of the influence.

Whether it be a teacher, a preacher or a pastor, we should ask 'What is the long-term influence of their ministry?' Jesus told us, 'A student is not above his teacher, but everyone who is fully trained will be like his teacher' (Luke 6:40). The main question to ask about the sermons is not, 'Are they intellectually stimulating?' or, 'Are the stories funny and the headings memorable?' Rather, we should be asking, 'Are they bringing people closer to God?'

I regard Sandy Millar, whom I worked with for thirty years, as the greatest preacher I've ever heard, because of his influence. Paul says, 'Everyone who prophesies speaks to people for their strengthening, encouragement and comfort' (1 Corinthians 14:3). I never heard a talk given by Sandy from which I didn't leave strengthened, encouraged, and comforted. Furthermore the impact of his teaching was to produce a wonderful group of people and a flourishing ministry.

Recently I met Gary Haugen, founder of the International Justice Mission (IJM). The moment he walked into our house, I had the impression of extraordinary grace and humility. Then I discovered some of the things that IJM do: rescuing people from enforced prostitution, bonded slavery, illegal detention, and unprosecuted rape. They are responding to God's call in Isaiah to 'seek justice, encourage the oppressed. Defend the cause of the fatherless, plead the case of the widow' (Isaiah 1:17). As he spoke over lunch about his wife and children I noticed his love for them; and not just for them but also for the poor and the oppressed. I read an article in *The New Yorker*, which described how he would go and pray for the people that he was trying to rescue. Gary is a very influential Christian. He has inspired many, many, young people by his example to go out to all parts of the world and rescue people from oppressive situations.

So let's watch out for the false prophets. But let's also be inspired by the true prophets, whose lives reveal this fruit.

How to Build a Secure Future

'Therefore everyone who hears these words of mine and puts them into practice is like a wise man who built his house on the rock. The rain came down, the streams rose, and the winds blew and beat against that house; yet it did not fall, because it had its foundation on the rock. But everyone who hears these words of mine and does not put them into practice is like a foolish man who built his house on sand. The rain came down, the streams rose, and the winds blew and beat against that house, and it fell with a great crash.'

When Jesus had finished saying these things, the crowds were amazed at his teaching, because he taught as one who had authority, and not as their teachers of the law.
Matthew 7:24-29

What does the future hold in store for you? We all have our dreams, hopes, aspirations, and longings (as well as our fears) for ourselves, our families and our society.

Futurologists predict what will happen in the future. For example, it is being predicted that some babies born today will live to the age of 150. Some of these predictions may come true, others may not. In 1876, the head of the British Post Office said, 'The Americans have need of the telephone but we do not. We have plenty of messenger boys.' In 1932, Albert Einstein said, 'There is not the slightest indication that nuclear energy will ever be obtainable.' In 1943, Thomas Watson, chairman of IBM, said, 'There is no reason anyone would want a computer in their home.' In 1962, Décor Recording Company rejected the Beatles, saying,

'We don't like their sound and guitar music is on its way out.' In 1974, Margaret Thatcher said, 'It will be years, certainly not in my lifetime, before a woman becomes Prime Minister.'

People also want to know what their personal future holds; hence many consult horoscopes. There is a website that promises the 'Secret of Abundance', offering 'your free personal horoscope'. You are asked to fill in a form to indicate your hopes and aspirations, in order to help them tell you about your future. Among the options you can tick are:

- I would like the chance to win a large sum of money from lottery games
- I would like to meet the great love of my life
- I would like to destroy the suffering in my life and find again confidence in myself
- I would like to ward off fate but succeed brilliantly in my life
- I would like to know success, how to succeed and how to gain a lot of money

Jesus tells us that our decisions will shape our future. The last three sections of the Sermon on the Mount are all about such decisions. Which road are we on: the broad or the narrow? Whom will we follow: the true or the false prophet? Now, finally, Jesus requires us to decide on what we will base our lives: on rock or on sand. Once again, Jesus presents us with only two alternatives. In the current climate of pluralism and permissiveness, we would like to think that there are many different ways to build our lives. Yet Jesus tells us here that there are ultimately only two alternatives. In the previous section he contrasted 'doing' and 'saying', but in this one he contrasts 'doing' and 'hearing'.

A long time ago, soon after Pippa and I were married, I decided I would like to take up windsurfing. It looked fun, and relatively easy to learn. I bought a book all about it and learned the theory. We booked a holiday by the sea and I hired a board for an hour. It was a hot day, so I covered myself in sun oil, which is what we used in those days! The first time I fell, the sun oil came off me and onto the board. Thereafter, I fell first forwards and then backwards, time and again. Soon word spread around the beach that something amusing was occurring and a crowd gathered and began to cheer. Even my wife joined the crowd, roaring with laughter at me, and when I finally came out of the water they gave me a round of applause! I have never been windsurfing since. I learned that there is a great difference between hearing about how to windsurf and actually doing it.

Similarly, there is a great difference between hearing the words of Jesus and putting them into practice. Jesus illustrates this by telling us about two men, two houses, two foundations, two results and two responses to Jesus.

1. Be prepared for storms

Both the wise man and the foolish man 'built his house' (vv.24, 26). Jesus knew all about building houses. He was a craftsman by trade and had practised as a carpenter. The illustration he uses is the down-to-earth one of a practical man. Two men decided to build a house. No doubt they intended to live in and enjoy them, perhaps with their families. Both were building something of long-lasting significance. Our lives are like the houses, yet their significance is for all eternity.

The houses they built differed little in appearance. At this stage no one looking on from outside, in a purely superficial way, would have been able to tell them apart. Similarly, two lives can look very similar. Superficially they may be the same, but the difference is evident when, inevitably, the challenge comes. In both cases 'the rain came down, the streams rose, and the winds blew and beat against that house' (vv.25, 27).

All of us, sooner or later, face the inevitable pressures of life in this world. The challenges of life come in many forms: misunderstandings, disappointments, unfulfilled longings, doubts, trials, temptations, and satanic attacks. Success, too, can be a test. There are also pressures, setbacks, suffering, sickness, bereavement, sorrow, trauma, tragedy, persecution, and failure. Ultimately, all of us will face death and God's judgment. The image of 'rain... torrents... winds' is used in Ezekiel to refer to God's judgment (Ezekiel 13:11), but the language of judgment is not confined to the Old Testament. C. S. Lewis wrote, 'All the most terrifying texts came from the mouth of our Lord.'[1] Here, and elsewhere, Jesus warns of the coming judgment, as do the other New Testament writers.

However, we need not live in fear. It is not easy, but there is a way to be sure that when the foundations of our houses are tested, they stand the test. It is possible to know that our future is secure.

2. Think

Although there are superficial similarities between the two houses, the underlying differences are so great that Jesus can describe one of the builders as 'a wise man' (v.24), whereas the other is 'a foolish man' (v.26). The Greek word that Jesus uses for the foolish man is such a strong word that translators avoid translating it, because in today's world it would cause offence. The distinction between the two men is that the foolish person does not use his mind; he does not think.

The foolish man, possibly in a hurry, does not stop and ask the farsighted questions of life. He takes a short-term view and does not think ahead. Indeed, he hardly seems to think at all. The wise man goes to a great deal more trouble, thinking and planning for the long term. A foolish person takes the path of instant gratification, whether from money, sex, power or relationships.

Yet Jesus encourages us to *think*. He wants to ensure that we do not miss out on all the amazing things that God has in store for us. In our climate of pluralism and permissiveness, it is assumed that there are many different ways to live. As before, Jesus' teaching here is very countercultural – he tells us that there are only two alternatives: either we are wise or we are foolish; there is no 'third building'.

3. Build strong foundations

The difference between the two houses is in the foundations. The wise man built 'on the rock' (v.24), whereas the foolish man built 'on sand' (v.26). It is not entirely clear in this version of the parable whether Jesus is speaking of a difference in location or a difference in depth. In Luke's version, it could be a difference in location. The wise man goes on looking until he finds rock on which to build, whereas the foolish man 'chooses an attractive stretch of sand, not realising that it is a dry wadi which in winter will become a raging torrent'.[2] Or it could be that the fool builds on sand, but the wise man digs until he finds the rock beneath it. Certainly, in Luke's version of the

parable, Jesus speaks of a man 'building a house, who dug down deep and laid the foundation on rock' (Luke 6:48), as opposed to the man who 'built a house on the ground without a foundation' (Luke 6:49).

It is foolish to go through life without thinking about the foundational questions regarding the meaning of life. Unless we answer questions about why we are here and what the point of life is, we will never know whether our plans are right or wrong, good or bad. If we don't know what life is for, we'll use it wrongly. Bishop Lesslie Newbigin tells the story of when he was a schoolboy:

> There was a great Scout jamboree in Liverpool and about the same time a new substance had been unleashed on the world, said to be edible, and called 'shredded wheat'. One day [of the camp] this shredded wheat was issued as rations for all the jamboree troops and after breakfast there was a complaint in the camp office from [one group of scouts]... 'These pan-scrubbers are no use!'[3]

Until we know the purpose of something, we cannot tell whether or not it is of any use. God's purpose for us is to be living in a relationship with him. When we have established this, everything else begins to take its place.

4. Consider the long-term

Because the foundations of the men's houses (which represent our lives) are so different, the results are equally different. When 'the rain came down, the streams rose, and the winds blew and beat against that house' (vv.25, 27), the house built on the rock 'did not fall' (v.25), but the one built on sand 'fell with a great crash' (v.27). These are solemn words of warning. The trial may be during this life or it may come on the day of judgment. What is certain, according to Jesus, is that it will come.

Again, this is not a threat, but a warning from Jesus. He warned of the danger of 'destruction' (v.13), of the 'fire' (v.19), of being told, 'Away from me, you evildoers!' (v.23), and now he warns of a 'great crash' (v.27). Jesus knew that, in the long run, it is more loving to warn people by telling them the truth. On Wednesday, 13 March 1991, there was a disaster on the M4 motorway. Ten people died and twenty-five people were injured on a foggy day in one of Britain's worst road accidents. One man, Alan Bateman, was hailed as a hero after he climbed out of his damaged car and ran along the central reservation to try to warn oncoming vehicles of the wreckage ahead. Some drivers sounded their horns at him, however, and drove on towards the crash.

Jesus warns us, not in order to frighten us, but because he loves us and wants us to avoid the crash. He wants us to be like the wise man whose house 'did not fall' (v.25), but stood the test. The promise of Jesus is that a house built on the rock will withstand the storms of life. A life founded on obedience to Jesus is safe, no matter what the storms of life may bring. The nineteenth-century evangelist, D. L. Moody, wrote in his Bible alongside this verse, 'Build on the rock and fear no shock.'[4]

The apostle Paul testified to how this was true in his own life.

He did not avoid life's problems. He wrote to a church which was questioning his qualifications for Christian leadership:

> I have worked much harder, been in prison more frequently, been flogged more severely, and been exposed to death again and again. Five times I received from the Jews the forty lashes minus one. Three times I was beaten with rods, once I was stoned, three times I was shipwrecked, I spent a night and a day in the open sea, I have been constantly on the move. I have been in danger from rivers, in danger from bandits, in danger from my own people, in danger from Gentiles; in danger in the city, in danger in the country, in danger at sea; and in danger from false believers. I have laboured and toiled and have often gone without sleep; I have known hunger and thirst and have often gone without food; I have been cold and naked. Besides everything else, I face daily the pressure of my concern for all the churches.
>
> 2 Corinthians 11:23–28

Amazingly, Paul could also write, 'Our light and momentary troubles are achieving for us an eternal glory that far outweighs them all. So we fix our eyes not on what is seen, but on what is unseen. For what is seen is temporary, but what is unseen is eternal' (2 Corinthians 4:17–18). Paul knew that, as Jesus had promised, a life built on him would stand not only in this life, but for all eternity. The wise man takes the long view.

The coming storms refer not only to the trials of this life, but also to the ultimate trial of the day of judgment. The wise man looks forward to 'a new heaven and a new earth' (Revelation 21:1). He will spend eternity in the presence of Jesus (Revelation 21:3). He knows that on that day he will receive a glorious resurrection body and that, as Jesus rose from the dead as the 'first fruits' (1 Corinthians 15), he will experience intense joy which goes on for ever. 'No eye has seen, no ear has heard, no mind has conceived what God has prepared for those who love him' (1 Corinthians 2:9).

Even in this life we get glimpses of this joy. The Holy Spirit has been given to us as a down payment, guaranteeing what is to come (Ephesians 1:13–14). It is not just a guarantee; we actually begin to experience some of the joys of heaven here and now.

5. Take action

Jesus tells us that the key difference is that the wise man not only hears the words of Jesus, he 'puts them into practice' (v.24). The foolish man, on the other hand, although he hears Jesus' words 'does not put them into practice' (v.26). We need to be clear that Jesus is not saying that we earn our way into the kingdom of God by good works. This would be contrary to what Jesus says elsewhere in the Sermon on the Mount. It is those who recognise their poverty of spirit to whom the kingdom of God belongs (Matthew 5:3). The rest of the New Testament underlines this and, in the book of Romans, Paul expounds why no one can be justified by their own works, but only by grace through faith in Christ.

Second, Jesus does not mean that a person who puts his 'words into practice' leads a sinless life. Paul summarises his argument in the first three chapters of Romans thus: 'All have sinned and fall short of the glory of God' (Romans 3:23). John tells us, 'If we claim to be without sin, we deceive ourselves and the truth is not in us' (1 John 1:8).

If, then, Jesus is not teaching justification by works or sinless perfection, what is he teaching here? He is teaching what he taught elsewhere and what the rest of the New Testament affirms, that listening alone is not enough. Hearing must lead to action (see also Romans 2:13; James 1:22–25; 2:14–20; 1 John 1:6; 2:4). Today, many people hear the words of Jesus; they are taught in Religious Education lessons at school and millions of people have their own Bibles. They may have been baptised and confirmed. However,

Jesus says that hearing his words is not enough; it needs to make a difference. Knowledge must lead to action, theory must be put into practice, our theology must affect our lives – or else we are building our lives on sand.

In the Sermon on the Mount, Jesus describes this different life of the kingdom of God. It will be seen in who we are: living a life of blessing, as children of God, being peacemakers, being pure in heart, having fullness of life, living in right relationships with God and with each other. It will be seen in how we live: as the salt of the earth and bright lights in a dark world. It will be seen in our righteous lives: instead of revenge, there will be reconciliation; and in following the radical teaching on faithfulness in relationships, not being a slave to sexual desire, but upholding sanctity in marriage. It will be seen in complete integrity, going the extra mile, loving our enemies, being full of light, not afraid of death and being part of God's plan to redeem the world.

It will be made evident by our secret life of giving generously, being a community that prays and in not being consumed by hatred and unforgiveness, but forgiving one another. It will show itself in the fact that we store up treasures in heaven and not on earth, not being dominated by worries and fears or obsessed by money, but seeking God's kingdom. It will be revealed in our relationships, that we are not judgmental about others, that we seek God with all our hearts and that we do to others what we would have them do to us. Finally, it will show itself in our commitment to enter through the narrow gate, and to build our lives upon the rock.

6. Respond to Jesus

Jesus says, 'Therefore everyone who hears these words of mine and puts them into practice is like a wise man who built his house on the rock' (v.24). Through the centuries, people reading the Sermon on the Mount have tried to summarise its message. There are three main ways in which this has been done and I think each one is helpful.

First, it is a call to repentance. As we look at the standards set in the sermon, we see how desperately far short we all fall. Each time I have worked on one of the eighteen chapters of this book, I have felt deeply challenged as I have been reminded that my life is so far from where it should be. Sometimes people say to me, 'I live by the Sermon on the Mount', and I know then that they can't have read it. When we read we feel deeply challenged and so it becomes a call to repentance and living differently.

Second, people suggest this sermon is Jesus putting forward who he is. Again this is true: these are the greatest words ever spoken. The people who heard Jesus were 'amazed, because he spoke as one who had authority' (v.28). Jesus was not producing second-hand stuff. He was 'not like their teachers of the law' (v.29) who taught derivatively. Unlike them he did not teach with an endless string of quotations from commentaries and famous names. He did not even teach like the Old Testament prophets who began, 'Thus saith the Lord.' Rather he declared, 'I say to you.' He did not teach by authority, but taught as one who had authority (v.29). As John Stott pointed out, he claimed the authority of a teacher, the Christ, the Lord, Saviour, Judge and criterion of judgment; Son of God, and indeed of God himself. 'He teaches with the authority of God.'[5]

Furthermore the name Jesus means 'saviour'. Matthew tells us earlier in his Gospel that the angel of the Lord told Joseph, his father, 'You are to give him the name Jesus, because he will save his people from their sins' (Matthew 1:21). Jesus alone can save us. That is why he came to earth to die on the cross and rise again – so that we could be forgiven and set free. He came 'to give his life as a ransom for many' (Mark 10:45).

Third, many have pointed out that when reading the Sermon on the Mount we recognise that we cannot possibly live up to it without help from outside. The standards it sets are unattainable and therefore we need the power of the Holy Spirit in our lives. He alone can enable us to live up to the pattern of life Jesus has set out. Jesus promises us that God will give his Holy Spirit to those who ask him (Luke 11:13). Only as we repent, put our faith in Jesus and receive the Holy Spirit will we be able to put into practice the words of Jesus.

One person who made the decision to live the Jesus lifestyle recently told her story at our church:

> In my past I've been a prostitute. I took drugs, I sold drugs, imported them and manipulated them. I was on antidepressants, anti-psychotics and mood-stabilisers, more medication to counteract the side effects of those – so I was pretty glued together, really. I couldn't really go to the toilet; I'd taken to urinating in cups that were overflowing. Metaphorically, I would say I had a black tongue, I had a black heart and I had black blood that ran through me. There was no oxygen. I was absolutely and completely dead. But my physiology was working. I wasn't breathing; I was drawing breath.
>
> I have a chihuahua who eventually needed walking, so I sort of scraped myself out of my pit and went to Battersea Park. I sat down by the lake and I started to talk to this man called Chris, and he told me about church [she later came to Alpha at our church].
>
> I heard these words; that 'Jesus loves you, and that if you had been the only person in the world, Jesus would have died for you.' It broke this kind of concrete underground bunker that I was. Nothing could penetrate me, but those words completely and utterly destroyed me. It completely broke down all that anger, all that rage, that sort of self-disgust and everything. I prayed: 'Jesus, this is who I am. This is who I've been. And I now turn away from this'. And I asked Jesus to come in.

Slowly, slowly, since... Alpha... my life has been completely transformed. I say slow, but it's been really rapid. It's not been that many months – I guess it's about four months now. But Christ did come into the most polluted, most toxic, most self-serving person and he's filled me with love, and he's forgiven me. All this anger that I felt towards people who had abused me, and the parents who've never cared for me, I just feel love and compassion and insight, and I feel so cleansed! I am truly, truly restored.

I really do want to tell you about what Jesus has done for me and why I just love this man. Now I'm so forgiven that the life I've led is a memory of a memory. I feel so cleansed. If I look back over my life, I can see my sin, I can see those who've sinned against me, and I just feel the most overwhelming love for people who've really hurt me. I no longer 'draw breath'; I have a heart that beats, that pumps, and I now have really red blood! When I go to the park, I smell the weather. When I prepare a salad, the colours are so living. I can smell the rain hours before it rains. Now I really know what grace is. Handing my life over, experiencing complete surrender, I've been given the grace of God. So anything that I am now is not because of me; it's because of Christ and the love of Christ and the heart of Christ.

Endnotes

1. Michael Green, *Matthew for Today* (Hodder & Stoughton, 1988), p.69.
2. A. B. Bruce, *Commentary on the Synoptic Gospels* (Hodder & Stoughton, 1987), p.95.

Chapter 1

1. A. A. Gill, 'Fame, Who'd Want It?', *Style, The Sunday Times,* 8 October 2006.
2. According to researchers from marketing firm The Henley Centre.
3. The opinion poll by GfK NOP for BBC 2's series *The Happiness Formula*.
4. George Michael, 'Freedom! '90', *Listen Without Prejudice Vol. 1* (1990).
5. St Augustine, *On the Morals of the Catholic Church and on the Morals of the Manichaeans* (De moribus ecclesiae catholicae et de moribus Manichaeorum).
6. G. K. Chesterton, 'When Doctors Agree' in *The Paradoxes of Mr. Pond* (Courier Dover Publications, 1990), p.35.
7. Dietrich Bonhoeffer, *The Cost of Discipleship* (SCM Press, 2001), p.61.
8. D. Martyn Lloyd-Jones, *Studies in the Sermon on the Mount* (IVP, 1976), pp.72–73.
9. John Bunyan, *Pilgrim's Progress* (Barnes and Noble, 2005) p.261.
10. William Barclay, *The Daily Study Bible, Matthew 1–10* (The Saint Andrew Press, 1975) p.99.
11. Ria Higgins, 'Sister Wendy', *The Sunday Times*, 8 October 2006.

Chapter 2

1. Martin Luther King, *The Measure of a Man* (Fortress Press, 2001), p.43.
2. Fiona Gibson, *The Daily Mail*, 9 February 1992.
3. Sarah Sands, 'Sir Richard Dannatt: A Very Honest General', *Daily Mail*, 13 October 2006.
4. Paul Burnell, 'Victim's Widow's Faith in Future', *BBC News,* 13 April 2005.
5. Robert Wright, *A Memoir of General James Oglethorpe* (London: Chapman & Hall, 1867), p.102.
6. Dietrich Bonhoeffer, *The Cost of Discipleship* (SCM Press, 2001), p.64.
7. William Shakespeare, *The Merchant of Venice* (Act IV, Scene I).
8. J.B. Phillips, *The New Testament in Modern English* (Collins, 1958), p.7.
9. Shane Claiborne, *The Irresistible Revolution* (Zondervan Publishing USA: February 2006), p.254.
10. Alistair Cooke, *The Vintage Mencken* (New York: Vintage, 1955), p.231.
11. H. G. Wells, *The History of Mr Polly* (Collins, 1910), p.19.
12. Jim Wallis, *A Call to Conversion* (San Francisco: HarperCollins, 2005), p.135.

13. From Ronald Reagan's First Inaugural Address as President of the United States, 20 January 1981.

14. Every effort has been made to trace and acknowledge the copyright holders of this quotation. We apologise for any error or omission and would ask those concerned to contact the publishers, who will ensure that full acknowledgment is made in the future.

Chapter 3

1. Richard Dawkins, *The God Delusion* (Blackswan, 2007), pp.31, 248, 250.
2. Nicky Gumbel's reflections and commentary on the One-Year Bible readings are available for no cost on our website, and can also be subscribed to as a daily email. See: bibleinoneyear.org
3. Abraham: Genesis 11:10–25:11; Joseph: Genesis 37–50:26; Moses: Exodus and Deuteronomy; Ruth; David: 2 Samuel 16 – 1 Kings 2:12; Daniel.
4. Much of this material is gleaned from Chris Wright's *Knowing Jesus Through the Old Testament* (Marshall Pickering, 1992).
5. John Wenham, *Christ and the Bible* (IVP, 1984), p.37.
6. For further reading see Gordon Wenham, *The Book of Leviticus*, New International Commentary on the Old Testament Series (Grand Rapids: Eerdmans, 1979), especially p.32.
7. Karl Barth, *Church Dogmatics*, Vol. 1.2, pp.488–89.
8. 'The same things, to be sure, are in the Old and the New, there concealed, here revealed, there prefigured, here made clear.' St Augustine, *Quaestiones in Heptateuchum*.
9. Dietrich Bonhoeffer, *The Cost of Discipleship* (SCM Press, 2001), p.75.
10. Chris Wright, *Knowing Jesus Through the Old Testament* (Marshall Pickering, 1992).

Chapter 4

1. Tim Rayment, 'The Age of Rage', *The Sunday Times*, 16 July 2006.
2. C. S. Lewis, *Letters to Malcolm: Chiefly on Prayer* (Mariner, 1991), p.95.
3. Martin Luther, *The Table-Talk of Martin Luther*, tr. W. Hazlitt (London, 1883), p.cccxix.
4. Aristotle, *Nicomachean Ethics,* (Cambridge University Press), p.78.
5. Richard Chartres, BoL Lent Lectures 2007, *Missing God – The Wrong Pathway*, p.2.
6. Letter to Charles Clay, 12 July 1817.
7. Matthew Henry, *The Life of Mr. Philip Henry* (London, 1825), p.184.
8. *The Times*, June 1992.
9. Stanley Hauerwas, *Matthew* (Brazos Theological Commentary on the Bible) (Grand Rapids: Brazos Press, 2007).
10. C. H. Spurgeon, *The Gospel of the Kingdom* (Pilgrim Publications, 1974), p.27.

11. Stephen Gaukroger and Nick Mercer, *Frogs in Cream* (Scripture Union, 1990), p.95.
12. Corrie ten Boom, 'I'm Still Learning to Forgive', *Guidepost Magazine*, 1972.

Chapter 5

1. Will Iredale, 'Children Film Sex on Their Mobiles', *The Sunday Times*, 4 February 2007.
2. Rob Bell, *Sex God* (Zondervan, 2007), p.62.
3. *Ibid.*, p.164.
4. Copyright material is included from Common Worship: Pastoral Services; copyright © The Archbishops' Council 2000.
5. Sadie Nicholas, 'Guess how many lovers we've had?', *Daily Mail*, 30 June 2007.
6. Lewis Smedes, *Sex for Christians* (Triangle, 1993), p.220.
7. Graham Tomlin, *The Seven Deadly Sins* (Lion, 2007), p.128.
8. John Diamond, *The Times*, 21 May 1992.
9. John Stott, *Christian Counter-Culture* (IVP, 1993), p.89.
10. Lewis Smedes, *Sex for Christians*, p.188.
11. Leadership Today, November 1987.
12. Graham Tomlin, *The Seven Deadly Sins*, p.131.
13. William Martin, *A Prophet with Honour*, (Hutchinson, 1991), pp.597–98.
14. Rob Bell, *Sex God*, pp.83–84.

Chapter 6

1. Christians of different denominations hold varying views on this subject. Even Christians within the same denomination can find it hard to agree. I regret that there is not space to give weight to all these views in this chapter. I approach the issue from the perspective of being a minister in the Anglican Church, and I can only tell you the conclusions I have reached.
2. National Statistics, Summer 2007, No. 128 and National Statistics Online 'Divorce in 2005'.
3. John Diamond, *The Times*, 21 May 1992.
4. Dr Patrica Morgan, *The Catholic Herald*, 9 June 2000.
5. *The Times*, 22 February 2007.
6. R. Berthoud and J. Gershuny (eds.), *Seven Years in the Life of British Families* (Policy Press, 2000).
7. Karl Barth, quoted in Lewis Smedes, *Sex for Christians* (Triangle, 1993), p.220.
8. Rick Warren, *God's Strategy for a Stable Marriage: How to be at peace under pressure and finding the love of your life*, 'Marriage Matters'.
9. Raneiro Cantalamessa, *Come, Creator Spirit* (Liturgical Press, 2003), p.92.
10. Lewis Smedes, *Sex for Christians*, p.193.

11. See Christopher Compston, *Recovering From Divorce: A Practical Guide* (Hodder & Stoughton, 1993), pp.40–45.

Chapter 7

1. Shane Watson, 'Sins ain't what they used to be', *Sunday Times*, 18 February 2007.
2. Rick Warren, 'Living with Integrity: Making a Difference in Our World', Part 2.
3. For further reading, see Ken Costa, *God At Work* (Alpha International, 2013).
4. Matthew Parris, *The Times*, 22 December 2007.
5. William Barclay, *The Daily Study Bible, Matthew 1–10* (The Saint Andrew Press, 1975), pp.160–61.
6. C. H. Spurgeon, *The Gospel of the Kingdom* (Pilgrim Publications, 1974), p.29.
7. Rick Warren, 'Your Integrity and Your Influence – Living God's Way', Part 4.
8. Dietrich Bonhoeffer, *The Cost of Discipleship* (SCM Press, 2001), p.89.
9. John Stott, *The Contemporary Christian* (IVP, 1992), p.117.

Chapter 8

1. Martin Luther, 'The Sermon on the Mount', in *Vol 21 of Luther's Work* (Concordia, 1956), p.110.
2. Christopher Hitchens and Alister McGrath Debate, Georgetown, USA, 12 October 2007.
3. John Stott, *Christian Counter-Culture* (IVP, 1992), p.107.
4. St. Thomas Aquinas, *Summa Theologiae* (Cambridge University Press, 2006), II/II.40.1.
5. Dietrich Bonhoeffer, *The Cost of Discipleship* (SCM Press, 2001), p.94.
6. Charles Colson & Nancy Pearcey, *How Now Shall We Live?* (Marshall Pickering, 1999), pp.482–87.

Chapter 9

1. G. K. Chesterton, 'The Irishman' in *The Selected Essays of G. K. Chesterton*, ed. E. C. Bentley (Methuen, 1949), pp.182–83.
2. David Hannay, Don Emilio Castelar (BiblioBazaar, 2009), p.85.
3. From a private conversation with Canon Oestreicher.
4. An idiom is a phrase or expression that has come to mean something particular, and so should not necessarily be taken literally. An example in English might be the expression 'cut to the chase'. Various idioms also exist in the Hebrew language. This is an important example. The word for 'hate' is sometimes used as a Semitic (Hebrew) idiom. It does not literally mean hate, but rather means 'love less'. In Luke 14:26 Jesus says 'If anyone… does not hate his father and mother, his wife and children, his brothers and sisters – yes, even his own life – he cannot be my disciple' (See also Matthew

10:37). He does not mean that we should hate, but rather that we should not love anything more than him.

5. G. Vermes, *The Dead Sea Scrolls in English* (Penguin Books, 1987), p.62.
6. R. T. France, Matthew (IVP, Eerdmans, 1985), p.128.
7. The sayings 'bless those who curse you' and 'do good to those who hate you' aren't in the better manuscripts of Matthew 6:44 as the NIV footnote indicates. But they are definitely part of Jesus' teaching. See for example Luke 6:27–28 where Jesus says, 'Do good to those who hate you, bless those who curse you.'
8. Dietrich Bonhoeffer, The Cost of Discipleship (SCM Press, 2001), p.98.
9. J. D. McClatchy (ed.), *Longfellow: Poems and Other Writings* (Library of America, 2000), p.797.
10. W. F. Arndt and F. W. Gingrich, *A Greek–English Lexicon of the New Testament* (University of Chicago Press, 1957), p.651.
11. Dietrich Bonhoeffer, *ibid.*, p.103.
12. R. T. Kendall, *God Meant It for Good*, (Paternoster, 2003), p.62.
13. Carol Midgley, *The Times*, 22 March 2006.

Chapter 10

1. Gordon MacDonald, *The Life God Blesses* (Nelson Word Ltd, 1994), pp.29–33.
2. John Stott, *Christian Counter-Culture* (IVP, 1992), p.126.
3. A. H. McNeile, *The Gospel According to St Matthew* (Macmillan, 1949), p.73.
4. See Dr and Mrs Howard Taylor, *Biography of James Hudson Taylor* (Hodder & Stoughton, 1965), pp.50–53.
5. D. Martyn Lloyd-Jones, *Studies in the Sermon the Mount* (IVP, 1976), p.333.
6. John Stott, *Christian Counter-Culture*, p.130.
7. A. B. Bruce, *Commentary on the Synoptic Gospels* (Hodder & Stoughton, 1986), p.116.
8. C. S. Lewis, *The Weight of Glory* (HarperOne, 2001), pp.26–27.
9. From a sermon by Russell H Conwell, 'The History of the Fifty-Seven Cents', 1 December 1912.

Chapter 11

1. Martin Luther, *A Simple Way to Pray* (Westminster John Knox Press, 2000).
2. Mother Teresa, *Everything Starts With Prayer* (White Cloud Press, 1998), p.35.
3. Philip Yancey, *Prayer: Does it Make Any Difference?* (Hodder & Stoughton, 2008), p.46.
4. St Teresa of Avila, *The Life of St Teresa of Avila* (Cosimo, Inc., 2008), p.51.
5. C. S. Lewis, *Mere Christianity* (Collins, C. S. Lewis Signature Classics Edition, 2012), p.196.
6. Martin Luther, *A Simple Way to Pray* (Westminster John Knox Press, 2000).
7. C. S. Lewis, *Letters to Malcolm: Chiefly on Prayer* (Mariner, 1991), p.80.

8. Philip Yancey, *Prayer: Does it Make Any Difference?* (Zondervan, 2006), p.134.

9. For further reading on this subject I recommend Pete Greig, *God on Mute* (Kingsway, 2007).

10. *Dark Night of the Soul* is the title of a poem written by the sixteenth-century Spanish poet and Roman Catholic mystic, Saint John of the Cross.

11. C. S. Lewis, *A Grief Observed* (Faber & Faber, 1961), p.7.

Chapter 12

1. Julian Borger and Duncan Campbell, 'The Governator', *The Guardian*, 8 August 2008.

2. Oliver James, *Affluenza* (Vermillion, 2007).

3. *Esquire* magazine, October 2008.

4. *The Week,* 6 September 2008.

5. Kate Muir, 'The Dark Ages', *The Times*, 27 September 2008.

6. John Stott, *Christian Counter-Culture*, (IVP, 1992) p.155.

7. William Shakespeare, *Othello* (Act III, Scene 3).

8. Jackie Pullinger, *Renewal*, no. 161, October 1989.

9. Lynn Barber, 'Simon Cowell: The Interview', *The Observer*, 9 December 2007.

10. James Dobson, *Marriage and Sexuality* (Kingsway, 1982), p.86.

11. Dietrich Bonhoeffer, *The Cost of Discipleship* (SCM Press, 2001), p.121.

12. Barry Humphries, *More Please* (Penguin Books, 1992), p.xiii.

13. N. T. Wright, *New Tasks for a Renewed Church* (Hodder & Stoughton, 1992), p.131.

Chapter 13

1. Title taken from a book by Dale Carnegie (Cedar, 1953).

2. Rob Parsons, *The Sixty Minute Father* (Hodder & Stoughton, 1995), pp.36–37.

3. Another health issue relating to this subject is depression. In October 2015 the World Health Organisation estimated that 350 million people worldwide suffer from depression (see who.int/mediacentre/factsheets/fs369/en/). Sadly two out of three never seek help. It is important to state that depression is not a sin. If you are suffering from anxiety or depression it is wise to seek help from your doctor or a counsellor.

4. Winston Churchill, *Their Finest Hour: The Second World War,* vol. 2 (Houghton Mifflin Harcourt, 1986) p.418.

5. William Barclay, *The Gospel of Matthew,* p.259.

6. Corrie ten Boom, *He Cares, He Comforts* (F. H. Revell, 1977) p.83.

7. Dale Carnegie, *How to Stop Worrying and Start Living* (Cedar, 1953), Chapter 1.

8. *Alpha Magazine*, May 1995.

9. Graham Twelftree, *Your Point Being?* (Monarch, 2001), p.114.

Chapter 14

1. Letter to Munich critic Rudolph Louis, responding to a savage review in 'Münchener Neueste Nachrichten', 7 February 1906; in Nicolas Slonimsky 'Lexicon of Musical Invective' (1953) p.139.
2. D. Martyn Lloyd-Jones, *Studies in the Sermon on the Mount* (IVP, 1976), p.484.
3. Leon Harris, *The Fine Art of Political Wit* (1965).
4. Dale Carnegie, *How to Enjoy Your Life and Your Job* (Pocket Books, 1990), p.77.
5. John Stott, *Christian Counter-Culture* (IVP, 1992), p.180.
6. Edythe Draper, *Draper's book of Quotations for the Christian World* (Tyndale House, 1992).
7. Martyn Lloyd-Jones, *ibid.*, p.497.
8. Quoted in Jamie Buckingham, *Coping with Criticism* (Bridge Publishing, 1978), p.71.
9. Gordon S. Jackson, *Never Scratch A Tiger with a Short Stick, and other quotes for Leaders* (NavPress, 2003), p.53.
10. Quoted in Johann Christoph Arnold, *The Lost Art of Forgiving* (Plough Publishing, 1998) p.27.

Chapter 15

1. Graham Twelftree, *Drive the Point Home* (Monarch, 1994), pp.109–11. Lee Harvey Oswald was himself killed before his trial. Hence, it was never conclusively proved that he carried out the assassination.
2. The Good Childhood Enquiry, quoted on *BBC News*, 2 February 2009.
3. Decca Aitkenhead, *The Guardian*, 9 February 2009.
4. Barack Obama, *The Audacity of Hope* (Canongate Books Ltd, 2008), p.202.
5. *Ibid.*, pp.206, 208.
6. Barack Obama, speaking at the National Prayer Breakfast, Washington DC, 5 February 2009.
7. Joachim Jeremias, *The Prayers of Jesus* (SCM, 1967), pp.96–97.
8. William Barclay, *The Daily Study Bible Matthew 1–10* (The Saint Andrew Press, 1975), pp.271–272.
9. Martyn Lloyd-Jones, *Studies in the Sermon on the Mount* (IVP, 1976), p.513.
10. Obituary of Odette Hallowes, GC, *The Times*, 17 March 1995.
11. J. C.Ryle, *Expository Thoughts on the Gospels: Matthew* (William Hunt and Co., 1878), p.66.
12. Jonathan Sacks, *Faith in the Future* (Darton Longman & Todd, 1995), p.50.

Chapter 16

1. Michael Green, *ibid.*, p.89.
2. *The Times*, 4 May 2009.

3. Walter Bauer, *A Greek-English Lexicon of the New Testament* (The University of Chicago Press, 1957).
4. *Hello!* No.3224, 1 October 1994 (Hola, S.A., Spain).
5. G. K. Chesterton, *All Things Considered* (BiblioBazaar, LLC, 2008), p.156.
6. *Post* magazine, *South China Morning Post*, 12 April 2009.
7. Rachel Lewis & Jo Upcraft, 'Hymn Books and High Heels – Meet the Religionistas'.
8. G. K. Chesterton, *Orthodoxy* (Arc Manor LLC, 2008) p.87.
9. A. N. Wilson, 'An Easter Essay', *Daily Mail*, 11 April 2009.

Chapter 17

1. *Sunday Times Magazine*, 14 June 2009, p.46.
2. John Wesley, *The Works of John Wesley*, vol. 1 (Baker Books, 1996) p.294.
3. John Stott, *Christian Counter-Culture*, p.200.
4. 'It is clear that Matthew by no means polemicises against prophetic proclamation, exorcism and acts of power, even though according to 7:22 the false prophets appeal to these. On the contrary. The fact that their emergence is so emphatically described as a sneaking in, as wolves in sheep's clothing, shows how like the other sheep their actions are. There must therefore be proper prophets who behave in similar ways, the difference being of course that these proclaim and perform love for one's neighbour which is no longer taught and practised by the false prophets... Not only healings of sick persons and exorcism, but even raising the deadre expressly promised to his disciples at 10:8, as they are reported of Jesus at 9:18–26. All these charismatic deeds should continue in the community as "deeds of Christ" and serve to answer all questions of doubt.' (Edward Schweizer, *The Interpretation of Matthew*, edited by Graham Stanton [Fortress Press/SPCK, 1983], pp.130–31.)
5. *The Big Issue*, no.29.
6. Caryl Matrisciana, *Gods of the New Age* (Marshall Pickering: 1985), p.220.

Chapter 18

1. C. S. Lewis, from the Introduction to J.B. Phillips, *Letters to Young Churches* (Fontana Books, 1947), p.9.
2. G. B. Caird, *St. Luke* (Penguin, 1963), p.107.
3. Lesslie Newbigin, *Faith in a Changing World*, ed. Paul Weston (Alpha International, 2012), p.68.
4. D. L. Moody, *Pleasure and Profit In Bible Study and Anecdotes, Incidents and Illustrations* (Read Books, 2007) p.129.
5. John Stott, *Christian Counter-Culture*, p.122.

Alpha USA
1635 Emerson Lane
Naperville, IL 60540

800.362.5742

questions@alphausa.org
alphausa.org

@alphausa

Alpha in the Caribbean
Holy Trinity Brompton
Brompton Road
London SW7 1JA UK

+44 (0) 845.644.7544

americas@alpha.org
caribbean.alpha.org

@alphacaribbean

Alpha Canada
#101-26 Fourth Street
New Westminister, BC V3L 5M4

800.743.0899

office@alphacanada.org
alphacanada.org

@alphacanada

What is Alpha?

Alpha is a series of sessions exploring the Christian faith, typically run over eleven weeks. Each talk looks at a different question around faith and is designed to create conversation. Alpha is run all around the world, and everyone is welcome.

Find out more

alphausa.org | alphacanada.org | caribbean.alpha.org

"Alpha was the best thing I ever did. It helped answer some huge questions and find a simple, empowering faith in my life."
Bear Grylls, Adventurer

Millions of people have tried Alpha in over 100 countries and over 100 languages.

What to expect

A typical Alpha

Alpha runs in cafés, churches, universities, homes, bars—you name it. No two Alphas look the same, but they generally have three key things in common: food, a talk, and good conversation.

Alpha Topics

Alpha explores the following topics over 11 weeks, including a weekend or day away. We recommend beginning and ending each Alpha with a party where guests can invite their friends who might be interested in attending the next Alpha. Alpha is free of charge to guests.

Session 1:   Is There More to Life Than This?

Session 2:   Who is Jesus?

Session 3:   Why Did Jesus Die?

Session 4:   How Can I Have Faith?

Session 5:   Why and How Do I Pray?

Session 6:   Why and How Should I Read the Bible?

Session 7:   How Does God Guide Us?

Alpha Weekend or Day Away

Session 8:   Who is the Holy Spirit?

Session 9:   What Does the Holy Spirit Do?

Session 10:   How Can I Be Filled with the Holy Spirit?

Session 11:   How Can I Make the Most of the Rest of My Life?

Session 12:   How Can I Resist Evil?

Session 13:   Why and How Should I Tell Others?

Session 14:   Does God Heal Today?

Session 15:   What About the Church?

CONNECT WITH ALPHA

Let's connect

We welcome any opportunity to speak with you. Whether it's hearing your vision, or simply assisting you with a question, our team is waiting to talk with you.

alphausa.org/contact
800.362.5742

alphacanada.org/connect
800.743.0899

carribean.alpha.org/contact
868.671.0133

Go deeper in the Word

Start your day with the Bible in One Year, a free Bible reading app with commentary by Nicky and Pippa Gumbel. Receive a daily email or audio commentary coordinated with the Bible in One Year reading plan.

alpha.org/bioy

Connect with us on Social Media

@AlphaUSA | @AlphaCanada | @AlphaLatAm

Join the conversation: #TryAlpha #RunAlpha

Getting started with Alpha

PREPARE: We're here to help you

We are eager to help you get your Alpha started. Contact us to connect with a network of experienced Alpha coaches and leaders in your local region.

PLAN: Go online to build your Alpha

Within Alpha Builder you will find team training videos and resources both for you and for your Alpha team. Oh, did we mention they are all free?

It's crucial that you make sure that all of your hosts, helpers and other team members are trained. Alpha small groups are different from other small groups that they may have participated in before, so they need to know how to run their group well.

PROMOTE: Easily promote your Alpha with our tools

Easily promote your Alpha by customizing our tools within Alpha Builder. You can post your Alpha on our website so guests can find you online. You can also download free resources to invite guests to your next Alpha. In the USA you can also find many promotional tools in our print shop at alpharesources.org

PRAY: Lay the right foundation

Prayer is the foundation of Alpha. Gather a team to pray and go for it. You are part of a global story and we cannot wait to hear how it goes.

"(Alpha) is one of the greatest evangelistic tools a church could use.... because there is this underlying dependence on God to transform."

—Pastor Harvey Carey, Senior Pastor at Citadel of Faith, Detroit, MI

One Alpha, three ways to run

The Alpha Film Series

Begin the greatest adventure with us. The *Alpha Film Series* is an updated, relevant and engaging way to experience the Alpha talks. They are designed to take the audience on an epic journey exploring the basics of the Christian faith.

Alpha with Nicky Gumbel

Filmed live at HTB London, Alpha pioneer Nicky Gumbel delivers a complete set of 29-minute Alpha talks.

The Alpha Youth Series

Thirteen video sessions filmed all around the globe, designed to engage students and young people in conversations about faith, life and Jesus.

Related Alpha resources

Run Alpha Kit

Includes two DVD options for the Alpha talks as well as copies of each of the key resources to plan, train, promote and run Alpha.

Searching Issues

Nicky Gumbel tackles the seven most common objections to the Christian faith, including suffering,other religions. Recommended reading for all small group hosts and helpers.

Alpha Guide

Essential for every Alpha guest, the guide serves as a companion to the talks. The guide is an invaluable resource to guests during Alpha and as a reference for individual reflection long after Alpha is over.

Alpha Team Guide

This essential tool for Alpha small group hosts and helpers can be used with team training videos. It contains outlines for each training session as well as sample questions for hosting each session of Alpha.

30 Days: A practical introduction to reading the Bible

God has given humanity the extraordinary privilege of knowing Him through His word. Nicky Gumbel has selected thirty fascinating passages from the Old and New Testament, accompanied by an insightful commentary and suggested prayer.

Marriage Courses

These courses can be run either before or after Alpha and are an excellent way to reach out the wider community.

The Marriage Course

The Marriage Course is for any couple who wants to invest in their relationship, whether they have been together 1 or 61 years and whether they have a strong relationship or are struggling.

The Marriage Preparation Course

Most couples spend countless hours preparing for the wedding, but little, if any time preparing for married life. The Marriage Preparation Course can help couples develop strong foundations for a lasting marriage.

**For more information in the USA,
visit alphausa.org/the-marriage-courses
or purchase materials at alpharesources.org**

**For more information in Canada,
visit themarriagecourses.ca**

ALPHA TITLES AVAILABLE

Why Jesus?   This booklet may be given to all participants at the start of Alpha. "The clearest, best illustrated and most challenging short presentation of Jesus that I know." – Michael Green

Why Christmas?   Why Easter?
The Christmas and Easter versions of *Why Jesus?*

Questions of Life   Alpha in book form. In fifteen compelling chapters Nicky Gumbel points the way to an authentic Christianity which is exciting and relevant to the world today.

Searching Issues   The seven issues most often raised by participants on Alpha: suffering, other religions, does religion do more harm than good, is faith irrational, new spirituality, science and Christianity, and the Trinity.

The Jesus Lifestyle   Studies in the Sermon on the Mount showing how Jesus' teaching flies in the face of modern lifestyle and presents us with a radical alternative.

30 Days   Nicky Gumbel selects thirty passages from the Old and New Testament which can be read over thirty days. It is designed for those in Alpha and others who are interested in beginning to explore the Bible.

All titles are by Nicky Gumbel, pioneer of Alpha

The Jesus Lifestyle